Planners on Planning

Planners on Planning

Leading Planners Offer Real-Life Lessons on What Works, What Doesn't, and Why

Bruce W. McClendon

Anthony James Catanese

Editors

Foreword by Eugenie Ladner Birch

Afterword by Ted Gaebler

Jossey-Bass Publishers • San Francisco

Substantial discounts on bulk quantities of Jossey-Bass books are available to corporations, professional associations, and other organizations. For details and discount information, contact the special sales department at Jossey-Bass Inc., Publishers (415) 433–1740; Fax (800) 605–2665.

For sales outside the United States, please contact your local Simon & Schuster International office.

TCF Manufactured in the United States of America on Lyons Falls Pathfinder Tradebook. This paper is acid-free and 100 percent totally chlorine-free.

Library of Congress Cataloging-in-Publication Data

Planners on planning: leading planners offer real-life lessons on
   what works, what doesn't, and why / Bruce W. McClendon, Anthony
   James Catanese, editors.—1st ed.
      p. cm.— (The Jossey-Bass public administration series)
   Includes bibliographical references and index.
   ISBN 0–7879–0285–3
      1. City planning—United States. 2. Regional planning—United
   States. 3. Planning—United States. I. McClendon, Bruce W.
   II. Catanese, Anthony James. III. Series.
   HT167.P5 1996
   307.1'2'0973—dc20   96–10091

FIRST EDITION
HB Printing 10 9 8 7 6 5 4 3 2 1

The Jossey-Bass
Public Administration Series

Contents

Foreword

We can be proud of our profession as we read the contributions of the twenty-two authors in this collection. We can celebrate the expertise that is apparent in every word. We can be secure in the knowledge that the testimony of these planners demonstrates the firm foundation of their academic training—90 percent of them hold master's degrees in planning—and their professional growth; collectively they represent many decades of practice. This anthology is witness to a delicious combination of knowledge and action in planning, a link that some believed broken but that is proven here to be securely in place. A critical strength of this book is its demonstration of how practicing planners adapt and apply their academic training to their work.

A valuable aspect of *Planners on Planning* is its recognition and affirmation of the inner workings of planning practice. It systematically dissects the phenomenon into four important areas: evaluation of the personal qualities needed for success, recognition of the political nature of the field, affirmation of the values and principles of effective planning, and suggestions for a realignment and new orientation of the profession that emphasizes customer service, empowerment, and entrepreneurship.

This book helps eliminate an enormous void in planning literature, one that some scholars have attempted to fill with journal articles and oral histories but that until now remained stubbornly empty. Part of that void had to do with the failure to explore the heroes of planning. A few years ago, I asserted in a *Festschrift* for the renowned planner, teacher, and scholar Chester Rapkin, published in the *Journal of the American Planning Association,* that today's heroes are unlike those of yesteryear. They are not brash and outspoken. They are not grand or prepossessing figures and are less obviously noticeable than their predecessors. Nevertheless, they exist and have special valuable qualities. I wrote: "They have vision, but it is tempered by expertise and realism born of experience. Their vision is not brash, it is possible. . . . They possess expertise that they gained systematically and pass on to their successors. They are concerned with the public interest and subscribe to ethics used to regulate practice" (Birch, 1988).

With the publication of this book, I can now admit that I based these assertions on intuition, not fact. Today I can make this confession shamelessly because my intuition is now shown to be fact. This book brims with planning heroes. They have much to teach us.

New York, New York   Eugenie Ladner Birch
May 1996

The Editors

Bruce W. McClendon is the director of planning and development for Orange County, Florida. He has an M.C.R.P. degree from the University of Oklahoma and over twenty-five years of local government planning experience in Florida, Texas, Oklahoma, Kansas, Missouri, and Montana. McClendon was national president of the American Planning Association (APA) from 1983 to 1984 and a recipient of the APA's Distinguished Service Award. He is a charter member of the American Institute of Certified Planners (AICP) and is the author of two books and more than one hundred published articles.

Anthony James Catanese is president of Florida Atlantic University. A practitioner and educator in urban planning and development, he received his Ph.D. degree in planning and land economics from the University of Wisconsin–Madison, an M.U.P. degree in planning and public administration from New York University, and a B.A. degree in planning and civil engineering from Rutgers University. Before assuming his post at Florida Atlantic University, Catanese served as provost of Pratt Institute in New York City and dean of the College of Architecture at the University of Florida and the School of Architecture and Urban Planning at the University of Wisconsin–Madison. In addition to many years of teaching and research at various universities, Catanese has had an active professional practice, consulting on projects in such places as Hawaii, Alaska, Florida, Georgia, Europe, and South America. He has published eleven books, more than sixty-five journal articles, and thirty-five research monographs. Like his coeditor, Catanese is a charter member of the AICP.

The Contributors

Robert W. Becker is currently senior vice president of the Audubon Institute and former executive director of the New Orleans City Planning Commission (1982–1988). He received his M.A. degree in urban and regional planning from the University of Iowa and has over twenty years of public sector planning experience. Becker has been active in the American Planning Association (APA) and has served as president of its Louisiana chapter.

Paul A. Bergmann is senior director for the Department of Planning and Development Services for Lake County, Florida. He has over twenty-five years of experience, including ten years as director of planning and development for the Louisville and Jefferson County (Kentucky) Planning Commission and eight years as planning director for Clearwater, Florida. Bergmann has a B.S. degree in architecture, a B.S. degree in urban planning, and an M.C.P. degree from the University of Rhode Island. He has served as president of the Florida and Kentucky chapters of the APA.

Richard C. Bernhardt has been director of the Department of Planning and Development for the City of Orlando, Florida, since 1982. Previously, he was planning manager for the City of Gainesville and director of the Hophinsville–Christian County (Kentucky) Planning Commission. Bernhardt has a B.S. degree in economics from Auburn University and an M.C.P. degree from Ohio State University. He is a two-term past president of the Florida chapter of the American Planning Association and previous chairman of the American Planning Association's Chapter Presidents Council.

Gene Boles is director of planning and development for Hillsborough County, Florida. He has worked in both the public and private sector for over twenty-five years and has nine years of experience as a planning director in Florida, Oklahoma, and Missouri.

Boles has earned a B.C.E. degree from Auburn University, as well as an M.C.P. degree and an M.S. degree in civil engineering (transportation) from the Georgia Institute of Technology.

William W. Bowdy is currently executive director of the Northern Kentucky Area Planning Commission. He has previously served as assistant director of the Tri-County Regional Planning Commission in Akron, Ohio. He graduated from Michigan State University with B.S. degrees in landscape architecture and in urban planning and an M.U.P. degree. Bowdy has been active in APA chapter capacities in Ohio and Kentucky, serving two terms as Kentucky chapter president and having received the Kentucky chapter's Highest Honors Award for Distinguished Professional Achievement. Bowdy was elected to the American Institute of Certified Planners (AICP) Commission and is now president of that organization.

Keith L. Cubic has been the planning director of Douglas County, Oregon, since 1976. He has worked in county government in Oregon since he graduated from Portland State University with a B.S. degree in urban studies. He has been an active participant in the development and subsequent revisions of Oregon's statewide planning program. Cubic's career has been distinguished with special recognition in planning, including three Oregon chapter APA awards of special merit, four National Association of County Officials awards for achievement, and two county awards for distinguished service.

Linda L. Davis is a planning consultant with the firm of Cogan Owens Cogan in Portland, Oregon. Previously, she was community development director, planning and building director, and planning director for the City of Beaverton, Oregon, for almost fifteen years. She has also held public sector planning positions in Ada County and Boise, Idaho, and in Oregon and Michigan. Davis has a B.S. degree in geography from Portland State University and has served as vice president and president of the Oregon chapter of the APA.

V. Gail Easley is president of the Gail Easley Company and has over eighteen years of national planning experience in growth management, land use planning and development regulations, and visioning. She served six cumulative years as assistant director and community development director for the City of Largo,

Florida. She has been a planning consultant since 1987 and has worked for over fifty local governments in Florida, Washington, Tennessee, and Kentucky. Easley has an M.S. degree in planning from the University of Tennessee and is working on her doctorate in planning at the University of Florida. She was president of the Florida chapter of the APA and has authored a Planning Advisory Service report on growth management.

Angela N. Harper has over twenty-five years of experience in local government and has been serving as the director of planning for Henrico County, Virginia, since 1990. An active member of the APA, Harper has been president of the Virginia chapter and a member of the national board of directors and of the board of the Chapter Presidents Council. She has a B.A. degree from Memphis State University and an M.P.U.D. degree from the University of Virginia.

Elizabeth L. Hollander has spent over thirty years in public service in government and nonprofit settings in the Chicago area. She was the commissioner of planning for the City of Chicago between 1983 and 1989 and the executive director of the Metropolitan Housing and Planning Council from 1980 to 1983. Since 1994, she has been the executive director of the John Egan Urban Center with De Paul University. Hollander has a B.A. degree in political science from Bryn Mawr and attended the Senior Executive Program of the Kennedy School of Government at Harvard in 1986.

Norman Krumholz earned his M.C.P. degree at Cornell University and has served as a planner in Ithaca, New York; Pittsburgh, Pennsylvania; and Cleveland, Ohio, where he was planning director from 1969 to 1979. Since 1985, he has been professor of urban planning at Cleveland State University. Krumholz has published widely in books and professional journals, and his book *Making Equity Planning Work,* written with John Forester, won the Paul Davidoff Award from the Associated Collegiate Schools of Planning. He served as president of the APA in 1986 and as a member of the APA board from 1992 through 1996.

Floyd Lapp, having majored in urban and regional planning, holds M.P.A. and D.P.A. degrees in public administration from New York University. He has more than thirty years of experience at virtually every level of government. Lapp is presently the director of transportation planning for the New York City Department of City Planning and has served in the past as director of the Bronx office of the New York Planning Department and as executive director of the Kingsbridge–Riverdale–Van Cortlandt Development Corporation in the Bronx. He has served as the chairman of the AICP, as an APA board member, and as president of the New York chapter of the APA. Lapp received APA's National Planning Award for Distinguished Service in 1988.

John A. Lewis is the economic development administrator for Orange County, Florida. He holds an M.S. degree in economics from Florida State University, and he has thirty years of experience in urban economics, visioning, goals-setting, and strategic planning. For twelve years, he was executive director of the Goals for Dallas program. Either as staff director, coordinator, or consultant, he has been intimately involved with visioning and goals-setting programs throughout the United States, including San Diego, California; Memphis, Tennessee; Rochester, New York; Tucson, Arizona; Pensacola, Florida; Carlsbad, New Mexico; and Corpus Christi, San Antonio, Wichita Falls, Graham, and Jacksonville, Texas.

Marjorie W. Macris has an M.S. degree in journalism and planning from the University of Illinois at Urbana. She currently practices as a planning consultant. She was planning director for Marin County, California, between 1978 and 1984 and for the City of Berkeley between 1984 and 1989. Macris has taught at the University of California at Berkeley and serves on the editorial review board of the *Journal of the American Planning Association.* She has consistently promoted the role of women in planning and raised the importance of women's issues to planners. She was a founder of the APA's Planning and Women division and received the APA's Distinguished Service Award in 1991.

Robert W. Marriott Jr. is the assistant executive director of the National Capital Planning Commission. He was the director of planning for Montgomery County, Maryland, from 1991 to 1995. He has an M.S. degree in rural and regional resource planning from the University of Aberdeen (Scotland). Marriott has international experience but has spent the majority of his professional career in local government planning in Maryland, including five years as deputy director of planning for Baltimore County and three years as assistant director of planning for the City of Baltimore. He is a past president of the Maryland chapter of the APA.

Stuart Meck is the principal investigator for the APA's Growing Smart project, intended to develop the next generation of model planning and zoning statutes for the United States. A former national president of the APA, Meck has twenty-four years of experience as a practicing planner and public administrator and has written widely on planning and land use controls. He was the assistant city manager and planning director for the City of Oxford, Ohio, from 1982 to 1994. Meck holds B.A. and M.A. degrees in journalism, an M.C.P. degree from Ohio State University, and an M.B.A. degree from Wright State University. He has taught planning, public administration, and organizational behavior and decision making at the graduate and undergraduate levels.

Ray Quay is assistant director of planning for the City of Phoenix, a member of the faculty at Arizona State University, and a principal in McQuay Technologies, a software development partnership. He has seventeen years of experience in the public sector, predominantly in Texas and Arizona. Quay has an M.R.C.P. degree from the University of Texas and a B.S. degree from Baylor University. He has written and lectured extensively on the concepts of mastering change, technology and innovation, and customer service.

Jim Reid is president of the Southern Dallas Development Corporation, a nonprofit agency established to promote small and minority business, job creation, and economic development in southern Dallas. Previously, he was Dallas's assistant city manager for about six years and assistant city manager in Miami, Florida. Reid has held planning and development positions in Washington, D.C.; Fairfax County, Virginia; and Prince George's County, Maryland, and worked in the private sector for the Rouse Company. He has an M.A. degree in public administration from George Washington University.

Sergio Rodriguez is an assistant city manager for the City of Miami and has been director of the building and zoning department since 1990. Between 1983 and 1990, he was director of the Miami Planning Department. Previously, he worked for the Maryland–National Capital Park and Planning Commission and Anne Arundel County Planning and Zoning Office. Rodriguez has an M.R.P. degree from the University of North Carolina at Chapel Hill and a bachelor's degree in architecture from the University of Florida. He has been a member of the APA board since 1992 and is chairman of the Hispanic Planners Network.

Norman Whitaker is executive director of the Knoxville–Knox County (Tennessee) Metropolitan Planning Commission. He has an M.C.R.P. degree from the University of Texas and over seventeen years of professional experience in Texas, Virginia, and Tennessee involving land use, transportation, parks and recreation, downtown revitalization, historic preservation, economic development, capital projects management, coastal zone management, and land use regulation.

Paul C. Zucker has thirty years of experience in public and private sector planning and management. He was planning director for Brookline, Massachusetts; Marin County, California; and Tucson, Arizona. He was also assistant county administrator for San Diego County, where he headed one of the largest planning, building, environmental, and transportation agencies in the country with a staff of over 300. He has been president of a private development company and is currently president of Zucker Systems, a planning, management, and development consulting firm established in 1982. Zucker has an M.C.P. degree from the University of California at Berkeley and has written and lectured extensively on planning agency management.

Planners on Planning

Introduction

Bruce W. McClendon and Anthony James Catanese

Thomas Jefferson observed over 200 years ago that "as new discoveries are made, new truths discovered, and manners and opinions change, institutions must advance also to keep pace with the times." Probably at no time in our history have we experienced social, political, and economic changes occurring as rapidly as today as we move relentlessly toward an uncertain future. At a dizzying pace, both planning practitioners and public officials are being asked to do more in our communities—better, faster, more efficiently, and with fewer resources. President Clinton could have been speaking to planners during a nationally televised address on September 4, 1993, when he stated, "I want to say to my fellow Americans, when you live in a time of change, the only way to recover your security and to broaden your horizons is to adapt to the change, to embrace it, to move forward." In an environment where change is the only constant, planners must learn to do a better job of seeing the future, changing the way they practice, and positioning themselves to be masters, rather than victims, of change.

Over the years, the practice of city planning has evolved from an emphasis on physical determinism (such as the City Beautiful movement), to planning for people (social reform), to planning with people (advocacy planning), and now to people planning for themselves (empowerment and self-help). At each transition, there was much sound and fury as some well-meaning planners bravely defended their past and others called for change. All, in reality, were fueling evolution; planning theories and practices have evolved and continue to evolve as the profession adapts to changing social, political, and economic forces. While this has enabled

the profession to reinvent and sustain itself, something important
has been lost in the transition: no one has documented planning's
anchors, traditions, core values, and agreed-upon theoretical foundations of practice.

For many years now, John Freidmann has been attempting to
call attention to what he views as a pervasive crisis of confidence
within the planning profession. In *Planning in the Public Domain*
(1987), he said: "Talk to planners and nine out of ten will describe
their work as a 'failure,' or of 'little use.' They will say: 'We no longer
know what to do. Our solutions do not work. The problems are
mounting.' If they are right—and who would quarrel with them?—
we are forced to conclude that mainstream planning is in a crisis.
Knowledge and action have come apart. The link is broken" (p. 311).

Others argue that the news is even worse. According to Howell Baum, associate professor in the School of Social Work and
Community Planning at the University of Maryland at Baltimore,
planners are in trouble with the general public. From his surveys,
Baum has found that in the public's mind, planners are part of the
multitude of government employees who cost vast amounts in taxes
and accomplish little (Baum, 1983). He is not alone in his conclusions. In the early 1990s, Thomas Miller and Michelle Miller (1991)
carried out a meta-analysis of 261 citizen surveys of local government services in forty states conducted over the past decade. Meta-
analysis is a statistical method of combining findings from many
smaller studies, rendering a more accurate and reliable overall
assessment. The Millers found that planning and zoning services
collectively were rated last in the cumulative ratings and rankings
of public satisfaction. Furthermore, they noted that the service
quality ratings were relatively stable from community to community, and not appreciably affected by the method, type, or quality of
the survey techniques used. Planning has drifted to the bottom
of the local governmental food chain. In many communities it is
one of the first programs targeted for reductions when budgets
have to be cut.

Heroes of Planning

On the Fox network's trendy show "The X-Files," which premiered
in 1993, dead-serious FBI agent Fox Mulder tells viewers, "The truth
is out there" (Genge, 1995, p. xii). Of course, the show is fiction, but

then, much of the pessimism that shrouds the planning profession is based on false perceptions. Michael Brooks (1988), professor of the School of Community and Public Affairs at Virginia Commonwealth University, laments, "The seminal thinkers of the profession are now largely historical figures; few 'heroes' have emerged to replace them" (p. 242). This is not true, according to Eugenie L. Birch, former coeditor of the *Journal of the American Planning Association* and now associate provost at Hunter College. She contends that the conditions and circumstances surrounding the practice of planning have changed dramatically, and that planning is well established as an important government service. The number of planners has grown geometrically. Our new heroes, part of a much larger group, are just not as visible as their predecessors. But though they are less noticeable, argues Birch, they are no less important just because there are more of them. She reasons that while these new heroes may not be so grand or overtly prepossessing as the earlier ones, they are effective and they do deliver significant results (Birch, 1988).

The overwhelming good news is that in the face of almost insurmountable obstacles, many planners have figured out—the hard way, day-by-day, one step at a time—how to become more effective. Obsessed with learning and dedicated to continuous self-improvement, these new heroes of planning have learned from their victories and their mistakes. They have learned that traditional theories and practices do not always work. In response, they have adapted and created new principles and practices with outstanding results. They know, as the saying goes, that "second place is first loser." They quit whining years ago, and they don't rationalize failure. You can almost hear them saying, "We're not good enough! We can do better! We're not there yet!"

In Lewis Carroll's classic, *Alice's Adventures in Wonderland*, Alice too is on a journey. Early in her travels she is confronted with two pathways. When she asks the Cheshire Cat which path to take, he replies that it depends on where she wants to go. Alice says that she does not really care where she is going, and the Cat explains that under those circumstances it does not matter which path she picks. But there is more to the story. Alice asks the Cat for assurance that eventually she will get somewhere. "'Oh, you're sure to do that,' promised the Cat, 'if you only walk long enough'" ([1865] 1985, p. 54).

Like Alice, most of the planners who contributed to this book really did not know where they were going when they began their professional journeys. However, just as in the Cheshire Cat's promise to Alice, by persevering long enough these planners have each arrived somewhere. And the advances in their journeys have advanced the profession. If practitioners have learned anything from their experiences, it is that the planning profession is by nature in constant flux.

Fortunately, they have not had to carry on the fight for change by themselves. Many prominent academics have also recognized the inadequacies and failures of such traditional planning theories as the rational model, and they too have been leading the call for change. Most planning schools have dramatically changed their core curricula and course content since the accreditation process began in the mid 1980s. In recent years, practitioners and educators have joined forces to aggressively embrace change, share ideas and experiences, adapt, and collectively reinvent why and how planning is being practiced. This book is the result of one such collaborative effort.

Peak Performers

The phrase "peak performers" was defined by management guru Charles Garfield (1986) in a book he wrote with that title. A peak performer, he said, is "a kind of everyday hero whom many of us admire: the man or woman who possesses the ability to achieve impressive and satisfying results, not just once or twice but repeatedly, consistently" (p. 15).

As members of the profession, we have much to learn from innovative, peak-performing planners who see change as an opportunity, not a threat, and who have transformed themselves and their organizations. These planners are leading the way to a stronger, more vital, and more effective profession. They welcome change, are excited about the opportunities it brings, and are optimistic about the future. These innovators share the characteristics identified by Denis Waitley and Robert Tucker (1986) in their book *Winning the Innovation Game:* "Innovators are unique hybrids. They have the visionary's ability to look ahead, the inventor's ability to combine and create, and the entrepreneur's ability to sell customers. Above all, innovators have a burning desire to make their ideas manifest in the world. They are not content to imagine the future; they want to create it. Nor are they content to develop prototypes that gather dust on shelves. They want to connect their ideas with a customer group" (p. 30).

Innovative planners are also unique hybrids. Along with the visionary's ability to imagine the future as it could be, they have a burning desire to get plans off the shelf and into the hands of those with the capability to implement them. The chapters in this book, prepared by some of the most innovative and respected peak performers and visionary leaders in the planning profession, reflect these attitudes. The planners we invited to contribute are some of the most visible, successful, and respected frontline practitioners in the profession. These planners—with significant diversity in education, background, and professional experience—have practiced in a great variety of geographic settings. All of them have held high-profile directorships or senior-level management positions in local government and have proven track records of crafting successful planning programs. Almost without exception, they have been actively involved in professional associations and have shown that they possess outstanding leadership ability.

For planners of every persuasion, these chapters offer an opportunity to receive one-on-one advice, guidance, and insight from some of America's most experienced and respected practitioners. No other book offers practitioners, students, and academics the chance to go straight to the source and learn first-hand about the realities of day-to-day practice. Where else can you learn about the core values and philosophical beliefs that have sustained planners or about the key principles, practices, and strategies they have come to rely upon for their success? Using specific and personal real-world examples, these planners tell the reader what works, what doesn't, and why.

Lessons

This book has four parts. Part One focuses on personal success for planners. Norman Whitaker discusses specific strategies and tactics he has used, or has seen others use, to increase effectiveness. He notes that while specialists from other fields may encroach on planner territory, planners can make themselves indispensable to both the public and private sectors by capitalizing on the profession's traditional strengths and by developing new competitive advantages. Sergio Rodriguez follows by urging planners to build on the profession's enduring fundamental principles and strengths, to uphold the trust placed in them, and to become more skilled in public relations. The inability or reluctance of planners to engage in organized public relations efforts is one main reason, he says, why planning receives such low satisfaction ratings from many citizens. Richard Bernhardt then offers his ten personal habits for success. He demonstrates that personal success depends on understanding that continuing education is an essential aspect of professional development and practice. Next, Paul Bergmann outlines five commitments that will enable planners to increase their effectiveness and produce better results. One of his most important commitments is the maintenance of high ethical standards. Jim Reid follows by sharing the lessons he learned from years on the planning battlefield—lessons he did not learn in school. Most significant, he has learned that implementation is not an afterthought of the planning process but rather the ultimate objective. Next, Paul Zucker describes how to become what he calls a "Bravo" planning director—a tenured leader who is a change agent with ideas and, most important, who gets things done. He argues that on-the-job longevity is the unappreciated key to both personal success and professional effectiveness. Keith Cubic concludes Part One by concentrating on the specific skills of organizing and managing for success. In his view, planners cannot be effective unless they have first organized for success, set the stage for the development of trusting relationships, and established a standard of excellence for themselves and their programs.

Part Two focuses on the politics of planning and the importance of planners assuming the roles of facilitator, caring advocate, and consensus builder. Linda Davis starts it off by providing a guide to survival and success when dealing with the politics of planning. She has found that taking things too personally compromises the ability to come up with worthwhile alternatives, leading to a loss of effectiveness. Gene Boles discusses community alignment and empowerment, suggesting that a guiding paradigm of alignment and empowerment gives values and emphasis to notions of diversity, flexibility, teamwork, networking, commitment to results, a sense of community, and collaboration. Norman Krumholz, the guru of the equity planning movement, shares the lessons he learned as planning director of Cleveland and describes the strategies and tactics that should be used by aspiring equity planners. Based on personal experience, he argues that equity planning can be done, that it can produce benefits for poor and working-class city residents, and that planners can do it and survive, even prosper. Finally, Elizabeth Hollander advocates a new vision of public service that assigns planners the critically important role of collaborator responsible for linking citizens with resources. In her view of public service, government agencies must have a clear vision of what they want to accomplish and a work ethic that focuses on outputs, goals, and performance, not on tasks and processes for their own sake.

Part Three concentrates on effectiveness and the principles and values that can make a difference and produce results. Robert Becker discusses the core values and overriding principles and qualities of practice that are essential to effective planning. He urges planners to conserve their personal professional capital, using it sparingly on significant issues rather than exhausting it on lesser matters. John Lewis offers the most important principles and practices for effective visioning and goals-setting. He reminds us that the only time achievement comes before work is in the dictionary. Next, Gail Easley shares her views on the five principles of effective practice in a participatory democracy. These principles are based on her belief that citizens have a right and a responsibility to be both informed and involved in the practice of planning. Angela Harper follows with ideas for creating a toolbox that will enable planners to become more effective. The people skills in her own toolbox include listening, caring, persuading, supervising, counseling, negotiating, facilitating, leading, following, and team building. Marjorie Macris recounts her trailblazing career in a male-dominated environment and offers unique insights on the practice of planning. She has learned that there are no universal right answers for every situation and that people often cannot or will not do what planners think they should be doing anyway.

Part Four emphasizes the importance of developing and integrating such private sector principles and practices as customer service, excellence, and entrepreneurship into local government. Robert Marriott Jr. argues that the keys to effectiveness can be found in teaching, patience, and timing. He believes that patience is the single most important characteristic of effective planners and that in achieving ultimate objectives you must stay focused and constantly rethink how to get there, how to get it done, and how to achieve it. Bruce McClendon explains the six operating principles of effective customer service and how to instill a customer service orientation into day-to-day operations. He contends that the ultimate expression of customer service is to empower customers by involving them in all aspects of the development and delivery of products and services. Next, Ray Quay advocates a philosophy of customer service that emphasizes trusting and allowing citizens to make decisions for themselves. To be more effective, planners must learn to act strategically and with a sense of urgency that meets the timetable of their customers. Floyd Lapp then explains how an entrepreneurial approach to developing and delivering needed and valued products and services can make a difference in professional life. He believes that to ensure continued success, planners must continuously re-create their job tasks and constantly seek new funding sources and new customers. William Bowdy follows by contending that attitude, ethical professional conduct, and positioning oneself to be able to act on opportunities are the three primary determinants of effectiveness. He reckons that the more planners and the general public meet face-to-face, the greater the opportunity for development of the mutual trust that is an essential prerequisite to effective planning. Stuart Meck concludes this part by explaining why and how planning departments differ from other government departments and by suggesting management practices that can help planners get the job done. He calls for managers of planning agencies to recognize and respond to the contemporary pressure to be relevant, to produce results, and to have a "bias for action."

As in any anthology written by a large assemblage of diverse individuals, there are some redundancies and a few conflicting opinions in this book. We consider this a strength, not a weakness. Consistency of views from a diverse group obviously validates and lends collective support to the ideas expressed. But contradictory advice is healthy; it offers alternatives and identifies areas that warrant further analysis, discussion, and debate. Every successful planner has had to search for answers, just as you may be doing right now. What works for one planner may not work for another whose circumstances differ. You must evaluate the information in this book according to your particular situation. Flexibility and creativity are hallmarks of effective planning; we encourage all planners to get out of the box and learn to adapt and innovate for themselves. Will Rogers once quipped, "Even if you are on the right track, you'll still get run over if you are standing still." No one will ever accuse the planners who wrote this book of standing still.

There are many planning heroes and peak performers other than those selected to write this book, but we believe the ones on these pages truly represent the best the profession has to offer. Other planners deserve recognition; we hope that this is just the first in a series of books that will provide increased access to the vast reservoir of useful, pragmatic knowledge accumulated by some of the most effective, successful, and respected practitioners in the country—the peak performers of the planning profession. This book is not offered as the last word but rather as part of the ongoing process of reinventing the field and increasing the effectiveness of planners. This reinvention is a necessary and important step that must be taken as practitioners and academics collaborate to develop reality-based theories for effective planning practice.

Part One

Lessons on Personal Success

Planning is an institution of American life. It is a process with principles, methods, and techniques, and planners lead the process. As leaders, they have beliefs, attributes, and behaviors that usually lead to personal success and the implementation of their plans. It's safe to say that every major planning achievement in history was based upon the personal success of planners.

The authors of the seven chapters in this part of the book suggest dozens of ways you can be a successful and effective planner, even in an era where, it seems, few people trust government employees. They demand that you use your most powerful personal tools, including imagination and will, to accomplish many things: build trust and credibility, plan for change, empower communities, commit to innovation, focus on implementation—all these and more, and all within a strict ethical framework.

Chapter One

Pursuing Effectiveness and Personal Success in the Next Era

Norman Whitaker

Once or twice a year, I am confronted with a particularly scary situation: giving someone, usually an idealistic young person, advice on whether to become a city planner. I have found planning to be rewarding, interesting, and fun, but I've definitely concluded that it is not for everyone. Usually I tell prospective planners that they should consider entering the profession only if they are willing to make a commitment to an unpredictable, demanding career that is not especially well paid. I also explain that there is no real need for merely adequate planners—that they must be either exceptionally talented or exceptionally persistent to make a difference. On the bright side, I suggest that those who are willing to work hard and learn from success and failure can be rewarded with careers that are rarely boring and often present opportunities to contribute, in big ways and small, to a better future for the communities in which they work.

The first time I remember hearing about city planning was around 1960, when I read a newspaper article about a comprehensive plan for Port Arthur, Texas. I was nine years old and did not know what a comprehensive plan was. It fascinated me that there were people who had somehow figured out what Port Arthur would be like in 1980 (bigger! better!) and that they got paid for seeing into the future and coloring maps. Seventeen years later, I too was getting paid for coloring maps, although I never quite got the hang of seeing into the future. By the early 1980s, I'd had enough exposure to the ups and downs of planning to find myself in the early stages of burnout.

Around this time, a couple of sessions at an American Planning Association conference in Dallas helped me. One of the sessions focused on alternate careers for planners. Judging by the overflow crowd, there was lots of interest. But the two speakers, who had escaped from the dead-end grind of public sector planning, had also become two of the most humorless, depressed people I've ever seen. One of them worked exclusively concocting rows and columns of numbers to try to get real estate loans. He was kind of like an accountant, but less charismatic. The other had apparently landed a position that involved firing a lot of people. He'd walk up to them and say, "You're not working out. It's time for you to leave." They'd say, "Do you want me to work out two weeks notice?" "No," he'd reply, "I want you to leave today—right now." I left that session with a renewed appreciation for my job, which at the time involved everything from developing comprehensive plans to preparing Urban Development Action Grant applications to taking phone calls from interesting people with questions like "Someone is digging a hole on my property; what are you going to do about it?"

At the same conference, I heard a truly inspirational speech by the late Stephen Bollinger, the federal Department of Housing and Urban Development's assistant secretary for community planning and development. There had been a few other Reagan administration speakers on the conference program, and their comments had ranged from condescending to threatening. Bollinger was different. Speaking to the planners in the audience who were dispirited by cutbacks in federal urban programs, he challenged us individually. "Think back to your original decision to become a planner," he said. "What were your ideals? What were you hoping to accomplish? You should renew your faith in those original ideals and hopes. Rely on your own commitment, your own ideals, your own talents and energies to make your community a better place." Bollinger recognized that changes in the federal budget being proposed at the time were threatening to many planners, but suggested that the profession would probably be better off with less reliance on federal grants. And he was right. Within a few years, planners were spending more time solving local problems and less time dancing at the end of the strings attached to federal categorical grants.

Periodically, I think back to Stephen Bollinger's challenge to remember my original idealistic motivations for becoming a planner. In my case, city planning seemed like a profession that was both creative and socially useful. I was particularly interested in the physical and economic development of cities and neighborhoods and in the protection of coastal environments.

At this point in my career, I know that the planner's opportunities to make a difference are very real. Early on, I didn't understand that the process of building better communities is extremely incremental, or that planners, though important to the process, are seldom central to it. But when it involves a wide spectrum of community interests and is pursued with creativity and confidence, the planning process actually works.

The Next New Era

Planning is a profession that always seems to be entering a new era. At least since I began studying the field in the mid 1970s, planners have been talking about preparing for the twenty-first century. Now, whether we're prepared or not, it's almost here. And as I write this in 1996, we really are entering a new era in planning. As the century winds down, some powerful trends are obvious:

- Citizens are fed up with centralized government, at least on the federal level; people clearly want more control over governmental affairs at the local level.
- Citizens want more services and more responsive government but want to pay less for them.
- Courts are no longer willing to presume that local land use decisions are automatically valid. The 1994 *Dolan* v. *City of Tigard* decision has brought an element of uncertainty into some of the most routine aspects of land development regulation.
- Electronic communication promises to replace some of the need for travel for business, entertainment, shopping, and education, giving businesses greater latitude in choosing locations.

- Some planning methods and concepts that guided development in the second half of this century are being called into
  question by responsible people concerned about the unin-
  tended effects of such development.

These trends mean simply that there will be both opportunities
and risks for planners in the new era. Risks include declining effectiveness as access diminishes to major implementation tools such as
land use regulations and capital improvement funds; fewer job
opportunities as financially stressed governments hire fewer staff
members and consultants; stagnation of the profession as a large
supply of aging baby boomers preempts opportunities to bring new
blood into the profession; and loss of a clear professional identity
as other professions encroach on the planner's turf.

More optimistically, the new era may allow the planning profession to expand on some of its traditional strengths: an interdisciplinary approach, the dual focus on long-range thinking and
short-range action, the ability to analyze complex problems and
propose pragmatic alternative solutions, a tradition of working with
a diverse range of interest groups to develop consensus solutions,
and access to public decision-making processes that influence the
quality of our communities.

This chapter looks at the effectiveness of planning from two
perspectives: that of the planning organization, whether a government agency or a private firm, and that of the individual planner.
I outline strategies and tactics that have worked for me, and those
of other practicing planners who have influenced my approach to
planning.

What Is Effective Planning?

Effective planning produces results that meet important needs of
communities, constituencies, or other clients. It often takes years
to evaluate the effectiveness of planning, and that which is initially
well received may later prove to have been ineffective. Because
planning that advances one interest group's objectives may be damaging to another's, individual planners must weigh the ethical
implications of their planning recommendations and actions.
Without compromising their personal or professional ethics, they

must respond to complex challenges by anticipating at least some of their client's most important needs before the needs become serious problems, be sensitive to politics without allowing their recommendations to be unduly influenced by politics, and maintain the capacity to learn and prepare for new challenges throughout their careers.

What Should Planners Be Doing?

What unique services can you, the planner, offer clients? Mapping can be done by anyone with access to, and technical knowledge of, a geographic information system (GIS) or desktop mapping setup. Many variations on visioning and the nominal group technique are being used in creating strategic plans—some good, some bad—by professional trainers, management consultants, and community organizers. Architects using charrette techniques are doing very effective planning for developments ranging from themed subdivisions to new communities. Environmental engineers command significantly higher salaries than environmental planners. Are planners in danger of losing all their turf? I don't think so.

Although other specialists may encroach on their territory, planners can make themselves indispensable to the public and private sectors by capitalizing on the profession's traditional strengths and developing some new competitive advantages. I suggest the following roles and strategies for planning organizations as well as individual practitioners:

- Focus on the relationships between population, economics, public facilities and land development.
- Work on three levels: long-range (conceptual), mid-range (specific), and short-range (implementation). Think on these levels and present recommendations to clients based on them, whether the project is a regional comprehensive plan or a site plan for a single infill housing unit. Make sure you know what implementation tools will be needed and available very early in the planning process. This will sharpen the focus of the plan, even at the long-range (conceptual) level.
- Look beyond the two-dimensional, schematic view of your proposals. Get urban designers, architects, landscape architects,

or graphic artists involved in your projects to show the implications of your ideas in three dimensions.

- Look at development proposals in their larger contexts—block face, neighborhood, city, region—to make sure they relate logically in terms of aesthetics, traffic, economics, markets, utilities, and environmental factors. The ability to visualize large or small plans in their various contexts and evaluate them on several scales is a powerful skill possessed by the best planners.
- Embody seemingly contradictory personal traits. Successful planners are pragmatic but visionary, assertive but sensitive, focused on the big picture but also the fine details, self-confident but humble, action-oriented but reflective.
- Capitalize on your generalist knowledge of the whole urban system. Being able to visualize whole neighborhoods, cities, and regions and their component infrastructures, natural and built environments, and socioeconomic fabrics makes planners key players.
- Continually rethink, reinvent, adapt, and synthesize what you know about planning principles, concepts, and techniques. Every successful planner and planning organization tries to redefine the state of the art with each new project. There is currently an explosion of new thinking in planning and a growing rejection of the conventional wisdom of the last few decades.

Strategies for Effective Planning Agencies

Much of this section may appear aimed at planning directors or administrators, but all planners contribute to the effective management and strategic planning of their agencies or firms. The following sections contain suggestions for increasing organizational effectiveness.

Minimize Layers

Many governmental and business structures of today were adopted from hierarchical and organizational models developed long ago by the military. But, as anyone knows who has been observing the effects of economically driven downsizing in the private and (more recently) public sectors, "flat" organizations are now in favor. Advances in office automation and computer-aided manufacturing have contributed to the flattening of hierarchies by broadening the span of control—that is, increasing the number of employees one supervisor can oversee effectively. Having too many hierarchical layers in an organization drains creative energy and reduces the number of people available to provide services to clients. Reassigning middle managers to the front lines is the equivalent of putting more police officers on the street by taking them out from behind desks. Once organizations have been flattened, old hierarchical channels of employee advancement should be replaced by new ones based on employee performance.

Have People Own Projects, Not Functions

Computer Associates (CA), a software company, is definitely not afraid of innovation. CA has launched bold, seemingly crazy initiatives, such as giving away software, confident that they'll make money by selling upgrades to users who become hooked on the free programs. In *21st Century Management,* Hesh Kestin (1992) outlines some of the organizational management philosophy of Charles Wang, CA's founder, who says the company's success is simply due to good people. "Succeed or 'bye" is an important part of the organizational ethos. Wang believes in continuous reorganization. People are given ownership of projects, not functions, and their level of performance is considered to be the same as their last project's level of success. This is what Tom Peters, in *Liberation Management* (1992), calls "projectizing" the organization. Good people are given as much responsibility as they can handle without much regard to their professional credentials. Wang also believes in creating open pathways to advancement for high achievers, regardless of job title or credentials.

Applying these principles to a planning organization promotes continuing professional development for both novice and veteran planners. Instead of a given function's being the acknowledged turf of a long-tenured section head, an idealized planning organization would consist of teams that are restructured for each new project. This also promotes rapid and continual professional development.

Elevate the Status of the Practicing Planner

I once saw a high-paying planning job in the Seattle area advertised as having no supervisory duties. The planner would be responsible for developing policies and strategies. The ad also stated that the successful candidate would have to be comfortable producing innovative, high-quality results under totally unreasonable deadlines. Aside from its honesty, the ad was unusual because it reflected an understanding that the best planners may not be the best managers, and vice versa.

Advancement to high levels in a planning organization has usually been tied to supervisory duties. With middle management becoming an endangered species, what will the planning agency of the future offer high achievers to entice them to stay? One thing, at least: a career path for excellent nonsupervisory planners that ensures recognition and good salaries.

Have a Few Good Supervisors

Most planners learn supervisory and management skills on the job, so their training in this area may be hit and miss at best. Thus, rewarding star performers by promoting them into supervisory roles may not be the best move. Not only are the best and brightest planners not always cut out for management, but pushing productive planners into supervisory jobs may diminish the available pool of creative talent.

Accumulate Diverse Talents

City planning is highly interdisciplinary, benefiting from the inclusion of people with a wide range of talents. The medium-size staff of my agency, the Knoxville–Knox County Metropolitan Planning Commission, includes planners with social science backgrounds; planners with architectural design backgrounds; a traffic engineer; transportation planners; GIS specialists with backgrounds in geography; graphic artists; an accountant who serves as budget and personnel officer and also maintains our computer network; a librarian who also manages demographic data, development trends studies, and desktop mapping; and other specialists in communications and historic preservation. A landscape architect is on our shopping list. We round out our talent pool by hiring interns with exotic skills such as traffic modeling and database design.

Even in small organizations, adding a few nonplanners with special skills broadens the scope of work you can tackle and results in better planning products. It's especially important to have someone with physical design skills.

If plans are to have meaningful impact, it's also necessary to look beyond the organization to businesspeople and any other citizens interested in the process. Of these, some may have specialized talents not available on your staff. Many more will have knowledge of the community and its people that will improve plan effectiveness.

Practice Continuous Improvement

Total quality management (TQM) is a system of empowering workers, reducing mistakes, and quantifying achievement. Developed by Dr. Edwards Deming, an American, TQM caught on first in Japan and is often credited as a major force behind Japan's ascendancy as a modern industrial power. TQM programs are now commonplace in American business and industry.

TQM is also being used by many local governments, with mixed results and disagreements about its effectiveness. The process was originally designed for manufacturing, where errors and deviations from quality standards are easy to quantify. But government provides services, not products, including services such as long-range planning that are not very tangible. Another difficulty with adapting TQM to government is the level of commitment required from everyone involved. Training needs are very substantial and it may take years for the TQM process to become fully operational. Before then, the effort may be abandoned with a change in administrations or budgetary priorities.

If TQM has been embraced where you work, you should obviously commit to its success. If not, there is a simpler alternative. Instead of the formal TQM process, focus on creating a culture of continuous improvement in your organization. To do this, each individual and work group must internalize and act on the idea that each employee is personally responsible for finding ways to improve quality and efficiency, meet customer needs, and eliminate waste. Managers in particular must learn to create a work environment that nurtures and amplifies the positive, creative energy of workers. *Zapp! The Lightning of Empowerment* by William C. Byham and Jeff Cox (1988) is a good tool for explaining and instilling continuous improvement concepts without the technical framework of TQM.

Downplay the Professional–Support Staff Dichotomy

I've stopped referring to my coworkers as "professional staff" or "support staff." Calling themselves professionals is a point of pride with most planners, and that's certainly not something to be discouraged. I have found, however, that many technicians, graphic artists, and word processors consider themselves professionals because they are specially trained, set high standards, and take pride in their professional attitudes. Nothing positive is accomplished by labeling these key players as anything less than full partners in realizing the organizational mission.

Teach Everyone to Be a Project Manager

Obviously, everyone in your office needs to be able to work as part of a team. I believe that everyone in the office also needs to be able to be a team leader at one time or another. Aside from developing project management skills, leading a team builds confidence and stretches capabilities. Having a long roster of potential project coordinators also gives managers more flexibility in delegating assignments.

Assign "Whole People" to Critical Projects

Planners must be capable of taking on multiple projects with overlapping deadlines. Experienced planners will tell you that crazy workloads go with the territory. It is not unusual for one planner to be assigned five, ten, or more special projects, plans, or parts of projects at once. When, as an overburdened midlevel planner, I questioned the wisdom of this setup, I was told that to think of it as "advancing on a broad front." Managers sometimes get too comfortable with this idea, especially in the public sector. An alternative is to reorganize the workload so that planners can concentrate exclusively on completing one or two projects at a time.

Recently, my agency struggled for a year with an ambitious public-access desktop mapping system, with unsatisfactory results. The project was funded by a nonprofit foundation grant; failure would have been very embarrassing. We finally got a handle on it by making it the only responsibility of one capable intern. She was assigned to experiment with the software for a couple of weeks and then get on with the work program. Within a few months, we had met all the terms of our grant agreement and had also learned how to use the mapping system to streamline our sector planning process. If you really want a project to succeed, put it in the hands of someone who arrives at the office each morning with only that project to worry about.

Use Quarterly Reporting

I use a "quarterly objectives" reporting cycle to review progress on work programs. Three months is long enough to measure progress on major projects and to completely knock off numerous smaller ones. As much as possible, I allow division heads or project teams to set specific start and finish dates once we've agreed on which quarter a project is to be completed.

Offer Apprenticeships

Apprentices "learn by doing" under the tutelage of a seasoned practitioner. According to current research on organizational learning, apprenticeship is the most effective technique for developing and retaining expertise. When new, inexperienced employees first arrive, they should meet everyone, read the personnel handbook, and study the zoning ordinance. Then, to develop good work habits and an action orientation, they should be assigned a real project immediately.

Veteran planners can benefit tremendously from "reverse apprenticeships"—working relationships with colleagues who may have less experience but more idealism, up-to-date computer expertise, and more recent academic exposure to planning theory and quantitative methods.

View the Entire Process from Start to Finish

Analyzing the ways your organization creates its major products— whether neighborhood plans, site development proposals, market studies, or zoning reports—can help identify needed changes. I've found more than once that no single person in my organization understood a particular process from start to finish. Enter the flowchart. Try diagraming a work process on a roll of butcher paper.

With all staff members involved in the process present, use a black marker to chart each step in the process in sequence. Use a purple marker to jot down particular problems or complications that occur, and where in the process they occur. The resulting annotated flowchart will probably be pretty chaotic. Next, redraw the chart with improvements in the sequence of events, elimination of redundant steps, and consolidation of related tasks. Develop action strategies to address the problems that were marked in purple. You may have to go through several iterations of this process with your team. When you're finished, you will have an improved process, well documented so all concerned know where their efforts fit into the overall picture. You will also have an action plan for making further quality improvements.

Personalized Strategies for Effective Planners

Although planners spend most of their time working as team members, the ultimate responsibility for professional excellence and professional growth falls on the planner as an individual.

Never Stop Learning

A planner's education can be divided into two phases. Phase one ends with graduation from planning school. Phase two ends with retirement. A planner who stops learning has effectively dropped out of the profession, even if still employed. Unless you are a narrowly focused specialist (not advisable in today's job market), you need to keep abreast of developments in a wide variety of fields, including economics; technology, particularly transportation, computers and electronic communications; real estate; politics from the local to international levels; organizational management; and social and environmental sciences.

Reinvent Yourself

As an individual, you are unlikely to transform your community, reinvent government, or change the world. One revolutionary act you can perform, however, is to reinvent yourself as a planner. After five or ten or more years of professional practice, consider that *everything you know may be wrong!* Sure, you've acquired street smarts and have learned the way your organization does things, but have you kept up with the state of the art in planning theory and practice? Are you doing anything to advance the state of the art?

Tom Peters, author of *In Search of Excellence, Liberation Management,* and *The Peters Seminar,* suggests that the fundamental facts and assumptions underlying the culture of business organization become obsolete every five or six years. In business, hanging on to yesterday's conventional wisdom buys you a first class ticket on the S.S. *Extinction.* The negative feedback may not come as quickly for planners in public agencies, and this is truly dangerous. Here are some of the warning signs that your skills and knowledge have outlived their shelf lives:

- You consider yourself an expert.
- You are confident that you have reached the pinnacle of your career.
- You think you have "seen it all."
- You pass up chances for professional development seminars because the material is too elementary.
- You are amused by the naivete of the ideas of neighborhood advocates and businesspeople who disagree with you.

Deliberately not included above are: occasionally feeling foolish in public; losing on an important issue and feeling temporarily discouraged; having to admit you were wrong; questioning the wisdom of your decision to join the planning profession; finding that you've overcommitted yourself; and realizing you could be replaced, at a cost savings, by any number of planners eager to prove themselves. These indicate, in a way, a healthy engagement in the real world of community decision making. If you are not periodically ticked off, discouraged, and overloaded, you have found a way to insulate yourself from the real action.

To start reinventing yourself as a planner, try the following:

- Ask some of your customers how you're doing and, in particular, what you can do to improve.
- Attend the American Institute of Certified Planners' annual Planning and Zoning Institute or other "skill renewal" programs.
- If you're usually a manager, get involved as a team member on a project managed by someone else.

- Ask yourself, as mentioned earlier, why you originally picked planning as your career. How true have you remained to your original ideals? Has your experience made you more effective or more cynical? If you can rekindle your idealism and combine it with what you have learned from years of professional practice, you will be happier and more effective.
- Learn new skills, whether or not they are currently required by your job. Some examples: computer-aided design, a foreign language, fundamentals of building codes.
- Make a list of planning innovations that you consider "mega-concepts." My list would include Victor Gruen's vision of the enclosed shopping mall or community center, Clarence Stein's neighborhood unit concept, and the Andres Dauan–Elizabeth Plater-Zybeck collaboration that produced neotraditional town planning and stimulated the new urbanism movement. After you've made your list, try to develop your own mega-concept as your contribution to your profession.

Use Your Most Powerful Tools: Imagination and Will

Creativity and the will to succeed can take you a long way. Among the best planners, professional growth has to do with developing these two commodities. I've known some planners who seem to have been strong-willed, creative dynamos from birth, but most of us have to work at learning to trust our imagination and exercising our determination. While it's essential for planners to know how to collect and analyze data, to understand the planning process, and to have a good grasp of planning principles and concepts, none of these guarantees good planning without the addition of imagination and will.

Imagination, to the planner, means being able to synthesize themes out of reams of research data and citizen input; to adapt proven planning methods to the local situation, or better yet to devise new solutions that redefine the state of the art; to provide creative leadership as a member of a multidisciplinary team (or an undisciplined mob) of planners, related professionals, and citizens; and to set aside one's ego and let the best ideas, mostly someone else's, emerge from the process. I didn't begin to fully appreciate my job as a planner until I realized that I was getting paid to use my imagination.

Will, to the planner, is the self-discipline and resolve to get the work done in spite of inadequate staffing, unreasonable bosses, citizens who have been disappointed by previous planning, and the multitude of other forces that make it seem like the project will fail. Sometimes it's much easier to find people who'll tell you why your project is doomed than to find encouragement or constructive advice.

A few other quick suggestions:

- Make yourself indispensable.
- Don't make excuses.
- Set high standards for yourself.
- Don't let anyone push you around.
- Be a team player.
- Care about your community and its people.
- Don't try to impose your own values on your community.
- Put something back into your profession.
- Don't pull your punches. Make the best recommendations you can.

This much is certain: effective urban and regional planning will be more important than ever in the twenty-first century. Planners will be dealing with more complicated issues, have more limited financial resources and regulatory tools to work with, and be held more accountable. The most successful planners and planning organizations will respond to these challenges quickly, creatively, and efficiently.

Chapter Two

How to Become a Successful Planner

Sergio Rodriguez

Many planners could claim that they entered the planning profession after considering all the alternative career paths and carefully deliberating what they really wanted to do with the rest of their lives. Not me! I did it almost by accident.

In my senior year studying architecture at the University of Florida, I was offered several scholarships to continue my education. At that point I decided to get a master's degree so that I could have the option of becoming a teacher in case the construction industry went into a slump.

I chose planning because I thought that it was a logical extension of architecture, more like the urban design courses I was taking at the time. I chose the University of North Carolina at Chapel Hill because it offered me the best scholarship. That was very important to me then, because I was a foreign student with a wife, two children, and no income.

Though I knew UNC had a good reputation, I was truly surprised when I met my classmates at Chapel Hill. Many came from Ivy League schools, were extremely intelligent, and spoke and wrote *English*. And my professors: they seemed committed to planning and their enthusiasm was contagious.

It is difficult for me to pinpoint when exactly I became hooked on planning, but I believe it was in my first year of graduate school—for sure no later than my internship in Norfolk, Virginia, under Phil Stedfast. I was extremely lucky to be there during the beginning of the Model Cities efforts, just after the 1968 riots; I had a great desire to serve the people, especially the needy people of the areas assigned to me. Perhaps my interest in planning actually started in Cuba, when I was 16 and worked in two Havana slums, and could be fulfilled by working in the profession here.

My career path has not always matched my interest in working directly with the needy. Throughout the years, as I have climbed the professional ladder, I have gotten closer to paper shuffling, meetings, administration, and politics. Still, in my innermost self, my desire is to fulfill my vocation and have a full and complete marriage of my volunteer work and my profession. When I daydream of an early retirement, after fulfilling my family obligations, I imagine utilizing my planning and design skills in working directly with the needy, helping them to empower themselves and build a better future in their immediate environment, without big fancy plans. It's only a daydream because this imagined future holds no board meetings or politics, just direct work with my clients, those that I am interested in serving. But the real world is different.

Today's planners are faced with a fast-changing environment. As we approach the twenty-first century, boundaries are shifting continuously. Technology advances speedily, steadied only slightly by the ability of users to absorb it. World events are communicated to us almost immediately. Locally, that gives us a raised consciousness of what is happening elsewhere and a basis to evaluate what we possess compared to others. Sometimes this leads to dissatisfaction and an aspiration for instant improvements. It also creates a desire among some people to get together with others of their same "type," partly as a defense mechanism. Often these groups, gathering to defend what they believe are their rights, demand immediate attention to their most important needs without much consideration to the needs of others. Within a framework of the breakdown of traditional ethical and moral values, and a growing disillusionment with politics, politicians, and the public sector in general, this all translates into an antigovernment mood. And planners working for the government are in the middle of it.

How can a profession that has attracted people who have high ideals and want to serve the common good best function within this environment? How can planners in this ever-changing, tense, diverse, even hostile environment exert leadership, given the tools and power at their disposal? Are not "planning" and "immediate solutions" at totally opposite ends of the spectrum?

Strengths of the Profession

In spite of change, some principles remain the same, and planners can draw from them in trying to deal with today's problems while adopting new approaches to cope with a fast-moving world. The following are two good bases for planners to work from.

Planners Are the Best Comprehensive Thinkers in Government Today

I believe no other group of professionals in government today is as well trained as planners to think comprehensively, to synthesize complex problems, and to arrive at clear solutions while taking into account their short- and long-range effects. Planners can consider the needs of many individuals and groups, translating them so they are understood by both policy makers and the people that will be affected by planning decisions. And planners have access to high-level decision makers, enabling them to do good things for the community.

Even today, some twenty-five years after I graduated from Chapel Hill, I credit my planning education for the ability to think in a particular way and approach problems in a particular fashion. It has been the sturdy foundation on which I have built a personal style that suits my professional needs within the framework of my Judeo-Christian values and my total persona.

Planners Need to Know Their Strengths and Weaknesses

Without this knowledge, strengths can't be used nor weaknesses compensated for. Obviously, though the profession requires training in a wide range of disciplines and demands excellence in both written and spoken communication, not everybody can be well rounded and outstanding in all areas. But planners need to keep abreast of the field in general, and stay knowledgeable enough in their areas of expertise to command respect from peers and other professionals while doing a decent job in selling their recommendations to clients.

I have found that the use of graphics has helped me compensate for my shortcomings in communicating my ideas. I have also found that my accent, though discomforting to some listeners as I start presentations, can actually help on the whole because it forces my audience to pay more attention. I think my sense of humor and personality help a lot in selling my ideas. I use my strengths and weaknesses to get my points across, to sell my "planning products."

Advice and Guidance

To do a good job in addressing today's problems, planners should consider the following points.

Planners Need to Uphold the Trust Placed in Them

Being trustworthy requires that one is first true to oneself. Planners are sometimes expected to be all things to all people, and that is of course impossible. But this does not preclude using their leadership to try to address the needs of all people toward whom they are responsible, from the poorest to the richest.

To accomplish this, planners do not need to be chameleons, or square pegs trying to fit round holes; but they must put themselves in other people's positions to understand other points of view, and then reflect those views in their planning efforts. This is quite difficult in today's diverse world, with each group comparing itself with, and pulling in its own direction without regard for, the others.

Typical of today's diverse and sometimes hostile society, and most specifically of cities like Miami, are decisions that must be made between two competing views of what is "good"; these are the most morally conflicting decisions for me. I often ask myself which position I should support in, for example, the location of a facility for the homeless. Should I prefer placing it where it will actually best help these "most needy of the needy," or should I take the side of the poor minority neighborhood, where the facility might be placed simply because of wealthier neighborhoods' NIMBY ("not in my backyard") sentiments? The temptation for some professionals is to cut ethical corners and sacrifice principles for the sake of expediency and to gain acceptance by at least one of the affected client groups. But there is no excuse for sacrificing one's ethical principles, whatever they might be.

· The best-sounding plan, even if it genuinely provides the best service to the most needy group, is no good at all if planners must violate their basic ethics to implement it. More than ever in these times of moral relativism, ends do not always justify means. Planners need to continuously question themselves about whether the day-to-day decisions they make fit snugly within the framework of what they consider to be *right*.

Planners Need to Remain Flexible in Their Use of Planning Tools

Too often, planners will hang on to a comprehensive plan as if it has Biblical status that only they can interpret, and use it as the "tool to plan"—that is, as the way to control or manage development. While I believe master plans have played an important role in guiding the growth of our cities and in protecting our environment, they have also been placed in an inflexible role that has created a backlash.

Comprehensive plans are important. They force planning staff and other public officials to think broadly about the city (or other area of responsibility) and its needs. They also take into account what the people who will be most affected by planning proposals say is really important to them. But the most important part of the comprehensive plan is the process—the exchange—not the document itself. It's the process that causes people in the community to focus, at least for a limited time, on what is really important to them.

Planners Need to Be Pragmatic

I believe that a lot of the really powerful planning done by agencies today is in the form of everyday decisions. These might not be "sexy," earthshaking, or important-looking, but the cumulative effect of a myriad of minor good decisions is significant, long-lasting improvements for the community. For the most part, such small decisions are made without political interference, following norms that have been the result of a comprehensive planning process.

I usually remind my staff of several points whenever we take a particularly painful loss during a hearing with the city commission. First, politicians are elected to make policy decisions; we planners are hired to give the best possible recommendations. They have one role, we have another; they operate in one time frame, we operate in another. Second, the planner's strength rests in the staff's staying power. Third, planners have to choose their battles. From time to time I ask myself if today's fight is the one over which I might choose to be fired. Fourth, it's okay to lose battles if we win the war. We have everyday minor wins, which are also important, as well as some good and difficult big battles under our belt. We are not there for the one short deal, but for the long run.

Planners Have to Deal with Politics

Planning, especially public planning, and politics are intrinsically intertwined. Sometimes, planners (myself included) twitch when the word *politics* is used in relation to public actions. The existing antigovernment mood in this country, the scandals by some politicians, and the failure of the political process to effectively deal with some of the issues important to the public have made the word "political" synonymous with "bad" and "corruption." But all planning-related laws—actually all laws and all public planning—are affected and effected by politicians. We, as planners, need to have the political savvy to use the system and work with politicians, without violating our principles, to benefit the people we serve—a difficult task indeed.

I remember my first year as planning director for the City of Miami, during which the planning department made zoning recommendations for individual petitions that were ignored by the city commission most of the time. Today, we get support for our positions most of the time. What has changed? First, we gradually changed the zoning laws to increase the number of cases requiring administrative approvals only (with notification to affected parties and possible appeals to the city commission). This eliminated unnecessary hearings before the commission, for which the members are grateful. Second, we now require that all controversial zoning cases have hearings before the city commission, but only *after* hearings with the planning advisory board or the zoning board. These early hearings, in turn, are preceded by extensive meetings with the applicants and the opposing parties; in some cases, we act in these early stages to broker a solution that supports our position as planners as well as the positions of the citizens we represent.

We have tried to achieve all this while being realistic about the possibilities of a "political" approval—one that makes no concessions to opponents. That can happen if our efforts to compromise are pushed too far. And we always keep in mind that we can accomplish little if we betray the trust that all parties have placed in us.

As the years have passed, I believe we have developed a reputation that the advice we give is reasonable, untainted by "bad" politics, and shaped by our best technical and political knowledge. All parties know that we don't play games. And at the end, if we have achieved a "win-win" situation, we leave the spotlight for the politicians and move on to the next job, always in the background.

Planners Need to Become Public Relations Experts

Public sector planners are no different than other professionals who need to sell their products. (How well planning consultants know this!) But somehow, many public sector planners still think that they need only to prepare their plans as best they can and then wait for approval at hearings in which citizens will only nominally participate. This old mentality, maybe the product of a formerly protected civil service status, now often fails.

In today's world, planning efforts many times start in the chambers of commerce where planners must rub elbows with the powerful, the "shakers," the decision makers, to gather support for funding even before plans are started. In a city as diverse as Miami, this means not only networking with the chamber types, but joining civic groups, serving on boards such as that of the American Red Cross, attending builders' banquets, participating in professional organizations, and meeting with church groups. In other words, working with the white, black, and Latin power brokers—and even with the powerless people of all backgrounds. Planners need to be everywhere, be known, be able to sell themselves as representatives of a planning product.

As good public relations professionals they should take advantage of good economic and budgetary times to prepare fancy documents to sell their products, and go after awards that can boost staff morale. In lean times they need to choose carefully a few major projects that can be done to professional standards, keeping the reputations of their departments untarnished.

Planning for Change

Planners today have to deal with tension, diversity, and an incredible rate of change. The world is moving fast; we find out instantly what is happening around us. Such speed creates a tremendous amount of tension, but planners nevertheless need to address changes as fast as they occur. Waiting for problems to settle down or for solutions to be perfected simply allows others to intercede, and they may be less equipped than planners to handle things, perhaps providing instant and politically expedient solutions that are neither comprehensive nor considerate of long-range consequences. The image projected by planning professionals should not be the frequent misrepresentation of "planners as dreamers," but one of good thinkers capable of delivering good products in a timely fashion.

Many cities have seen great change in the last thirty years; certainly in Miami the changes have been drastic. From a sleepy, southern, mostly Anglo town in the 1950s, it has evolved into a thriving cosmopolitan metropolis with a majority population derived from every country in Latin America and large groups of Anglos, African Americans, and Haitians. It is a population of extremes, of the very rich and the very poor, not unlike Third World countries. It is a city of Anglo outmigration to north Florida, followed by Cuban migration to the suburbs, followed later by young affluent Cuban migration to other cities and other counties. It is a city that has undergone so many political changes in such a short time that tension is an almost accepted ingredient in local politics.

If we planners limit ourselves in cities like Miami to tried-and-true planning approaches, we will fail. Instead there must be dialogue so we can hear what new clients are telling us as we keep listening to old clients; we need them all to build our city. We cannot afford most times the typical long-range approaches often required by state planning legislation for places as different as Appalachicola and Hialeah in Florida. On many occasions, the use of charrettes (another version of a short-range planning approach co-opted by members of our sister discipline, architecture) might be the most appropriate planning method. What might work in blue-collar Little Havana might not be acceptable in high-income Brickell or for newly arrived immigrants in Little Haiti. A zoning requirement that limits signage in commercial areas might be impossible to implement in most permissive Latin neighborhoods but might not be restrictive enough to please the residents of Coconut Grove, where the phrase "professional citizen" was probably coined. In some areas, pieces of a neighborhood may need to be reclaimed to establish oases of law enforcement, code enforcement, new business, and affordable housing; in higher-income areas, the problem may be to find solutions to preserve historic districts and obtain citizen support. Planners need to be instruments of adjustment and representation in the creation of the crazy quilts we call cities today.

Planners, in short, must now be trustworthy, flexible, pragmatic, politically smart, cognizant of their strengths and weaknesses, able in public relations, and capable of adjusting to fast change and adverse environments. They have the tools required to do the job, provided by their training; they only have to look within themselves and find the approach best fitted to their beliefs and styles.

Chapter Three

The Ten Habits of Highly Effective Planners

Richard C. Bernhardt

As a boy growing up in the South, I found hunting and baseball much more interesting than changes in our town. However, I developed an early fascination with buildings and cities. The more I wandered around Nashville, Atlanta, and other cities, the more I realized how the built environment and urban design could influence how we function.

At fourteen, I was sure that cities were simply collections of buildings and that the way to understand cities was to design buildings. Architecture became my entree into the field of urban design. Later I decided I wanted to study city planning even though I had no real understanding of what it involved. To me city planning was simply urban design; I had little appreciation or understanding for the relationship between places and people or between the natural and built environments. To this day, I believe that we are influenced significantly by the character of the places where we live.

Growing up in the 1960s, I was exposed to and challenged by a number of emerging issues. Urban renewal, environmentalism, growing citizen involvement, increased ease of travel, the birth of the information age, and instant communication were just a few of the factors that influenced me. In choosing a college, I simply assumed that the study of architecture was the prerequisite for a career in planning. After finally investigating the background necessary for entry into the profession during my second year in architecture, I transferred into liberal arts. With my early architecture training providing a basic design framework, I graduated with a degree in economics and minors in political science and sociology. Exposure to these fields gave me an understanding of the interplay between the physical, political, social, and economic forces that shape community.

My early professional training came in 1970–1972, working for the Metropolitan Planning Commission (MPC) in Nashville, Tennessee, under the guidance of Bob Paslay. He was a member of the American Institute of Planners Board of Directors during 1973–1976, and his influence was significant. The commitment of the MPC to totally professional work set a very high standard that I carry to this day. However, the inability to implement our planning products in a way that improved the community convinced me that there had to be a better way to approach the process.

In selecting a graduate school, I was faced with a choice that would mold my planning philosophy. Having worked in a planning agency for a couple of years, I had begun to realize what was important to be successful. Planning schools at the time were undergoing considerable turmoil. Curricula were changing. Physical design courses were being replaced by social and environmental classes. The increased availability of computers had many schools believing that technology was the answer to the issues facing our cities. Only now is the education planners receive becoming balanced, recognizing the importance of physical factors alongside social and economic forces.

I was fortunate to have chosen Ohio State University for my graduate study. OSU's planning program was led at that time by Professors Larry Gerckens and Jerry Vos, the former a member of the American Institute of Planners Board of Directors during 1973–1976. Their leadership combination was critical. My OSU education emphasized several important areas. It had a strong design element along with an almost technical-school emphasis on the practical tools and techniques of planning. Included was an emerging theoretical component designed to challenge students to focus their thinking between and among issues. Finally, the program provided a solid understanding of the historical context of planning, cities, and society; very few programs provide planners with the knowledge and awareness of our historical context. Without that understanding, planners are destined to repeat the mistakes of the past.

To guide my practice, I developed a personal mission statement. This statement is important in maintaining my focus. My mission as a planner is to utilize my training, skill, experience, and position to create a partnership and framework to enhance the quality of life for individuals, families, and society so that the future can be more complete than the past.

Ten Personal Habits for Successful Planning

To be consistent and effective, I rely on ten fundamental planning principles that have become habits in my life. They are based on the results of my work and the experiences of planners whom I consider successful. They do not cover all aspects of the profession, but I believe they are at the heart of most effective planning.

1. Credibility: To Care Is to Build Trust

It is said that people do not care how much you know until they know how much you care. A personal relationship and trust between planner and client is critical to building community. Personal credibility can be built in many ways, but it is essential if a planner is to be effective.

My first directorship was with a joint city-county agency in western Kentucky. The area was extremely conservative. Many people had endured bad experiences with the state and federal government in land condemnation cases related to military bases and the Tennessee Valley Authority. The last person many citizens wanted to see was a government planner. I represented nearly all they felt was bad about government.

To be effective, I had to establish credibility. The planning commission staff, though small, did represent the overwhelming majority of the professionally trained staff available to the city and county. During our first year, we spent most of our time helping out however we could. By using our research and analysis techniques, we assisted in everything from writing personnel policies to submitting grant applications to running a shuttle diplomacy service between the city and county elected officials who did not speak to each other. These activities, while far from planning, did give us the opportunity to gain respect and credibility. They opened the door to discussions of the community's future and to development of a vision that would lead us to that future. Over the next several years, we were able to develop a meaningful planning program, one that set in place a comprehensive plan and implementation ordinances for the first time. Though it was still very difficult, that project could never have been undertaken successfully without the groundwork we laid in the first year. Remember, people do not care how much you know until they know how much you care.

2. Listening: To Listen Is to Learn

Planning is the art of the political. Planning is not black or white but rather shades of gray. The planner must listen and, more important, understand to be effective. The most common complaint I hear from people is that government does not listen. The planner, of all people, must truly hear what is said. Many times we are too close to a problem or too self-confident in our training or title to really hear what is being said. This is especially true of planners right out of school who feel their degrees are a license to demonstrate how little others know.

One of the most difficult issues I faced early in my career in Orlando, where I am now, had to do with the large number of variances requested in older neighborhoods. Like many cities, Orlando had over the years "modernized" its land development regulations in an attempt to be on the cutting edge in planning evolution. The large number of variances frustrated neighbors, took up unnecessary staff time, and continually reminded commissioners that our codes did not appear to be working. During one hearing, a neighborhood resident made the offhand remark that when she had moved into her house forty-five years earlier, the neighborhood was well regulated and neighbors generally understood the city codes. This simple comment led to a rewrite of development codes based on the original 1926 city regulations. The community now feels that regulatory obstacles have been reduced and its neighborhoods protected while requests for variances have been all but eliminated, freeing staff for other projects. The best solutions often come from a casual remark that is overheard and then planted, nurtured and cultivated. Remember, the planner must listen and understand to be effective.

3. Research: To Research Is to Supplement, Not Supplant

One of the most common complaints I hear from other professionals is that they do not have the time to do thorough research.

There is never enough time to do all the research that we think is appropriate. Planners must balance the information available to do the job at hand. If we listen, and I mean truly listen, we can effectively blend research, community input, and our training and experience for an effective response.

A wealth of information and research skill is usually available if you have designed your project in a way that truly encourages participation by the people affected. Active and direct involvement gives the public actual ownership in the outcome of the project and relieves staff of research requirements while providing another opportunity to listen. Once we get over the belief that only we can do research properly, a number of new and creative research avenues open. Planners do not have all the answers. Citizen assistance in research is one of the best ways to get real community involvement in planning. Combining planners' training and meaningful citizen input provides the opportunity to find workable solutions to issues. Remember, planners must balance the information available to do the job at hand.

4. Thinking: To Process Information Successfully Is to Find Solutions

Planning is complex and is not an exact science by any means. The most critical talent or skill planners bring to the table is their ability to think horizontally or divergently as opposed to vertically or convergently. By this I mean we must use our ability to think beyond the obvious and understand the interrelatedness of ideas between issues, even when the linkage is not the most direct. Effective planners take every opportunity to use thinking skills together with their credibility and their listening and research skills to present realistic alternatives. More than professionals in other fields, planners must usually color outside the lines, seek innovative solutions, and find new approaches to problems.

One of the most time-consuming tasks many planners face each day is handling feedback from notice signs on property. This is often the case with NIMBY ("not in my backyard") opposition to special exception cases such as group homes or home occupations. In our attempt to be informative and seek involvement, we often increase the anxiety and tension people feel about a land use issue. By placing a public notice sign on a property, the local government says, in effect, that somebody wants to do something out of the ordinary on this property, or that somebody wants to change or get around the rules. The community immediately assumes that its responsibility is to oppose the request. An adversarial situation springs up regardless of the proposal's merits.

Home occupations are often considered a special exception or conditional use. Each case requires a public hearing, including notice to surrounding neighbors. Issues of concern at the public hearing are usually traffic, intensity of use, signage, and noise. Several years ago, we appointed a task force of neighborhood residents and small-business owners to consider the matter; they addressed it head-on, agreeing on a list of critical factors that affect neighborhoods as a result of home occupations. Most people recognized that such occupations are becoming more and more common, especially with evolving computer technology. Our community was able to define the appropriate level of intensity, traffic, and signage that would be acceptable. The zoning code was amended to allow review of this use through an administrative process. Staff reviews the request to ensure compliance with the conditions, the home occupation license is granted, neighbors are notified that a license has been issued, and a complaint process is in place to monitor conditions. This has resulted in much less controversy and has been very successful in accommodating the needs of a home occupation applicant while preserving the integrity of the neighborhood. The same approach has been used for group homes, mixed housing types, and day-care facilities, to name a few. By removing the controversy over an individual site and escalating the discussion to solving the broader problem, the community can establish reasonable guidelines that accommodate desirable land uses. Remember, the most critical talent or skill planners bring to the table is their ability to think horizontally.

5. Commitment: To Be Effective, Planners Must Be Committed

A commitment to planning requires more than just saying that you are interested. It requires your direct action. To me, it is important that the planner be part of the system, a player. Though there are effective planners in private practice and working in other capacities, I believe the best way to be a player is to be a local government planner. Once your credibility has been established, you have the opportunity to carry out your mission. As you gain tenure, you frequently acquire the freedom to become bolder in your approach. However, this does involve taking risks. Effective planners recognize the risks and strategically utilize their positions to bring forth issues that are important to the community. Not every issue is worth fighting about, but you can take a necessary stand with less risk of losing your job if you have established trust and tenure by being part of the system.

Your commitment as a planner is rooted in the professional ideals of your personal value system. While an individual ideal will be refined over time, it forms the foundation of your practice. Recognize what you stand for and understand whether your value system is consistent with the job you were hired to do. Insincerity created by incompatible values will undermine your commitment more quickly than anything.

Commitment can be translated into action on the part of your community. Properly presented issues can be most successfully debated and acted upon if you are prepared, have built the proper partnership, and act when the time is right. Use your ideals and commitment to push your community to face an issue that it has not addressed.

Your commitment, as well as that of the community, can be tested in a number of ways. For me, the time to put up or shut up came shortly after the 1992 Los Angeles riots. Orlando, over the previous few years, had been working to revitalize an area immediately west of downtown known as the Parramore neighborhood. Various planning efforts had been undertaken. The city had allocated a few resources for housing rehabilitation and had begun a relatively slow effort to revitalize this neighborhood.

Following the Los Angeles riots, I met with the commissioner for the area to discuss whether the city's actions were really going to result in meaningful change in this neighborhood. The city had shotgunned its resources, and the neighborhood suffered considerably as a result. To help much, the city would have to make a major investment of resources there at the expense of other neighborhoods, and the Parramore leadership would have to emerge in a true and unprecedented partnership with the city. But it did happen: a partnership was established, the Parramore Heritage Project was instituted, and the city made an informed and serious commitment that remains today.

While this project (much like the American Planning Association's Agenda for America's Communities) will not be an overnight success, continuing action by the planning department and city government, together with involvement by residents, will make a very real difference in this neighborhood. Remember, a commitment to planning requires your direct action.

6. Continuing Education: To Grow Is Constantly to Seek Education

The five principles above have to do with the planner's personal approach to the job. They come together in the ongoing and fundamental need for continuing education. Effective planning requires continuing education as a way of life.

As administrator of a large department (more than 120 employees), I could easily spend all of my time in administrative problem solving. However, I allocate plenty of effort to the important job of exposing myself to changes in my field. Conferences and other formal educational opportunities are excellent, but more casual learning channels are valuable as well.

Reading journals and publications on planning and affiliated professions is an outstanding way to keep aware of what is happening. My particular reading interests include the history of planning, the evolution of cities and neighborhoods, and the ways of establishing solid, viable communities. Often this research reemphasizes for me the importance of urban design. There are many other opportunities to learn, such as experiencing other communities and talking to others in the field about problems, issues, opportunities, and the ways they deal with them.

Planners need to be involved in continuing education from the giving end as well as the receiving end, however. They must help educate members of the boards and commissions they work with. Our department works hard to provide initial and ongoing training to members of our planning board. Fundamental to this is membership in the American Planning Association, which provides access to materials and conferences. Board members' knowledge can also be enhanced by publications such as the *Planning Commissioners Journal;* the more knowledge they have, the better, as they are your most direct tie to the community.

Continuing education about planning should extend into the community itself, for that matter, and planners should help provide it. Both in Gainesville and Orlando we have formed neighborhood councils to encourage neighborhood leaders to get together and learn from each other, share problems and solutions, and just communicate on ways they can protect and enhance the quality of local life. We have used national and local leadership councils to train neighborhood leaders and educate them on the relevant issues. Newsletters can also help. .

Look around, take time, involve your community leaders, involve your municipal planning board, and involve yourself. Remember, effective planning requires continuing education as a way of life. To be really effective requires a solid partnership between you, the community, the decision makers, and those institutions ultimately responsible for transferring the structure of the community to future generations. The next four principles reflect my approach to bridging the planners' skills and true community building.

7. Decision Making: To Build Community Requires Making Choices

A commitment must translate into solid decision making. Great communities, like great paintings, are created through many small, deliberate, individual decisions made over the course of time. Just as the artist decides on every stroke and color that will make up a painting, planners' everyday decisions will determine the quality and character of the communities we live in. Every true masterpiece is a combination of the artist's vision and the successful use of the tools, skills, persistence, and techniques at hand; every community that stimulates and enhances the lives of its residents is created by a vision that guides the planner's decisions.

Communities often avoid tough decisions. Making them takes political will, brings into question our effective use of resources, and requires us to be held accountable. To be effective, decisions must be based on a vision; for planners, that vision must be what the community and society eventually could become. Together we must develop a broad-based vision that leads to action, to the creation or re-creation of a sense of community that supports and encourages individuals to become positive, contributing members of society. Today's communities need to strengthen our shared cultural institutions such as the educational, religious, library, and recreational systems. These build and support the family so that all people can fully participate in the community of tomorrow.

During a major rewrite of its growth management plan, Orlando was faced with a dilemma. Neighborhoods to the east of downtown had deteriorated over the years into a concentration of boarding houses and substandard buildings; then pressure mounted to convert parts of these old areas into offices. Downtown growth had created some of this pressure (though downtown itself remained low-density), and well-connected speculators had created the rest by buying up nearby neighborhood property with an eye toward office conversions. But meeting with neighborhood residents, evaluating the amount of vacant land available for development, and recognizing the need for solid, affordable owner-occupied housing near downtown convinced us that preserving the area was the best option, from both a land use perspective and in concert with the city's overall goals and objectives.

To accomplish this preservation, a partnership was formed between city staff, a few concerned residents of the neighborhood, and the Downtown Development Board. The partnership developed policies, implementation tools, and programs to preserve the neighborhood. A series of public hearings on the future of the neighborhood were held as part of the city's Growth Management Plan update. Finally, and over the objections of the speculators, the city council decided to hold the line. It approved comprehensive plan policies and zoning intended to maintain the residential character of the neighborhood.

Since that fundamental decision in 1985, the city has further supported it by increasing code enforcement, designating the area a historic district, and enhancing public facilities through capital improvements. The result—a neighborhood once 80 percent owned by investors is now more than 50 percent owner-occupied—has spurred redevelopment of other adjacent downtown neighborhoods. A solid housing stock is in place for a mixture of income, social, and ethnic groups.

The decisions that led to this happy ending, though very difficult to make at the time, retain city council support today. Mayor Bill Frederick, upon his retirement, stated that protecting that neighborhood was one of the most important and successful decisions of his term of office. Remember, decisions are not easy or simple.

8. Implementation: To Implement a Proposal Is to Show the Community You Care

Plan development is only the beginning, and frequently the easiest part, of the planning process. Healthy communities spend much more time on meaningful implementation than on plan development. People care more about how a plan will improve their community and their lives than they do about the plan itself. Effective planning includes a sound implementation strategy which, though it may be time-consuming to come up with, must be considered at the beginning of the process. It requires teamwork, partnership, and an understanding of the tools and techniques at hand.

Frequently, the development of a growth management plan and its implementation are distinct activities. During our 1985 update of the growth management plan, we decided to combine the update with implementation. To be successful, the land development regulations had to be totally integrated with growth management plan policies. More than 300 citizens were involved in the plan's development; staff and the community came up with implementation ordinances that actually tracked the policies being developed. This hand-in-glove approach led to land development regulations which refined and sharpened the growth management plan itself. It helped the community understand the full impact of the policies and, more important, understand the framework behind the specific land development regulations. This approach continues today as a realistic check on policy development, and has made implementation as important as policy formation, if not more so. Remember, healthy communities spend more time on implementation than on plan development.

9. Empowerment: To Transfer Responsibility Is to Build Community

The planner, usually even local government, cannot build community without the consent and power of its residents. Just as parents must allow their children to grow up and move on, planners must let go. Our role is to ensure that we have transferred the skills and tools necessary to carry out the project. Furthermore, the planner must assist when asked and follow up to make sure the project is not forgotten. As projects evolve, a solid partnership must be developed that begins at project conception and continues through project completion.

To succeed in the implementation of any project, the community must be empowered to achieve the objectives of the program. Orlando faced this issue directly in the Parramore Heritage effort discussed above. Empowerment started at the first meeting. This meeting and all sessions since were run by the residents themselves, building their leadership skills to the point that they now can carry on the project without the day-to-day involvement of city staff.

The Parramore Heritage Foundation was formed as a chartered nonprofit corporation with an elected board of directors. As such, it has the stability to continue beyond what a bureaucratic city-led program could do. This empowerment has built the Parramore community and ensured a true partnership led by community residents. It is the heart of community building. Remember, the planner must let go.

10. Responsibility: To Build Community Requires Community Responsibility

Empowerment of the community by the city means little if the community does not accept the responsibility. Making more decisions is meaningless if nobody assumes the responsibility of implementing them. Neither the planner nor the local government can take responsibility for successful community building; the planner may be able to bring certain resources to the problem, but without community responsibility no amount of government involvement will bring success.

Responsibility is built through the implementation and empowerment process. I have seen this in my experiences with historic preservation planning. Early in my career, historic preservation was generally instigated by city staff. The planners, sure that they knew what was right, would move forward whether the community cared or not. This, of course, usually led to community backlash, lack of support, and the satisfaction of no one. In 1987, we changed our approach to encourage community responsibility and obligation. It has been a great success.

Basically, the city of Orlando decided that if historic district issues were important to the community, the community had to take responsibility. The planner and the planning board provide support, counsel, advice, and research; however, the decision-making process for a neighborhood and its historic district is under the general purview of the citizens who live there. A certain property-owning percentage of these citizens must sign a petition for a historic district even to be considered. Then a proposed historic district ordinance is developed by the neighborhood itself, giving residents an opportunity to decide what should be regulated in their neighborhood. We have seen widely differing levels of control come out of the ordinance development process. Finally, once an ordinance has been developed and subsequently adopted by the city, the neighborhood is responsible for providing the review council.

In a nutshell, the neighborhood institutes the process, defines issues of importance, and reviews all petitions. The planner provides support and appeals can be made to a broader city board in case of controversy, but the issues are defined, settled, and implemented by a community that has assumed responsibility for itself. Remember, if there is no community responsibility, no amount of government involvement will bring about success.

Our Social Bedrock

My ten principles allow me to focus on achieving my mission. To evaluate whether I am on track, I give close attention to three fundamentals that I believe are the bedrock of our society. They should be the ultimate objects of a planner's time and energy— even if we rarely acknowledge them directly.

The Family

There is no better or more fundamental shaper of community than the family unit. It has been the basic building block for society since the beginning of time. Many of the decisions we face every day, from the design and implementation of zoning codes to issues related to transportation and capital budgeting, have a direct impact on the ability of the family to function in our complex communities.

The questions I ask are these: How does this project affect the family? How can this project support and enhance the family? What should be in my work program that will remove any negative impacts on the family? What can I do to create a solid and productive family unit?

Our Shared Cultural Institutions

Planning involves resource allocation. Daily we make decisions that affect the shared cultural institutions that so significantly influence the evolution of society. Historically, the broad community (together with government) has, through various religious, social, and family structures, provided support, guidance, and accountability. The community has acted as the framework for our social, political, and religious structure. More recently much of this has fallen through. We have no definitive leadership, shared community values, or consensus on community action. There is little accountability and few consequences for actions taken. Ultimately, we must decide whether government or the community will direct our cultural institutions. Someone must be willing to establish our basic moral truths and beliefs and societal norms.

The questions I ask here are: What can I do to enhance our educational systems? Does this project help build safe and supportive gathering places and networks? Can my actions enhance or support our private cultural systems? Does this project move society forward and upward?

Pattern and Distribution of Power

How decisions are made tells a lot about our approach to community building. Planners must recognize diversity but acknowledge the need for a fundamental community culture. We must define and build our communities in a way that results in a society greater than the lowest common denominator. We must develop and utilize effective, honest, and open means to challenge and provide opportunities for meaningful citizen involvement in building supportive and positive communities.

The questions I ask here are: Who are the affected parties and how are they actively involved? How do our governmental structures measure up? Can this project empower people to become more involved and responsible for their actions?

Bases of Planning Success

To be effective, our planning processes must recall the strengths of the past while realizing the potential of the future. They should create a sense of history and place, establish a shared image or sense of identity, and rebuild the connections between our human and physical environment so that communities can become environmentally sensitive, aesthetically inspiring, and socially and economically integrated.

To succeed, planning must encompass more than just infrastructure and the creation of an easy market for real estate. The planning process we apply can enable us to rediscover the freedom known as community. Planning can provide a heart and soul for society through the physical environment and urban design. We are shaped and influenced by our physical environment. Together the physical, social, and personal elements of society form a community. There can be no more noble or desirable goal than to build a "state of social wholeness in which each member has their place and in which life is regulated by cooperation rather than by competition and conflict" (Abrams, 1971, p. 60).

Our goal, then, is to build a sense of community and provide opportunities for all people to grow, lead fulfilling lives, and contribute to a better life for future generations. Family structure establishes the basic personal belief system of an individual. Community structure establishes the basic cultural and societal belief system within which the individual operates. I do not believe we can separate these two elements. Planners indirectly influence the family structure through their direct involvement in the community structure. This is most commonly a result of decisions affecting the physical development of their communities.

We bring to the process an ability to think and to understand the connections between the issues and forces that can and do influence society, its values and morals, and the way we develop. Planners are responsible (though maybe not empowered) for using their training to enhance the ability of individuals to meet their own needs while contributing to the advancement of society.

I fear that we have lost the ability to celebrate our cities due to changes in their design, that we are no longer creating places where people can grow, learn, and develop a basic sense of cultural value. As a result, there has been a decline in shared institutions, a loss of our urban culture. We have seen a decline in the basics of society: individual responsibility, educational systems, religious and other cultural support systems, and the freedom to enjoy our parks, libraries, museums, and other civic places. Richard Sennett, the social historian and cultural critic, said it best: "The city ought to be a school for learning how to lead a centered life. The diversity, complexity, and connection to the past associated with cities is an essential need for individuals in a society" (Sennett, 1990, p. xiii).

The process of community growth and development can result in compact and defined communities. Communities with a cohesive sense of place. Communities with a fine-grained mix of land uses. Communities that support existing developed areas and recognize the need for safe public spaces for meaningful face-to-face interaction.

Much as when I was fourteen—in awe of the city, its buildings, and its excitement—I remain firmly convinced that urban design influences the advancement of society. Our planning and political approaches must consider and balance the difficult-to-define issues of design with the perceived benefits of social and economic development. We must find a way to better visualize, quantify, and display the advantages of solid urban design with social and economic development.

Planning, urban design, and citizen involvement are much more than add-on considerations! The real cost to society of inappropriate or inadequate urban design is a tremendous loss of human potential, support systems, and growth opportunities. If we do not realize the need for building community, we will lose our ability to pass on the basic cultural values of responsibility, concern for one another, concern for health, safety, well-being, education, and the potential for prosperity that positive human interaction can give.

As a planner, it is easy to get caught up in a day-to-day focus on specific projects. But I challenge you to consider whether, over time, you are painting that great picture . . . supporting the "new civics" through your actions. Are you doing your part to ensure that the future of our community is better than the past?

Chapter Four

Five Commitments That Can Make a Difference

Paul A. Bergmann

My introduction to city planning came quite by accident and quite early in my college days. I was an architectural student in a cooperative program where studies and work were linked in one curriculum. After the first year, the program required periods of work in an architect's office, or in a related field, rotated with periods of schooling.

My first "cooperative job" was with the City of Cincinnati Plan Commission. In the summer of 1957, I was introduced to urban design and the concept that, through planning, you could bring change to older neighborhood commercial centers. As a co-op student, I worked in several neighborhoods for the next eighteen months. The idea that you could influence where people lived, worked, and played was more exciting to me than influencing one or two building environments at a time. I was hooked. A few years later, my senior architectural thesis focused on urban design, neighborhood revitalization, and development. Based on my experiences and in the spirit of the 1960s, I decided to do graduate work in this profession. (It seemed like a third of my class went on to advanced studies in planning!)

Graduate work in community planning broadened my understanding of the field to include social and economic concerns, as well as the physical environment. Schooling, an internship in our nation's capital, and my first jobs in Maryland and Florida only strengthened my appreciation for planning. These experiences led to my early conclusion that planning was an integral part of local government, that it was supported, influential, and coming of age.

My conclusion changed after the period of the mid 1970s to mid 1980s. These ten years saw the loss of 701 Federally Assisted Community Planning funds and other federal support and the recession of 1982 to 1984. Community planning competed for limited dollars against more immediate needs of police and fire protection, the building and resurfacing of roads, drainage, and other concerns. We had to change and become more pragmatic. What did our clients (politicians and citizenry) want? Many programs and agencies had expanded to develop long-range and comprehensive plans, but then were cut back because "we had a plan." Traditional planning was oriented to the production of a document; we had sold the community on the need for a comprehensive plan through all the federal programs, but not (despite our assumptions) on planning as an integral part of local government. We had not been oriented to being day-to-day advisors on more pressing developmental issues. Successful planners saw that this reorientation was important. The shorter-range issues of neighborhoods and the quick response officials wanted (in contrast to years spent in the development of a plan) changed planning. The theorist idealist became the practical strategist. This change was pronounced in many states, but less so in states with mandatory comprehensive planning. Even then, once plans and codes were done, planners seemed lost unless they found a way to make themselves more valuable to the community.

Trends and Fads

Beyond the big picture noted above, planning has, in the past thirty years, evolved through many fads and programs. Throughout each cycle, planning has always focused on the central theme of influencing change for the betterment of the community. Programs such as 701 Federally Assisted Community Planning, 201 and 208 Water and Sewer Planning, New Town and New Town in Town Planning, Environmental Planning, Community Development Planning, Social and Advocacy Planning, Sector and Neighborhood Planning, Strategic Planning, Neotraditional Planning, and Visioning have all added to the profession.

All these programs and the theories behind them have contributed to reinventing planning and to gaining a measure of public support. Each program and theory has refined a part of the whole, and often refined concepts associated with traditional comprehensive planning. The idea that planners should use the natural environment was taught in schools in the 1960s and earlier and was always a given when planning for the use of undeveloped land. This idea became a fad using the McHarg *Planning with Nature* methodology. The existing manmade environment is equally recognized as the starting point of good planning. Planners must know the social and economic circumstances of their community so that they can identify needs in housing, open space, and recreation and, ultimately, their impact on the area's quality of life. This concern is reflected in advocacy planning, and in neighborhood and sector planning. Concepts such as short-range and focused project planning have merged with strategic planning to become an important implementation tool.

One of the latest fads, neotraditional planning, resurrects the best historical development patterns of towns and villages and applies them to new or redeveloping communities. This contrasts with the curvilinear planned unit approach or the "garden city" of the past. Another vogue, the communitywide "visioning" process, reminds us that planning with people has always meant learning the needs and wants of a community, whether through a nominal group that identifies goals or a communitywide effort. Planners need to understand and use all these programs and ideas as part of an education process, and to find direction to meet community changes.

Equally interesting to the planner is the wide range in the results of these efforts. Some communities have produced plans and documents so general as to give no clear direction. Often called policy plans, these are so flexible that a reason can always be found to support or deny any request. At the other end of the spectrum are plans that are so parcel and block specific that they look like zoning maps, with frequent amendments required to accommodate the normal flexibility needed for day-to-day work. In the middle of the spectrum is the comprehensive plan as advocated by T. J. Kent Jr. in *The Urban General Plan* (1964). A guide to the long-term growth of a community, this sort of plan gives form and direction but is flexible enough to accommodate real-world variations. Such a plan is best followed by short-range neighborhood and sector planning, including zoning proposals, that give definition to the long-term overall concept. Neotraditional, curvilinear planned unit, and other concepts can be used to implement these local area plans. Strategic planning can be used to address concurrency and timeliness of the proposal to cause the desired end result.

Principles and Strategies

Just what can planners do to increase their effectiveness and produce better results? It varies by locale, but several principles seem to apply regardless of the community and circumstances; they have to do with commitment to public involvement and ownership, implementation, flexibility and innovation, ethical standards, and being mission driven.

Constant One: Commitment to Public Involvement and Ownership

A community must see the benefits of planning and the planning process. For plans to be successful, the community must have ownership of the document and be a coproducer. This takes time and involvement. Historically, many jurisdictions' plans were directed by politicians, sometimes in pursuit of state or federal grants and sometimes when facing explosive growth or unwanted projects. Because such plans were not driven by citizens, they tended to change when the leadership changed. More recent and more effective planning recognizes and builds on the avowed political nature of the activity, but takes a grass-roots approach that involves and empowers the citizens. Thus, the agenda is set by the community for the leaders to carry forth.

Obtaining citizen input can be accomplished by ad-hoc groups meeting at hours when the working public can attend. At these workshops, planners give information and citizens comment, praise, or complain at each phase of the process. People naturally expect that the planners and other technical and professional experts who appear will treat them with respect and consider them partners in the process. The best examples of this level of involvement are when neighborhood and sector plans are developed through extensive sharing, where education is part of the process and consensus is created. The nominal group process encourages identification of a vision and community goals, possible alternatives, and the selection of the preferred solution. Each land use alternative requires a transportation alternative, and both require an environmental assessment to determine their level of acceptability to the community. This is often thought of as a systems approach. Based on my experience developing such plans in Clearwater and Pinellas County, Florida, and Louisville and Jefferson County, Kentucky, I can say that the grass-roots approach has proven most successful in empowering the community and guaranteeing coproduction and ownership. The citizens in these counties feel that they own the plans, and they defend them at hearings and at budget sessions.

Constant Two: Commitment to Implementation

Communities that help develop their own neighborhood and sector plans also must commit to follow through with implementation through areawide rezonings. In the counties mentioned above, each plan proposal included significantly lower urban density, commitment to open space and preservation of the environment, and reduction in commercial and industrial zoning to better reflect actual or proposed redevelopment. During the early 1970s, Clearwater decided to lower the maximum allowable density for redevelopment of areas on Clearwater Beach and the bluffs overlooking the bay. I drafted a code change reducing allowable density from fifty-four to twenty-seven units per acre. We worked with several property owners, giving notice of the ordinance change and of a grace period, so that those with "real proposals" would have an opportunity to complete their projects. This worked out quite well. Only one building plan was carried forward during this time; it was not built. To the best of my recollection, no lawsuits were filed.

In another Clearwater comprehensive plan action, the city downzoned a small area of upland land and a large marsh and mangrove area, moving it from commercial and high density to low-density residential and aquatic lands. The rezoning led to two lawsuits. The first addressed the facts of the rezoning. The second accused the city of violating the owner's federal civil rights.

The first suit went before the Second District Court of Appeals of Florida (383 So. 2nd), which upheld the city's position that it had the right to protect the lowlands and wetlands through rezoning, and that this did not preclude beneficial use of the property. The second case, based on civil rights, was the equivalent of one of the first Strategic Lawsuits Against Public Participation (SLAPP) lawsuits. It alleged collusion between the planning director, building director, city manager, and all council members, their objective being to take away the rights of the property owners. The case went to a jury, which exonerated the two directors but found the city manager, mayor, and each council member individually guilty. This finding, obviously very chilling to the officials and citizen politicians alike, was subsequently overturned by a federal court judge who questioned why the case should have gone to trial at all.

A Pinellas County example of a commitment to planning and implementation occurred in the northeast sector of the county. The area, a prime aquifer recharge area for the county's water supply, faced imminent development pressures; conversion of the land was under way. We worked with each owner-developer, creating the equivalent of a low-density planned community. The plan included lowering the allowable density across the board, creating vast areas of wetland preservation, identifying areas for golf course development, and allowing a reasonable transfer of density into several planned cluster development sites. Because the owners participated, they perceived the process as fair and above board. This is still the best-planned and most appropriately zoned sector of Pinellas County. Thirteen sector plans were done during the late 1970s; they became the basis of a countywide comprehensive plan.

From 1982 to 1992, the Louisville and Jefferson County Planning Commission developed more than twenty neighborhood plans. All led to subsequent areawide rezoning, neighborhood by neighborhood. During this period, the joint city-county commission saw a need and addressed it. Planning and implementation at a more local level was desired because the community's Policy Plan was considered ineffective in protecting these areas. Typical of older city neighborhoods, many areas of Louisville were changing due to old and very permissive zoning. The Old Louisville neighborhood wanted to retain and reestablish its residential character and prevent any further slide to office usage. Most other neighborhoods basically wanted to preserve their existing qualities and fend off changes that the old, permissive zoning would otherwise allow.

Accordingly, these neighborhood plans were the catalysts for rezoning, for improving roadways and sidewalks, and for requesting other changes from the board of aldermen, such as parkways and planting of street trees.

Constant Three: Commitment to Flexibility and Innovation

Planning requires flexibility, timing, and innovation because new problems often require new solutions. For example, I encountered uncontrolled tree removal and lack of planned open space in Clearwater. In Louisville and Jefferson County, I found a lack of landscape requirements and limited regulation of billboards.

A beautiful grove of oak trees was cut down for a strip mall at a major intersection in Clearwater; no permits had been required. After careful research, I determined that no Florida community had tree protection ordinances, but I drafted one for Clearwater modeled on those of Atlanta and other cities. It was adopted, and eventually other Florida cities copied it. Though it has been amended since, the ordinance has accomplished what the city intended: protection of stands of oaks and other trees indigenous to the area.

Another concern, also in Clearwater, was the lack of recreation and open space as identified by the comprehensive plan. The city addressed this and other needs by taking a general obligation bond program to the public, with the purchase of park land and open space as part of the package. Older neighborhoods would be brought up to park land standards by the bond program; however, as part of the presentation, new developments would be required to include land or cash in lieu of land to meet the same standards. Although not as complicated a formula as later adopted by other cities and counties, an ordinance I drafted for Clearwater was, I believe, the first in Florida to impose an impact fee. The formula was a simple percentage of all lands. It was not challenged (the city of Dunedin's later version was taken to court, however, thus deciding Florida law). Again, I saw the uniqueness of the moment, responded to the need, and moved forward with a proposal that met the city's wants.

In Louisville, we identified a need for the community's first landscape ordinance. We drafted one as part of a new unified development code and won the support of neighborhoods, business groups, and the local home builders association to get the ordinance accepted and adopted. It did not hurt that the chair of the planning commission was a businessperson and home builder.

Another example of timing and innovation was the redrafting of the city and county sign ordinance. Just a few years earlier, any planner trying to control the billboard industry would have been run out of town, figuratively at least. However, a rash of billboards along major corridors entering the community, in concert with renewed aesthetic concerns tied to economic development efforts, finally led to support for efforts to control them. An attorney for the city shepherded the merger of separate city and county ordinances for on-site signage control; I drafted the off-site (billboard) portion of the ordinance with his help, using the best research to date on regulation of the industry. Spacing between billboards was doubled along most roads and tripled along limited-access highways and parkways. Setbacks from the edge of rights-of-way were doubled. These standards, considered severely restrictive by some, have greatly reduced the number of new boards in the city and in built-up county areas. A new limited-access circumferential highway further out in the county, and roads radiating from the city to the county line, were prime areas for installing new signs. To regulate this, the ordinance divided the county into a metropolitan area and a nonmetropolitan area by drawing a line around Louisville from county boundary to county boundary and paralleling the new highway 2,000 feet inside its inner edge. From this line outward to the adjoining counties, the rural standard of the Federal Highway Administration would apply. The county commission became so enthusiastic about this proposal that it later made the circumferential highway a billboard-free corridor 4,000 feet across. The timing was right, and although some people wanted outright prohibition of billboards, imaginative and fair regulations managed to permit some signage while still responding to the community's economic and aesthetic concerns.

Constant Four: Commitment to High Ethical Standards

Planners often work in highly charged environments where the good of the overall community must be upheld while the rights of property owners are protected. We must treat all clients and the general citizenry with equity, openness, fairness, and honesty. We recognize our ethical responsibility to the public, our employer, the profession, and our fellow colleagues.

The routine activities of planners often revolve around two or three potential responses to an inquiry, any one of which could be considered correct. Whichever response will be perceived as most ethical should be the one presented, but often this isn't easy; one person's ethical viewpoint may lead to a different interpretation of the response than would another person's viewpoint. I can think of several examples to explain what I mean.

Many years ago a city planning director in Pinellas County sided with a neighborhood association against the city on a zoning issue. As he lived in the neighborhood himself, he immediately ran into trouble with his manager and the city council and was dismissed. He sued to regain his job and lost. Whether he was right or wrong on the zoning matter is not the point here; the significant fact is that he did not understand his ethical conflict. Because he was both a neighborhood resident and a city employee, he should have taken himself out of the issue. That would have been the only way to avoid the appearance of personal gain. He erred further by suing, which only earned him a reputation for litigiousness. For five years he tried to find a new job with local government, never understanding why every agency was so hesitant to hire him, before he ultimately gave up on public service.

Another example of ethical conflict, this one fairly well publicized, occurred in Baltimore County in the early 1970s. Several staff did volunteer work after hours in the city of Baltimore organizing neighborhoods to have a larger say in local government. Members of the county council felt this reflected poorly on the county since many people did not separate the volunteer workers from their daytime employer. In addition, Maryland had just put a number of ethics codes in place to address several recent problems. This and other issues came into play during the next budget cycle, when the deputy director and volunteer group staff positions were eliminated. The director resigned in protest. What had originally been only a concern about appearances escalated to lost jobs and the resignation of a director. And it got worse; lawsuits were filed and letters written to professional magazines urging outsiders not to consider working in the county. The leadership problems all this caused took awhile to repair. Which was the greater ethical issue, the setting of limits on outside volunteer work or the setback to the leadership and morale of this office? Could the matter have been diffused or handled in a less confrontational way? What was the best, most ethical action to take? The answers might not have been simple to come by, but clearly the problem could have been addressed well before it went as far as it did.

I have had to address several ethical issues in my own career. One involved a nearly seven-mile commercial corridor proposal. The highway in question was the only major facility in an area served by a few rural two-lane roads, and its commercialization was opposed by staff, neighboring jurisdictions, and the areawide planning council. It was supported, however, by a majority of the board, which sided with the property owners. The staff, of which I was a member, served both the planning council and the board. The proposal was modified to a residential-office and residential-office-retail mix; staff's opposition was noted and eventually resulted in my leaving that job. Fourteen years later, after some separation of powers and reorganization had occurred, even the chair of the board admitted "we could have done a better job of planning" for that major highway.

Another personal example of upholding high ethical standards centered on an important rezoning case. The proposal was for a major downsizing. When I received a request to meet with a niece of one of the property owners to discuss the case, it gained even greater magnitude. After discussing the request with the city manager and receiving his approval, I met with the niece after work hours. She made several comments about the zoning, but then, after some small talk, hinted at a sexual attraction. I did not respond and the issue was dropped. The next day I told the city manager what had happened. He consulted with the police chief and it was decided that I should set up another meeting, this time in the city hall and with me wearing a "wire." I called the niece and she came to the city building to review her comments with me and subsequently with the city manager. She restated most of her comments of the night before, minus the sexual overtures. After that meeting she had no further involvement in the zoning case, but soon I got an equally disturbing call from another relative of the same property owner, this one a federal judge in a nearby city. He also wanted to set up a meeting to discuss the case. I advised him of our rationale for the downzoning and suggested that his comments would be more appropriate at the hearing. He didn't show up, however, and neither did the niece. A sad footnote to this story was the subsequent suicide of the person whose two relatives had tried to help out.

The examples I've given here far surpass most ethical dilemmas I have encountered, but it is not unusual for even ordinary issues to be ethically less than clear-cut. I tell my staff that they should view their actions from several perspectives, but ultimately ethics is an area that requires a day-to-day sense of what is fair, equitable, and right for the community, the client, the profession, and one's own self-esteem.

Be familiar with the ethics code of your profession. Understand it and use it. Few things are black and white. Make ethical evaluations and actions a daily activity. It will be an approach that is a credit to you and your profession.

Constant Five: Commitment to Mission

The best planning agencies have learned that they need to work as a team, to be flexible, to be more responsive to the client, and to be committed to service. These agencies have evolved as teams because leadership roles are no longer hard and fast, but rather shift as needed. They are following in the footsteps of corporate America and, due to tight fiscal constraints over many years, are leaner and expected to do many more tasks. My experiences in Kentucky and Florida have shown a long-term need to upgrade staff standards, computerize operations, and do more with less.

Various staff may be specialists in demographic and social data, housing, transportation planning, or block grant programs, but they are also expected to be generalists. They may be required to lead neighborhood planning teams or commercial revitalization planning, or serve as staff to affordable housing or transportation disadvantaged committees. With so many dual roles for staff assumed, agencies have flattened organizational structures, putting fewer levels between entry and division head and director. With fewer levels of supervision, more people are empowered to be more responsive, less bureaucratic, and able to address issues more quickly.

Because of these shifts in responsibility, agencies have begun to focus on their purpose and goals, and many have developed mission statements. A mission statement is usually developed by a team, then presented for comment to the whole organization so that everyone will take ownership of it. After it has been revised to everybody's satisfaction, the statement is generally displayed as a credo of service for the employees to use and the public to see.

Retreats are common vehicles for the development of these statements. My first retreat was when the city manager of Clearwater took all his department heads and supervisors on a daylong break from city hall to develop his staff-generated issues statement for the future of Clearwater. As director of the Louisville and Jefferson County Planning Commission, I held early-morning staff meetings and luncheons to develop our mission statement. In Lake County, I brought the division heads and senior staff together for an all-day Saturday retreat. The county was in the process of updating its vision statement, so the timing was excellent; our mission statement as planners could help the board of county commissioners define its own statement. Most staff members probably do not have personal mission statements, but the agency statement can act as a personal statement if everyone accepts its value. More people will "buy in" if the statement is emphasized by posting it for public viewing and by frequent reference to it in the course of everyday business. I have heard of one agency that had various staff actually sign the document. When I presented this option in Louisville, one not-so-committed participant commented that it reminded him of the McCarthy allegiance-swearing approach. There's a skeptic in every crowd.

The mission statement should be a guide and be reflected in the agency's work program and budget development. Also, through the process of developing a statement, staff should realize the importance of a mission or commitment to a common course of action, of creating an environment that is product oriented, the product being implementation and service. Implementation includes commitment to update regulations to comply with the community's comprehensive plan, to make regulations user-friendly, and to simplify the process. Further, it means to assist in open space acquisition and roadway development, and to create innovative proposals for supplying low- and moderate-income housing, to name a few objectives. Eventually, dedication to carrying out the mission statement must lead to serving the community and the customers of the agency.

One way to foster a service orientation is to let customers evaluate your service by asking them, in random follow-up phone calls and conversations, how satisfied they are. In both Louisville and Lake County, service evaluation cards were created and placed in public areas for ease of access and use. Over 110 cards were received from May to December 1994 in Lake County. Many indicated that our service was excellent, but some made it clear there was room for improvement. The concept that the customer is always right needs to be stressed in planning offices as much as it is in department stores. Training may be needed to break down the "we-they" approach to client service that simply is no longer acceptable or permissible. When customers come to our office, I expect staff to find some way to satisfy them or, if that's not possible, to explain why not in such a manner that they leave knowing we cared about their problems and tried to help. Lake County's manager tells of a director who mandates that customers receive the answer "Yes, you can do it" whenever they ask if they can take any kind of action. Of course, if the customer wants to do something that is currently illegal, staff explains that first the customer must get a zoning change or a comprehensive plan change, or whatever, before proceeding. The customer may come to the conclusion proceeding isn't worth the effort, but still leaves convinced that the staff was very helpful!

Let Planners Be Planners

Planning is work, but it should also be fun. At the November 1994 annual conference of the Florida chapter of the American Planning Association (APA), I reminisced with Jim Duncan, a past Florida chapter and APA president, about our younger days twenty years ago in Florida. We recalled working hard but also having a lot of fun; it was an exhilarating, innovative time. Today seems to be a paper chase to meet state law, administrative codes, and state agency requirements. The flexibility that allowed each community to be a little different and to seek innovative solutions to its problems has been replaced by a maze of rules and code interpretations. The following two examples help make the point.

During a presentation I made at a September 1994 regional planning council workshop on intergovernmental coordination, I said that Lake County's 1991 Comprehensive Plan had been challenged by the State of Florida Department of Community Affairs

(DCA). The challenge went on for two years and was settled in 1993. A citizen's group also had challenged the plan. Their challenge was denied and the county's plan and settlement agreement with DCA had (that week) been upheld. These comments won the applause of the audience; apparently everyone there had experienced similar difficulties getting their plans approved.

The other example was at the fall Florida APA conference where a statewide compilation of county and city plans was displayed under the title "Statewide Future Land Use Map." Wayne Daltry, the Florida APA chapter president, gave it a more tongue-in-cheek title, "Florida, the State That Planning Made." It showed a lack of overall vision, no systems approach to areawide planning, and no consistency and coordination between counties. Probably it would lead to the kind of static future that an overly bureaucratic process can produce. It left little doubt what the current process can and cannot do. We need to be about what we can do; let planners be planners again.

Chapter Five

What They Don't Teach You in School

Jim Reid

After thirty years of public planning, I have learned many lessons about the profession that only experience, not education, could teach me. Here are the most important four.

Use the Power of the Open Participatory Process

Early in my career, I was named director of the Prince George's County (Maryland) Department of Community Development. At the time, it was not an influential position; the department consisted of myself and a secretary. But this was at the height of President Lyndon B. Johnson's Great Society initiatives, and three years later, with six major federal grants under our belts, my department had grown to 300 employees. The biggest grant was part of the federal model cities program.

Before my directorship in Prince George's County, I was director of programs for an antipoverty agency, the United Planning Organization, in Washington, D.C. One of the principles that job taught me was the importance of community involvement in the planning process. I was firmly committed to that principle, and as Prince George's County prepared its model cities application, we made sure residents of the affected communities were involved in a significant way. Our model area included both low- and middle-income African American communities as well as moderate-income predominantly white neighborhoods.

The planning process was truly participatory, with residents being involved in the documentation of needs, discussion of alternative strategies and programs for meeting those needs, choosing among those strategies and programs, and developing an implementation plan. Unfortunately, the neighborhoods we were now trying to help had for years been treated by Prince George's County with little more than benign neglect. The residents didn't trust us, and this climate resulted in a court challenge of our effort by the National Association for the Advancement of Colored People (NAACP). After the grant was awarded and detailed planning for implementation was under way, NAACP alleged that the county was doing business as usual and ignoring the needs and aspirations of the African American community. However, the accusation had not taken into account the power of our open planning process. On court day, observers were truly shocked when 300 African Americans showed up for the trial, 95 percent of them in support of our model neighborhood plan. It was a living testimonial to the power of an open process.

My definition of an open process also includes involvement of elected and appointed policy makers, technical experts, and a proper organization to carry out the process. An example of how these elements can be melded with the input of community and business stakeholders occurred in Texas between 1983 and 1985. At that time I was the Dallas assistant manager for planning and development, and we were developing a plan to rebuild North Central Expressway, a main artery connecting downtown Dallas with its northern tier suburbs. When it opened in the 1950s, Central was a shining example of modern freeway planning. By the early 1980s, it had become a traffic nightmare with a thirteen-hour daily peak load and a dismal safety record. Beginning in the mid 1960s, the city had studied Central Expressway several times without devising an acceptable solution. The state of Texas solution, developed in the late 1970s, was to "double-deck" the expressway, but this proposal satisfied no one but the bureaucrats who had devised it. In 1983, Mayor Starke Taylor asked me to address the problem. I informed him that the city would have to undertake an open planning process with policy makers, community stakeholders, and technical staff involved every step of the way; that $2 million would have to be allocated for the project's conceptual design phase (previous studies had been in the $100,000 range); and that the community and technical leadership of the project must be equal to the task.

The idea of an open planning process was embraced; it was agreed that policy makers, stakeholders, and technical staff should be involved in each step. On the funding side, the city put up $1 million and the Dallas Area Rapid Transit System, which proposed placing a rail line in the corridor, chipped in $750,000. Though the freeway is part of the federal interstate system, the planning process was managed by the city of Dallas; it may be the only interstate segment in the nation designed by a local government rather than a state highway department.

On the organizational side, two key steps were taken. First, Walt Human, the talented chief executive officer of Hunt Oil Company, was asked to chair the planning committee; he agreed and proved equal to this complex task. Second, Steve Lockwood, a veteran transportation professional who had been part of the famed Boston corridor transportation planning process, was hired as the project manager, reporting to me. He was compensated as an assistant city manager, but his only mission in the city bureaucracy was to successfully redesign Central Expressway. The planning process worked. In 1985, the state highway department allocated $600 million to completely modernize the expressway from downtown Dallas north to the Dallas beltway. Construction is now under way. When completed in 1998, the new freeway with its eight lanes and three continuous service road lanes will be testimony to the power of an open process.

Remember That Market Is Almost Everything

I believe it is safe to say that there are thousands of plans on shelves in this country that will never by implemented because no one took into account their financial feasibility or their economic impacts. As a public sector planner, I made a career decision to gain some direct experience working in the private sector. This, I felt, would help me to better understand the impact of profits, taxes, the time value of money, and the uncertainties created by the public that affect private investment. I chose to work for the American City Corporation, a subsidiary of the Rouse Company, on a project in Hartford in the early 1970s. This gave me exposure to private sector techniques of analysis and decision making. As a result, the first step I took in each of four subsequent city planning operations that I managed in Fairfax County, Virginia, Washington, D.C., Miami, and Dallas was to hire an economist–financial planner as part of the planning team.

Of course, taking such a step is in itself no panacea for a successful plan or project, but it certainly helps. Economists or financial planners, just like anyone else, can see the market as half empty or half full. To illustrate this point, consider the tale of two supermarkets in Miami. The first was in the Overtown area near downtown, a low- to moderate-income African American community served by small grocery stores but devoid of a substantial supermarket. With the prospect of a federal grant in sight to construct a small strip shopping center including a supermarket, I instructed our planning staff economist to push the definition of *potential market* to its limit as a justification for a $2 million grant from the federal Economic Development Administration (EDA). Based on this optimistic analysis, we received the grant and constructed a center that has been plagued with problems since its opening. But in another portion of Miami, Liberty City, we did not have to stretch the definition of market. Civil disturbances in the early 1980s had led to eighteen deaths and $100 million in property damage, mostly in Liberty City and Overtown, and among the casualties was the only major supermarket serving the 55,000 residents of Liberty City. The market message here was clear: the supermarket needed to be replaced. The only question was how to finance it.

Working with the Talcolcy organization, a local nonprofit, and the nationally known Local Initiatives Support Corporation (LISC), the City of Miami fashioned the Edison Plaza project, funded by EDA and other sources including LISC, Dade County, and the State of Florida. The project, managed by Talcolcy, included a Winn-Dixie supermarket. It has been a tremendous success for two reasons: it was truly rooted in a market need, and it benefited from the creativity and dedication of the members of the funding partnership, especially Otis Pitts of Talcolcy. (Incidentally, Pitts some years later received a "genius" award from the MacArthur Foundation in Chicago.) In this case, community leadership, tenacity, and dedication in response to a valid market need were properly rewarded.

Tapping markets in the inner city frequently requires both operational ingenuity and innovative financing. In researching how inner-city supermarkets could overcome problems such as theft and the difficulties of marketing in low- and moderate-income areas, we learned some excellent approaches from the Community Foods Corporation (CFC) of Baltimore. On the marketing side, CFC found that many people in the area it serves do not subscribe to local newspapers. They do listen to radio, but advertising multiple supermarket bargains in that medium is uneconomical. CFC overcame this problem by publishing a weekly flyer and hand delivering it to the 15,000 households in each market served. On the operational side, CFC addressed the shoplifting issue by placing all small, high-cost items in a "convenience area" of the supermarket where a clerk dispensed them to customers who paid for them on the spot. All other purchases were made in regular checkout lines.

Financing grocery stores in the inner city requires not only offsetting high operational costs but overcoming the timidity of investors. One way to do this is through low-cost financing. At times this financing can be secured through government or foundation grants. Another way is through a low-cost loan fund. In Dallas we financed a small office and retail center and an inner-city shopping center by providing $500,000 loans to each. Interest was 5 percent, with no payments for two years, interest-only payments for the next three years, and debt amortization over twenty-five years. This debt was also subordinate to any bank debt in the project and, therefore, took on the characteristics of a quasi-equity investment. Whatever your planning chores may be, pay attention to financial feasibility, take into account economic impacts, and stay ready to intervene if you must change market dynamics.

Learn from Others and Let Go

I currently work for the Southern Dallas Development Corporation, which has the mission of revitalizing the economy, assisting small business, and creating jobs in a distressed area of our city. Several years ago we decided to carry out a self-employment program for public housing residents on the "micro" business scale. Rather than simply research the literature or learn from our own mistakes, we decided to bring a group of nationally recognized program operators to Dallas, including the head of the micro program in Tucson, the director of the Woman Self Employment Project in Chicago, the head of Women's Ventures in St. Paul, and nationally known business consultant Kathy Keeley. Also invited was the director of the Resident Employment Assistance Program (REAP), run by the Housing Authority of Tampa. Each of these experts provided background and critiqued our program design. This process enabled us to carry out a moderately successful self-employment program in Dallas known as Business Owners Self-Supporting or BOSS. Under the program, twenty-eight people received business training and ten received loans.

Two years later we followed a similar process after deciding to aggressively enter the real estate investment field as a community-based organization. We held another backgrounding and critiquing session, this one attended by the head of the Bedford-Stuyvesant Restoration Corporation of New York City, a board member of a community agency from the Ogontz Avenue area of Philadelphia that owns a shopping center, the director of the Vermont Slauson community organization in Los Angeles that owns an award-winning shopping center, a representative of the East Los Angeles Community Union (TELACU), and the head of the LISC Commercial Investment Program in Chicago. Based on this workshop, we developed a policy paper for our board of directors and are now aggressively pursuing real estate investments.

The basic idea is to save time, energy, and dollars by learning from others. It is also one demonstration of the importance of "letting go" in the planning process. In my experience, many planners are petrified by the notion of circulating a draft planning document to others. Perhaps they are insecure or simply fear criticism, but they may also miss out on good ideas that could strengthen the document. Before I became a city planner, I worked for both houses of the U.S. Congress. I was a part of the lawmaking process by which draft bills are subjected to intense scrutiny and public input, a process that can make for better laws if the right people listen and learn from its results. The same process of scrutiny and input can and should apply to planning documents. It is much better to get draft ideas out early, listen to comments and critiques, and learn from the process than it is to prepare a plan that has no stakeholders and collapses under public scrutiny merely because those who could have strengthened it did not have the opportunity to do so.

Focus on Implementation

When I went to graduate school, planners were taught to be apolitical and not to concern themselves with implementation efforts. I remember reading the first line in Alan Altshuler's excellent book *The City Planning Process:* "The job of the city planner is to propose courses of action, not to execute them" (Altshuler, 1965, p. 1). But in the real world, planning is part of a continuous process that includes implementation and evaluation. In other words, ideas or policies should be viable enough to be carried out, and their impacts should be evaluated to determine if the plan assumptions, strategies, programs, or policies should be revised. There are many techniques for ensuring that plans are implemented; I will focus on two that are based on my experiences in Miami as director of planning and later as assistant city manager for planning and development.

One highlight of the 1970s was the rebirth of downtown retailing through the festival market concept as carried out by the Rouse Company, first in Boston and then in Baltimore. I was convinced that a downtown bayfront park near the Port of Miami would be an excellent site for a festival market. To implement such a concept, public and private partnership roles must be defined and carried out in the design, development, and management of the project.

Miami is governed by a five-member council, including the mayor. To gain support for the festival market concept, I arranged a trip for the mayor and several council members. We traveled to Boston to visit the Faneuil Hall Market Place and to Baltimore where we visited Harbor Place. In each city we talked to Rouse Company project managers, public officials who had negotiated the project partnerships, and key business and civic leaders whose views put the project in the context of the overall downtown economy. After the trip, the Miami council was prepared to support the steps that eventually led to the design and development of the successful Bayside Festival Market in downtown Miami.

Another case had to do with development next to the transit station in Overtown, the low- to moderate-income African American community adjoining downtown Miami. There is a myth that the mere existence of rapid transit changes local market development dynamics, but it is not always true. Overtown needed public intervention to assemble land and change market dynamics to stimulate development. Six key blocks adjacent to the transit station were inhabited by 400 low-income African American households, and over half the land was owned by several African Americans. Many of these people feared that they would be displaced without adequate housing, or that their land would be purchased without providing them the opportunity to invest in the redevelopment projects. Acquiring and redeveloping the land therefore required a realistic, sensitive relocation plan and an opportunity for the existing land owners to participate in the redevelopment process. To accomplish this, the Dade County Housing Authority identified replacement housing that was already funded and not simply planned, guaranteeing that every family would have access to satisfactory housing if and when displacement occurred. In addition, an equity participation program was developed with the assistance of the firm Hammer, Siler, George. This program guaranteed that every owner whose land was purchased could participate at the appropriate level as limited partners in real estate developments occurring later. The existing owners would sell their land to the government knowing that they were guaranteed an option to participate in the development process and potentially benefit from it.

Earlier, I discussed the power of an open participatory process and noted that in the planning process it is necessary to involve public policy makers, community stakeholders, and technical staff every step of the way. In the training of planners there is substantial focus on the technical skills required for competence and success, but very little emphasis on the people skills that are equally important.

Planners, especially in the public sector, have a tendency to disparage the political part of the decision-making process that inevitably surrounds such matters as land use, capital programming and budgeting, and development policy. They may adopt a "don't rock the boat" philosophy, or may propose policy choices that in reality appeal only to the lowest common denominators in a politically charged situation. These are mistakes. Planners who work with public officials must provide them with bold alternative courses of action and a clear statement of the consequences and benefits each alternative might bring. Only this enables officials to do what they were elected to do: set public policy based on analysis and impact. Recognize that the political process is essential but do not try to be a planner-politician.

Community stakeholders are also essential partners in a valid planning process. For members of the community to become enthusiastically and thoroughly involved in planning, they must feel that they are taking part in a process that emphasizes what I call responsive listening. Some planners conclude that they need to "educate" citizens regarding the proper choices to make for their community; actually they should be listening to their needs and aspirations and then responding to the issues they raise. This does not mean accepting bizarre ideas or acquiescing to policy choices that would be detrimental in the long run. I have sometimes found it helpful to receive community input in a sort of brainstorming session. You encourage everyone to speak freely, note that all ideas are open to consideration, and then listen without comment to all recommendations and statements of needs. When everyone has had their say, you give feedback based on your understanding of the community and your skills as a professional planner. You might comment on the feasibility of a proposal or the level of criticality of a stated need, putting each idea in its proper context. It is best to document your responses so that everyone can see that all the ideas you received have been responsibly evaluated.

On the technical side, planners must involve persons from other disciplines in preparing plans or making policy recommendations. These might include engineers, educators, economic developers, and others. Any or all of these disciplines can bring important insight and information to bear on planning choices. The planner thus acts as a facilitator, capitalizing on ideas from other disciplines and reflecting them in a coherent document or policy that has been strengthened by the skills of everyone involved. I have found it useful, in building good working relationships and credibility with other technicians, to make sure they are recognized for their role in the planning process, rather than dominating the spotlight myself. You might list everyone involved in a prominent spot in a finished document, or provide an addendum to a planning policy or recommendation describing the decision-making process and listing those who contributed to it.

Whatever techniques you use to cause it to happen, the essential goal is to make public officials, community stakeholders, and technical participants a part of the planning process. Planning occurs with people, not simply for people.

Chapter Six

Thirty How-To's for Success

Paul C. Zucker

An effective planning program requires the leadership of an effective planning director. There is no formal research to prove this premise, but I believe it to be true. In the private sector, the most successful corporations are usually led by the most effective executives. The business section of your local bookstore is filled with examples: Jan Carlzon, Scandinavian Airlines; Lee Iacocca, Chrysler; Sam Walton, Wal-Mart; Liz Claiborne, Liz Claiborne. In the planning field, the names of the most effective directors may be less known to the general public, but you can find them. Check the bylines on other chapters of this book for some good examples.

What makes for an effective executive or a successful planning director? After some thirty-five years in the planning profession and numerous directorships, I still can't give a complete answer to that question. I've had both good and bad experiences and, as in all things, I learned more from the failures than the successes. At any rate, I have some thoughts to share.

One of the country's top corporate executives is Harold Hook, chairman of the board of American General. He observes that while two executives may appear to be doing the exact same things in the exact same way, nevertheless one may become a great success and the other a failure. Why? Hook suggests simply that the line between success and failure can be so fine it cannot be measured.

Tom Peters, the national management guru, sometimes tells his audiences of hard-driving executives that success at high levels may be a matter of luck. This shocks some people, but many come to agree after they think about it. After all, Peters points out, the world is filled with bright, aggressive, capable leaders, all working to do a good job. The success of some over others may indeed be based on luck.

One might also wonder, in the case of planning directors, why some are highly successful in one community but fail in another. One possibility, besides luck, is the concept of "fit"—being the right person in the right place at the right time. Success in a given job is usually dependent upon others: coworkers, elected officials, city managers. The community's basic orientation—progressive, conservative, good-old-boy, change-seeking, or what have you—might also be a factor. All these things together determine if there is a fit between the planning director and the community.

Studies on leadership in general provide much insight into good leadership traits. One of the best is *The Leadership Challenge* (Kouzes and Posner, 1987). The authors suggest that most successful leaders have the following five practices and ten commitments in common:

Challenging the Process
  1. Search for opportunities.
  2. Experiment and take risks.

Inspiring a Shared Vision

  3. Envision the future.
  4. Enlist others.

Enabling Others to Act

  5. Foster collaboration.
  6. Strengthen others.

Modeling the Way

  7. Set the example.
  8. Plan small wins.

Encouraging the Heart

  9. Recognize individual contributions.
  10. Celebrate accomplishments.

All of these ideas are useful. Other leadership characteristics, however, may be unique to government and particularly to planning directors.

Leadership Styles of Planning Directors

I divide all planning directors between three leadership types, which I call the three *B*'s. Their characteristics follow.

Bureaucrat

The Bureaucrat director lasts a long time. He (it is usually a he) does not rock the boat, goes with the flow, is unknown in the profession, never accomplishes much, goes along with today's paradigm whatever it may be, and is rarely fired. As kindly suggested by an understanding friend following one of my firings as a planning director, only a competent person can get fired from government. The Bureaucrat neither understands nor practices leadership.

Boat Rocker

The Boat Rocker director is filled with ideas, is a forceful agent of change, has clear values (for better or worse), is well known in the profession, is generally a leader, and on the average lasts two to four years. He or she gets fired or knows when to move on. Although a few things get accomplished, lasting effectiveness is low.

Bravo

The Bravo director is also filled with ideas, is a change agent, gets things done, is a leader, and stays a long time. You'll read about some of these Bravo planning directors, such as Richard Bernhardt and Keith Cubic, elsewhere in this book. So how do Bravo directors do it? What are their characteristics? Can you become one?

Three Survival Skills of Bravo Directors

Studies of corporate managers show that they can be effective using any of several different management styles. However, irrespective of style, all effective managers are good leaders. The dilemma for planning directors is how to stay in the job long enough to be an effective leader. Through the years, I've seen at least three ways that Bravo directors solidify their positions. Some use all three, some survive on just one. The three survival skills are building personal relationships, buying into leadership, and creating one's own lobby.

Build Personal Relationships

Many planners naturally develop good relationships because of their personalities. Others find developing personal relationships more difficult. Some studies show that the only ways to change the adult personality are brain surgery, deep psychotherapy, religious conversion, or drugs, but fortunately you don't need any of them to become a Bravo planning director. Your present personality will do; you can learn to make better use of personal relationships.

I suggest you try to relate to your elected officials, planning commissioners, city manager, and others on a more personal basis. Let them know you as a person, and try to get to know them as people. It's much harder to fire someone you like. Ronald Reagan was a great recent example of this phenomenon; for many, it was hard to get mad at him even when he did or said what they considered crazy things.

To use this technique at the local level, you'll need to find a way to spend time with the power brokers. This can be difficult with busy elected officials. Look for opportunities to make informal nonbusiness connections, perhaps before meetings while waiting for a quorum. Some officials welcome casual drop-in visits; find out which ones do, then learn when they are usually in their offices. Discover what you have in common, and get to know about their families, hobbies, and idiosyncrasies. Speaking of families, one successful city manager told me he would never get fired because his wife always became friends with the wives of his elected officials (obviously, this technique isn't for everybody). In the corporate world, the master of personal relationships is Harvey McKay. Read his first book, *How to Swim with the Sharks Without Being Eaten Alive,* for some other good ideas.

You may also be able to develop relationships through one or more "boss interpreters." The boss interpreter (a term coined by Harold Hook as part of a copyrighted management program called Main Event Management/Model-Netics) is the person or persons in an organization who know what the boss said, wants done, or meant. There is virtually always a boss interpreter. He or she may be a secretary, assistant, campaign contributor, golfing buddy, another department head, or anyone else close to the person you want to cultivate.

Boss interpreters can be extremely useful. Not only can they help you understand the boss, but perhaps even more important, they can be used as a channel to educate the boss or sell the boss on proposals. Try to identify one or more boss interpreters for each of your elected officials. After you find them, continually check to make sure they remain accurate. If you get burned, it's time to find a more effective interpreter. And remember, the boss interpreter supplements, but does not replace, a relationship.

Buy into Leadership

A second skill of many Bravo planning directors is the ability to hook onto the star of a dynamic mayor. (It's almost impossible to do this unless you've already developed a personal relationship as discussed above.) Your tenure may not be as long as those of Bravo directors who use the other two techniques discussed here, but your effectiveness will likely be substantial while it lasts because of your relationship to the power structure. Many elected officials focus on short-term gains, but if you're hitched to somebody powerful enough, you should be able to introduce at least some long-term ideas that will remain effective long after you and the mayor leave the scene. If you're good enough at using the other two techniques, you may even survive after the mayor leaves. On the other hand, your odds of effectiveness will go up if you do not worry about long-term tenure.

Create Your Own Lobby

Otherwise known as building a constituency, this technique can be highly effective. But if your activities in this arena are too overt, some officials may think you are building your own empire, and they'll begin to see you as a direct threat to their own interests and power. So be careful how you go about it.

Since a planner's job involves providing information and education, building constituencies can actually help citizen empowerment. With the proper information, most constituent groups will arrive at a sensible planning direction. Older members of our profession will remember well a classic planner, Hugh Pomeroy. When Hugh took the podium at national planning conferences, he always had a camera and started off by taking pictures of the audience. I remember a session where citizen participation was being discussed. The planners were concerned that citizens would run off in bad directions, but Hugh would have none of it. He assured the group that given time, citizens would come to conclusions similar to the ones drawn by professional planners.

My most memorable experience with creating lobbies was as planning director of Marin County in the mid 1960s. After years of dormant planning, the county was ready for action. I was hired as a young, brash, wet-behind-the-ears, eager planning director. The department was given funds to expand the staff with the best and brightest from around the country. We held strong beliefs that were shared by many citizens. Citizen group after citizen group became our natural constituency. In many respects, we were too naive to be politically sensitive. We bought into neither personal relationships nor the elected leadership. After three years on the job, three of the five members of the board of supervision asked me to resign. The county charter allowed me to ask for a public hearing. Following a nine-hour hearing, the longest in the history of the county and attended by a packed house, I was given a 3–2 vote of confidence.

Some suggest that creating one's own lobby will not work in the 1990s. Yet, given the lack of good leadership at the local political level, the time may be better than ever for planners to build a constituency.

Incidentally, the end of the Marin County story is also worth telling. After four years, I took a leave of absence and ran for supervisor against the chair of the board. After losing the election, I was fired. It was an interesting lesson. Once I crossed the political line, although many individuals remained supportive my constituency no longer saw me as an independent-thinking planning director, but rather as one more political figure.

Bravo planning directors are needed regardless of the planning model being used. The best of them use all three of the techniques I have suggested. They develop personal relationships at all levels inside and outside of government, but particularly at the appointing level. Since they believe in democracy, Bravo directors also tie into the elected leadership and help to advance an agenda. And by creating their own constituencies, they provide stability and balance to the political arena. What does the Bravo director get from all this personally? Two things: greater longevity and greater effectiveness.

Thirty How-To's for Success

No one can tell you exactly how to succeed as a planner. But here is my list of suggestions that may add to your effectiveness, help you get to the top of the profession, and make it easier for you to stay there.

1. *Don't try to change your boss.* I used to believe that one of my jobs as a government manager was to change my elected officials. In thirty-five years of trying, how often did I succeed? Never! In traveling the country, I see too many burned-out planners and government officials who cannot change their elected officials and bosses. A better approach is to ask, "How can I learn to work better with this !%&#* elected official?" Call it democracy in action.

2. *Pledge yourself to excellence.* Strike the old phrase "good enough for government" from your vocabulary. Reread *In Search of Excellence* (Peters and Waterman, 1982).

3. *Create big ideas.* Planners seem to have lost the ability to come up with the big ideas. I was never fired for the big idea, only the small stuff or the style I was using. Daniel Burnham was right after all.

4. *Don't be afraid to act.* Try to accomplish things, not avoid criticism. Mistakes are an essential part of learning and action.

5. *Keep cool.* Use tact and keep cool under fire. Let everyone else make fools of themselves. You have done your homework so you do not need to get defensive.

6. *Don't hold grudges.* Carry no grudges. Treat each project as if it is a new one. When you get knocked down, get up again. But learn from your experiences. If you keep doing the same thing the same way over and over, you can expect the same results. A change in approach may be necessary.

7. *Don't take criticism personally.* Accept your role as one of "those government bureaucrats." Laugh more—at yourself!

8. *Give public information freely.* Public information belongs to the

public, so give it to them. There are no secrets in contemporary management. There are no secrets in government.

9. *Don't make recommendations based on politics.* Base recommendations only on your professional skills and judgment, not on politics. But be political with your strategy. Ask yourself: Is this the right time to make a recommendation? Have I spent enough time educating the elected officials or building the necessary support before I make my recommendations?

10. *Try to understand.* Officials have reasons for the positions they take. Try to understand what the reasons are. When you can make their argument better than they can, you'll come out a winner. Listen and try to determine what they really want, not just what they say they want.

11. *Admit that you don't know.* If you do not know an answer, admit it. But then go find the answer. Don't try to fake it.

12. *Admit that you blew it.* Nothing diffuses a bad situation faster than simply admitting a mistake when you make one. This is easier for most people to accept than some crazy excuse.

13. *Solve problems.* Try to solve your customer's problem, even if you think it isn't really a problem. And maybe it's not from your broader perspective. Still, getting it solved will gain you support for your bigger ideas. Don't sweat the little ones, just get them taken care of.

14. *Ignore political posturing.* Elected officials may feel they have to posture for the public, but you don't have to buy into it. Learn to separate posturing from the real issues. If your relations with officials are good, they may even give you prior notice of what they're up to.

15. *Do not assume.* When meeting with politicians, do not assume they have read a thing you have written. Also, be brief, be prepared to skip your presentation, and go with the flow. Get to their issues first, not yours.

16. *Mold pluralism.* Government is pluralistic and therefore consistency is often not possible. Your job is to help mold this pluralism into some reasonable policy framework.

17. *Respect political egos.* Most elected officials have enormous egos; in today's world, they may need them to get elected. Respect the ego even if you can't respect the politician.

18. *Make your idea their idea.* Be certain you have educated officials about the issues and that they know what you think should be done. Let them take the credit for good ideas.
19. *Help out, even if you disagree.* If elected officials decide to act against your recommendations, help them anyway. It's part of the job.
20. *Be modest.* Even politicians sometimes come up with the right answers, in spite of overwhelming reports and evidence that you have presented to the contrary. Give them credit.
21. *Understand that timing is everything.* Have a drawer full of ideas ready to go. Shuffle the deck to meet political timing.
22. *Lobby.* Build lobbies for your ideas in an indirect way. Let others carry the ball for you. Creating lobbies may be one of the most important things you do.
23. *Treat relationships as a full-time job.* In large cities or organizations, the planning director or community development director may need to consider building and maintaining relationships with elected officials as the biggest part of the job. Find a good assistant director to keep the trains running on time.
24. *Do your homework.* Be prepared. Your best tools are your knowledge and your grasp of the facts. Bring something to the negotiating table.
25. *Be careful.* Don't do anything you would not want to read about on the front page of your local newspaper.
26. *Have fun.* Life is too short to be a beat-up bureaucrat. If you can't have fun, find different employment.
27. *Don't surprise the wrong people.* You may be surprised at what occurs at a public hearing, but never surprise a public official yourself.
28. *Be speedy.* Elected officials like fast action. If you can respond to their requests the same day, terrific! If not, let them know when you will be able to respond, and stick to it.
29. *Avoid political involvement.* Don't walk precincts for your favorite candidate, contribute to the campaign, or show up in a picture in the campaign literature.
30. *Listen.* Consider with an open mind what public officials, private citizens, and organized opponents have to say. You might hear something valuable.

Empowerment and Leadership: A Note of Caution

Do the ideas I've presented here suggest a new paradigm for planning? Some other contributors to this book make a strong and compelling case for empowerment as a new planning paradigm. Intuitively, I too share much of the criticism of past planning models. But intuition and the real world may be two different things. I've heard much talk but seen virtually no solid research on the effectiveness of any planning model, including empowerment.

In my management consulting practice, I've had the opportunity to work with numerous planning departments throughout the country. I've interviewed hundreds of elected officials and planning commissioners. Many are interested in planning efficiency, but not effectiveness. There's a difference. A study of efficiency asks questions such as: How fast did we get out the permits? What were our costs? Did we produce the plans we said we would produce? An effectiveness study, should anyone be interested enough or courageous enough to make one, would ask: Were more people housed? Did their satisfaction with life improve? Did more people feel less alienated from government? Did anyone notice the special view that was preserved? Did crime go down?

Government is excellent at talking about a problem and proposing a solution. But generally there is little or no research to find out why—or even if—past remedies didn't work. Often an isolated incident can lead to an entirely new policy direction. Too often government engages in false logic known as the "fallacy of composition": event B follows event A, so event B must have been caused by event A. The witch doctor dances in the spring and the rain follows.

The current national political dialogue says it all. Crime will be solved if jail sentences are longer, the problem of unwed mothers will vanish if welfare is slashed, and immigration will be curtailed if benefits to immigrants are cut. Local planning debates are not much better. Transit will solve air pollution, inadequate transportation will be adequate when the balance of housing and jobs is restored, changing the color of a building will enhance our lives, and neotraditional planning will bring back old values to the community. In each of these cases, I say: maybe or maybe not. I'm not debating or defending any of the paradigms here, just raising some cautionary flags.

Empowerment as a paradigm is not something the planning profession needs to blindly embrace. Empowerment is here and will be here for a long time whether it is embraced or not. The forces of the information age radically changed eastern Europe; now they are creating part of the apparent havoc at city hall. More information gives citizens more power, so more and more cities decide that citizen empowerment is the right way to go. Some cities have established new bureaus, often at the expense of their planning departments, that focus on helping neighborhoods become empowered. Empowerment has arrived, full blown, from the information age. The genie cannot be put back in the bottle.

In some private companies, empowerment of employees and customers has led to remarkable results—improved productivity, higher profits, and more motivated employees. But some empowered companies seem to be losing their way and are not achieving these results.

In government, empowerment sometimes has led to single-purpose lobbies, discrimination, and a lack of social responsibility and justice. Increasingly, we deal with symptoms rather than the problems themselves. Why? What is wrong? I think the problem lies in some misconceptions about empowerment. Empowerment does not mean that everyone can do exactly as they please. It works only when core values and a clear mission continue to hold things together. To develop values and mission requires leadership, and most good leadership does not come from group thinking. Studies in the private sector illustrate that it generally comes from one or more top executives. It's easy to see how disastrous a lack of clear leadership can be in federal government. So can it be at the local level.

I've been working with a number of local governments who believe they are on the road to empowerment. The programs that seem to be doing well also seem to have clear values, missions, and leadership. Those that are floundering seem to assume that, in the presence of empowerment, leadership is no longer necessary.

This brings us back to the job of planning director. To be effective, a planning director must be a strong leader no matter what planning paradigm or agenda is in place, and that includes the empowerment paradigm in particular. Empowerment without leadership leads to chaos.

To survive as a leader, I suggest you become a Bravo planning director. Use everything at your disposal: luck, the right fit between you and your community, Kouzes and Posner's five practices and ten commitments cited earlier, personal relationships, leadership buy-in, and your own lobby. I cannot assure you success, but you will have the time of your life trying to achieve it.

Chapter Seven

Organizing and Managing for Success

Keith L. Cubic

In 1971 when I started my planning career, Oregon did not have a statewide planning program. Local planning was the only process for guiding change. I was a bright-eyed young planner who was dedicated to resource and development management and worked with subdivision regulations and with citizen participation programs. Making planning work in Oregon was hard. There were battles and wars. In my conservative rural county, planning was constantly under attack, but I continued to focus our program on tailoring it wherever possible to fit local need within the parameters of state law. I have grown with, suffered through, and lobbied for amendments of Oregon's planning system to ensure its success. I have observed statewide planning in Oregon from its beginnings. Guidelines for land use became a series of stringent rules and regulations governing all development. An advisory program became a sophisticated but complicated system of land use management.

After more than two decades of Oregon planning, I am now a bright-eyed middle-aged planning administrator who has learned that being on the cutting edge, focusing on clients, having a proactive program, and striving to be the best in the state directly relates to success. My planning career has been enhanced by working my way up in the ranks of planning positions, maintaining a statewide vision, advocating for my local planning program, and striving for excellence in everything for which I'm responsible.

There have been surprises in my career. First, I never expected Oregon's planning program to become so complicated and so top-down oriented; however, it is effective. Second, I never expected to be able to work for, and become the director of, one planning jurisdiction, Douglas County, for over twenty years. Finally, I did not realize how much fun the challenges of professional planning and planning administration could be and how rewarding a career field I had selected.

Doing the Right Thing

Our profession demands distinguished leadership. We deal with policy and shape future-oriented goals. We must ensure local, state, and national officials have vision and do not get bogged down in the maze of day-to-day operations and tasks. As planners and leaders, we must have high standards, respect, and do the right thing! The "right things" in leadership are self-awareness, vision, imagination, conscience, initiative, wisdom, independent will, and the power to base decisions on value-centered principles (Covey, 1989). Our success as leaders is shaped largely by our communication skills: writing, listening, and speaking. Planners have the special occupational privilege of influencing community behavior and gaining success through achieving common goals.

Planners are resource and development managers. We must conserve our natural resources and guide change to attain a desirable environment. Resource and growth management play an equal role in our challenge. Local governments can build credibility for state and federal programs. We must demonstrate a logical, thoughtful, and defensible decision-making process in our planning programs. We need to be sure our efforts have a solid foundation from which to make decisions and recommendations. It is possible to foster economic development as an urban, rural, and resource issue. The path planners chart in this process will set the stage for future generations.

As professional planners, we must build trust in both our personal and program actions. Fulfilling the challenges of good leadership and sound planning moves individuals and programs a long way in the building of trust. Additionally, planners must be honest and innovative in their activities, and must promote team opportunities. Planners can foster confidence in programs by embracing a "no surprises" philosophy with local, appointed, and elected officials. Trust is built by designing and placing emphasis on a process that offers options and is responsive. Trust does not just happen, but it is an evolved confidence in the local government. Trust will be decisive in our ability to attain the goals of planning in the twenty-first century.

Planners today must focus on customer service. Quality customer service is not always saying yes but rather understanding your clients' needs and providing services and assistance that build a program's credibility. It requires a goal-based program with expectations of excellence that promote teamwork and partnerships, and must include innovative approaches to planning solutions. A high level of personal and program integrity are also essential to successful customer service. Every planning professional must strive to implement planning programs with an emphasis on customer service.

Organizing and Managing for Success

To affect public policy successfully, a planning department must think well beyond the customary assignments associated with planning administration. Typically a planning department supports the governing body and planning commission, administers land use regulations, clears permits, conducts long-range planning and planning studies, provides public information, and coordinates at a variety of levels.

Management, work programming, forecasting, and conceptualizing skills must be applied to your work and must be integrated throughout your agency's activities. Often, the skills of a planner related to people, projects, and programs are needed but not used in other local government activities. Besides what you accomplish in your own department, emphasis should be placed on contributions you can make to management of your jurisdiction in general, internal and external coordination, and short-term goals-setting and work programming (three- to five-year) for the agency and jurisdiction.

It is essential for all planners to recognize that regardless of philosophy or principle, their objective is to *serve the governing body*.

In doing so, the planning department will serve the people (generally and individually) through consistent administration of plan policies and regulations and a priority on customer service. Service to the broad public of your jurisdiction by administering planning laws with a customer service focus enhances effectiveness. Planners must make their community a livable place for all by administering in a practical manner and promoting revision of existing regulations, plans, or programs within existing legal constraints while strengthening public support and acceptance. These responsibilities demand that the planning department be organized and managed for success.

Know Your Job

A first step in organizing for success is to know the major (critical) functions of the agency. This identification process should also be applied to every employee of the agency. There are a variety of techniques to identify an agency's major or critical functions. A most effective one is the Pareto principle (Imundo, 1991). This involves assessing your work to identify what generates the most significant results. The Pareto principle is commonly referred to as the 80–20 rule: 80 percent of your time is required to generate 20 percent of important results. By identifying the critical functions of an agency or job, the resources of the agency or individual can be focused on the important results. If you use the Pareto principle and connect it with a modified management-by-objective (MBO) approach to job assignments, the whole organization can be organized for success (McConkey, 1975).

On a department or agencywide basis it is essential to have a participatively developed mission, identify critical or major functions, and structure resources on those functions. Applying this process to an individual position within a planning agency can assist in monitoring efficiency and effectiveness, improving delegation of authority and responsibility, strengthening performance, and improving management. There are four steps to the job assessment process. (This *must* be a participatory process, with planning managers committing sufficient time and resources, for it to be effectively implemented.)

The *introductory phase* involves a review of the individual employee's job description, a detailed listing of duties, and a discussion of MBO concepts, management, and skills required in job performance. Second is the *analysis phase,* during which a critical function analysis is completed of each of the employee's responsibilities. There are normally between three and eight critical functions to a job; a higher number means the list is too detailed and needs to be reevaluated. The critical functions (major job responsibilities) are then evaluated to judge whether they affect external or internal operations. Then the duties are prioritized and an estimated work time percentage assigned to each. The process could stop here, but additional steps strengthen it.

In the *negotiation phase,* departmental goals are evaluated and discussed with the individual employee. Mutually agreed upon measurable objectives are established for the critical functions of each employee. Usually three to five measurements for each function are adequate. Measurable objectives are oriented to both the program and the individual. These objectives must be developed between the supervisor and the employee, and both must be in full agreement with the final statement. Finally comes the *application phase:* the list of major job responsibilities is utilized and the measurable objectives are achieved, with performance reviewed through a standard personnel evaluation but tied to the MBO process. (Ultimately you can develop your own unique evaluation reflecting the job's major functions.) During the application phase, timesheets are usually revised to reflect the major job responsibilities now identified.

This four-phase process is not fixed. It cannot be done once and considered complete. Each employee's critical functions and measurable objectives must receive an annual review. As work projects are completed, responsibilities change and, as experience dictates, modifications are appropriate to the program.

Program the Work
Managing activities strengthens success. Things often simply happen, new intervening factors crop up, and new assignments are common. Whatever the issue, knee-jerk reaction is rarely the best response; rather, a thoughtful, studied response tied to organization and budget abilities is required. Work programming is an important part of overall agency management and offers much greater accountability and certainty in operations. It improves the

provision of service and performance, but most important, it allows others to identify how and when to best coordinate activities. This is a real advantage in working with other agencies. Structuring operations and decisions to fulfill our duties is a part of our careers. We are responsible for making sure that planning takes place. We should use our planning process and project skills in overall program management. Placing a high premium on timely performance and product in your planning process leads your community to perceive your agency as results-oriented and effective.

Organizing for success also demands agency work programming. Work programming is deciding what must be done, when, by whom, and how. It means the process of integrating a manager's or governing body's plans or goals directly into the agency. It is communication! In a broad sense, work programming is planning. I program work because it allows me to develop a timetable of activities, provide control, determine resources needed to attain a project, communicate and coordinate, determine and delegate authority, aid employees in understanding what is expected of them, build commitment to the project or assignment, and identify and remove or reduce obstacles to it. In addition, work programming gives the supervisor, manager, or director the tools to manage. It becomes easier to place prioritized projects and activities before the governing body, schedule or avoid special assignments, measure staff performance, document and justify budget and staffing needs, and communicate the agency mission.

There are various systems or styles of work planning. Here is one that I use regularly that has proven simple and effective. First, establish achievable goals and objectives. Have a clear idea of where the agency or organization is going. Second, develop a list of projects to complete over a three-year period. This list should include projects currently in progress, those coming up in the immediate and near future, and ongoing programs and assignments.

Prioritize the project list into categories of high, medium, and low priority. Consideration should be given to goals, objectives, budget, and political reality. Select projects for completion during a specific period, usually a fiscal year. After reviewing the prioritized list, select those projects that are most important to complete during the period. Keep in mind the ongoing programs and assignments that should be part of the selected projects list. Establish time limits for each project. Be sure to account for ongoing programs and other assignments and leave ample nonproject time for them. Allocate manpower. Assign available staff to each project based on their special talents and abilities. Develop a Gantt chart based on the selected projects, time limitations, and manpower (American Management Association, 1970). A Gantt chart graphically illustrates the newly developed work program and helps to monitor progress at a glance. Implement the work program. Strive to ensure timely completion of each project. However, no work program is perfect, so you're bound to stumble over unforeseen circumstances that usually cause delays.

It is also important to maintain enough flexibility to meet the urgent and unforeseen needs of your organization or agency. Monitor at the third month for progress and possible delays. Review and revise, if necessary, at six months. Monitor at the ninth month for progress and possible changes. Develop a new work program before the twelfth month. With an ongoing work programming commitment, this renewal step will become a more in-depth "review and revise" step. The process should become circular: initiate the first steps for the next cycle before the final steps of the present cycle are completed so that the process can be continuous.

Note that more than one work program may be best for the overall planning department. Programs can be drawn up for divisions, sections, or project areas. Use the work program regularly. Advertise it, post it on the wall, and brief the governing bodies on it. Tie it to progress checks and obtain periodic reports. Build the work program into the agency's mission and major functions. Use the expertise of staff on scheduling and to make reality checks (can you actually accomplish what's on the agenda?). Delegate details; assign staff to carry out the work program. Build slippage (float time) into estimates. I recommend 25 percent! There are many intervening factors. Make certain that success and attainment is possible. Be satisfied with positive results. Do not be blocked by lack of achievement or completion. Be sure to celebrate success and recognize achievement. Planners must make work programming positive!

In successful work programming, planners must clearly recognize the parameters within which their program operates. This requires a team vision that expands beyond immediate staff. Always consider how you use teamwork in your activities. Once you have structured yourself and your agency it is crucial that you build trust in all aspects of your activity.

Build Trust

If you believe that your agency must operate as a team and those around you recognize that belief, it will increase your effectiveness in the formation and adoption of public policy, in successful work programming, and in gaining budget support. You must be able to discuss and disagree about any issue, then support whatever final decision is made even if you still disagree. People who are not afraid to state positions and make recommendations, but support the final position that policy makers select, are invaluable. Such a combination of integrity and pragmatism can remove many barriers between the professional planner and the appointed or elected official.

Building trust also requires the planner to incorporate a variety of agendas into departmental activities. Being able to solve problems, propose options, and create new systems is basic to building trust; being creative within general parameters and the constraints of state and local law will strengthen your ability to influence public policy. Trust building involves both personal and program performance behaviors. Trust in the planning program and in the planning professionals employed by your jurisdiction corresponds directly with effectiveness.

Diversify Program Responsibilities

Trust in a planning program can also be developed by diversifying program responsibilities. With the environment set by a clearly established department role, a consistent focus on strong communications at all levels, and a high standard of excellence, the opportunity to diversify your programs is considerable. A myriad of activities are associated with planning and could be organized or managed by a planning agency. These may be pet projects of the governing body, projects or activities not now being done (or being done elsewhere but poorly), prior failures, new grant opportunities, new requirements of law, activities forecast in a work program but undone; or anything another agency doesn't want to do that might be reasonably undertaken by planners. If the planning program has already built trust, it has established the perfect opportunity for the planning department to diversify. Diversification provides the ability to manage "white hat" nonregulatory programs. It offers new managerial and policy challenges and opportunities to a planning manager.

Diversification and involvement in a broader spectrum of planning activity enhances your planning effectiveness. Your policy-making expertise, developed in the planning program, can be applied to related areas and offered to the governing body. A trusted planner can serve as a staff consultant for policy and an expert on process issues. And diversification can prove a valuable asset in times of limited budgets or resource circumstances. Grants can be utilized to augment staff. Your agency's value is broadened. The typical regulatory "black hat" image is changed. When cuts are required, the diversification programs can be shed to demonstrate fiscal responsiveness and measurable reductions while protecting the planning and other core functions of your agency.

Set Quality Standards

Quality expectations are the standards you set for the performance of your planning program. They are critical to effectiveness and success. You should challenge your staff, program, and self with the quality standards you set. A realistic but high standard is the key to success. Your high quality standards should be a stated expectation and a philosophy of the department. If your approach is to make your planning agency the best it can be, your operations will thrive.

To ensure quality planning, our profession requires that we serve as educators as well as planners. We are challenged to inform, involve, and educate our clients, advisory committees, governing body, and staff. Formal and informal activities serve as special opportunities to educate. Planners must take advantage of as many as possible. A planner's leadership is instrumental to the education process and must be flexible and adaptive to be successful.

Communicate Effectively

One measure of a planning program's quality is your ability to communicate about planning issues. Quality communication is a vital ingredient in effectiveness. Seldom has a planning director lost a job when poor communication did not play a substantial role. Constant attention must be given to positive, two-way communication between you and three audiences: governing body, public, and staff.

Effective communications reduce surprises. Given the complexity of planning administration, it helps to be prepared before entering the arena of public decision making; you should at least know what issues may be discussed and the possible direction a decision may take. This empowers you to offer professional leadership to the planning process. Prehearing communication is an indispensable tool to help guide policy and reduce uncertainty. It can serve to focus issues and assist the governing body. Have no fear about offering assistance and information; in fact, fear *not* offering them. Pre-hearing issue resolution, informational appointments or workshops, endorsement requests for work programming, and town hall reviews are all excellent grounds for communication. Every planning professional should adopt the strategy of alerting governing bodies to hot spots, significant issues, and informational conflicts before the decision-making process begins. This is not lobbying but informing, and it contributes significantly to effectiveness.

Communication is not just verbal! An agency's success and effectiveness are often achieved through reputation and message delivery. Program promotion is important! Tools such as newsletters, press releases, special articles, and published positive answers to difficult or intricate issue questions can all be used to promote a program. Handouts are effective tools. Use them both informationally and promotionally. Be sure they are simple and understandable. Push the white-hat aspects of your programs. Staff reports, letters, and forms all communicate about your program. Always remember that communication is elementary and yet the most fundamental function of good leadership. Also make sure to "walk the talk"—actions always speak louder than words.

Emphasize Customer Service
Another way to build effectiveness is to create a strong service orientation in your department, which includes developing expedient ways of responding to the public. This will lead to positive feedback from the community to your governing body and subsequently assist your effectiveness. Planning agencies should set the stage for effectiveness when they design their missions. A mission

is a major communication tool, and customer service should be a part of it (McClendon, 1992).

Aim for Excellence

Quality means excellence, and excellence in your planning program, in management and employee performance, is a reasonable expectation. Excellence can be measured by five key components. One is a record of attainment, how well tasks have been done. Second is a mission to help others (governing body, staff, and public), which means demonstrating a public service orientation. Third is a consultative supervision or participatory management style that demonstrates your internal strength and ability to delegate. Fourth is intellectual maturity, reflected by your ability to change; adaptability measures excellence. And fifth is emotional stability, a nonreactionary style that allows you to deal effectively with both wins and losses.

A top-notch planning manager also has strong technical capabilities, integrity, loyalty, industry, and honesty. These characteristics are vital if the planning manager is to achieve the level of excellence necessary to heighten effectiveness. High performance standards go hand-in-hand with effective communication. As a planning manager, you have a position of authority and opportunity, but one that involves risk, making decisions, and being held accountable. Demonstrating excellence in all aspects of your work allows your planning program to be valued, used as a resource, and effective in bringing about desired change.

Provide Leadership

I'm discussing leadership last because planners cannot be effective leaders until they have first organized for success, set the stage for trust, and established a standard of excellence for themselves and their programs. This preparation enables effective leadership. Becoming a leader affords many opportunities, but also brings the burden of major responsibilities. To be a good leader is to make good decisions, to be a role model, and to work at guiding others. A good leader must be willing to take a stand even at the risk of offending some people. As a leader you must be convincing and often do not have anyone to delegate the decision to, to share the responsibility.

There is a difference between leading and managing. Leading is "doing the right thing"; managing is "doing it right." Leadership is a personal and professional commitment to value-centered actions. It is modeling. It is an earned respect. Leadership is influence. Management is bringing things together, determining how to accomplish goals but not necessarily setting them. Planning directors both lead and manage, so we need to remember these differences. Effective leaders must accept their responsibilities and commit the necessary time to their duties. Time management is an important skill for leaders; you must be able to control yourself before attempting to control others.

If you lead a planning program, or aspire to do so, you must deal with policy, be visionary and see the big picture, set goals, do the right thing, have high standards, demonstrate respect, master a package of behaviors that you can adapt to particular situations, and listen and speak well. It's a long list. Fundamentally, planners must use their expertise, their knowledge, and the excitement they feel for the profession to demonstrate their leadership. No one style is right for all occasions; leadership means deciding which style will best influence the planning program today. Henry Ford once said, "Whether you think you can or you think you can't, you're right." If you think you can, you're a step ahead in the journey toward successful leadership.

I'm sure this chapter makes it clear that there is no single secret to becoming an effective planning manager and leader. I've discussed organizing for success, building trust, demanding excellence, and providing leadership. Beyond these things, I recommend and adhere to a philosophy characterized by this statement: "As a planning manager, I am totally responsible." Whatever planning action takes place, whether by me or a staff member or a higher official, it is my responsibility.

There is, I admit, one final element to planning success: luck. The dictionary defines luck as "a force that brings good fortune or adversity; the events or circumstances that operate for or against an individual favoring chance; also . . . success." Perhaps we can shape our luck to an extent, but the saying "no amount of planning will ever replace dumb luck" is true. So . . . good luck!

Lessons on Politics

From the very beginning of organized planning early in this century, there has been a clear relationship to the political process at the national, state, and local levels. Curiously, the first half of the century was marked by efforts to isolate planners from politicians— usually through the creation of buffers called independent planning commissions. Today most planners have learned that success can only be attained when planning is a vital part of politics and the political life of the nation. Planners have learned that advocacy and collaboration are crucial to effectiveness within the political process.

Not that collaboration is easy. The four chapters in Part Two have to do with survival as well as success; after all, planners cannot be effective if they do not survive the political process. In part, survival is a matter of helping communities help themselves. This empowerment creates alliance between planner and public, which is good for both sides. Chapter Ten, in particular, deals with giving special help to those who cannot help themselves; this represents the evolution of 1960s-style advocacy planning to today's more acceptable equity planning. Put it all together and, as the final chapter in this part suggests, collaborative public service may be the key to achieving your planning visions.

Chapter Eight

Guidelines for Survival and Success

Linda L. Davis

Surviving the political arena is not something you learn in planning school. You learn it on the job, sometimes through terrible mistakes but more often by watching others to see what works for them and by experimenting to see what works for you. You do not have to love politics to be in planning, but you have to be sensitive to the politics of planning to survive. If you plain dislike politics and politicians, then you should consider getting out of planning. You cannot do your profession justice without understanding and accommodating the politics of planning.

Like most planners of my era (the 1960s) I entered the profession full of idealism. In those days, many planners felt like evangelists carrying the message of good planning to the council chambers and county courthouses of this country. Almost no one could disagree that if we conducted this rational, objective process called comprehensive planning our communities would be better. But at the same time, no one really cared about the results very much. While planning was the politically correct thing to do at the time, most plans sat on the shelves and had little real effect. Politicians could salve their sense of correctness and do the planning but still let business go on as usual, not hurting anyone. In the early 1970s this all began to change. Along came the environmental and antigrowth movements and then some significant court cases, especially here in Oregon, that gave meaning to comprehensive plans. Suddenly, politicians began to take notice of the plans and planners that seemed to be the center of all the controversy. A lot of planners I knew did not survive those tumultuous years because they were not prepared for this aspect of their profession.

The world of planning will never be the same as it was back then—and let's be thankful for that. While we do not want to lose forever the sense of idealism that most planners still have when they enter the profession, it has to be tempered with a large dose of pragmatism. An understanding of the politics of planning is crucial to the planner's survival in this volatile, contentious, and litigious society in which we now live.

This chapter is a checklist for political survival, reflecting some of the things I have learned about the subject. I have included some of my own experiences as examples. The stories have been simplified to more effectively illustrate particular points; the real situations were usually more complex.

Know Who You Work For

In all my various public sector planning positions, I have never had only one boss. There has always been one person directly responsible for supervising me, evaluating my work, and meting out rewards and admonitions, but I have had to answer to many people. There were the city managers, planning commissions, elected officials, and, most important, the public. Today we refer to these constituents as our "customers." The public is ultimately the planner's customer and boss, if you will, and the planner's primary responsibility is to work in the public's interest. This is also one of the most important tenets of the American Institute of Certified Planners Code of Ethics and Professional Conduct.

What is the "public interest"? Admittedly, this is hard to define, and the longer you are engaged in the profession the more you see that the world is not black and white, but shades of gray. It has been debated at many planning conferences over the years, but I do not hear it discussed as much as I used to back in the early days of idealism. Today I like to think of public interest more in terms of "community interest." This is because the "public" is indefinite geographically and increasingly diverse socially. There is no way we can know all the values and beliefs of this public. However, we can come to know and understand the values and beliefs of our community, our "local public." Thus, when faced with a difficult situation, ask yourself, "What is good for the community?" This will be an effective guide that will serve you well.

Theoretically, the community's interest is well represented on appointed and elected bodies with which you work. However, the planner is sometimes in the uncomfortable position of being pressured by politicians to make decisions that seem to work toward the benefit of particular individuals or interest groups, but may not serve the community's interest.

What to do in these cases is not easy to decide. First, try to see whether there are some redeeming values to the proposal that could benefit the community. Sometimes we have a knee-jerk reaction against something when, upon closer examination, it really is not so bad. See if there is some way to steer the proposal toward the benefit of the community. For example, if a park is needed in the neighborhood, and this seems like something that could mitigate opposition to a project, suggest that one be incorporated into the plan. Second, point out that you understand opposing viewpoints, directing attention to policies or other actions that have already been adopted and with which this new proposal would be in conflict. You can try to come across as someone who is trying to help the proponent to make the best possible case in favor of the proposal.

Know the Values and Culture of Your Community

What is good for the community? The worst mistake any planner can make, either as a consultant or a new employee, is to come into a community and pretend to know all the answers—to tell people what is good for them! I have seen it happen many times, and it is a sure-fire way to bring down the wrath of the community.

Whether starting a new job (with long-term ambitions) in the public sector or landing a new consulting project, the planner must learn what makes the community tick. What are the underlying values and beliefs that drive the community in the direction it is heading and have driven it in the past? What is causing the underlying problems that you have been asked to solve? The planner can gain enormous knowledge and credibility by getting to know the values and culture of the community. Get out and talk to people and ask direct questions like, "Why is it that people here have such a dislike of River City? Why are people so against apartments?" Before you step out in a new situation, or maybe even one that you think you are familiar with, do some local background work.

People's values and attitudes are often shaped by past events that can come back and haunt you if you are not prepared. Soon after I started a new job for a city where I worked for many years, I was asked to speak to a neighborhood group just outside the city limits. I knew that the city had desires to annex this area, but I had little idea of the animosity that these people had for us. Their purpose in inviting me to the meeting was not really to get to know me but to put me on notice that they had taken a stand many years before on annexation and I should not get any new ideas. I was not prepared for this agenda. Later I found out that one of my predecessors had visited this group many years before and told the group that "sooner or later we will annex you and there will not be anything you can do about it!" This lore had been passed down to more than one generation of neighborhood activists and had colored the relationship between the city and this group for many years. We were the city they loved to hate!

This knowledge and understanding paid off in the long run, however, in helping me establish a new relationship with these folks. Over the next year we changed one important city annexation policy that garnered a new level of trust. We formed a positive relationship on many local and regional issues. One day, I have faith that the old lore will be forgotten and replaced by a new one I worked so hard to foster. And maybe they will even decide they should join our fair city!

Know Your Constituency and Adversaries

While planners need to get to know their immediate customers, it is equally important to find constituencies in the community. This does not mean that the planner needs to be a politician, merely that it is necessary to get to know and establish a rapport with the leaders of the community.

Find out who influences decisions. They may be organized groups, like the Chamber of Commerce or League of Women Voters, or they may be neighborhood leaders, environmental organizations, or a few savvy citizen activists. These contacts can be invaluable when times get tough. At other times, it is good to have a few folks with whom you can test ideas and strategies.

It is also important that you get to know your adversaries. This is particularly hard for me; my inclination is to avoid people who disagree with me or outright oppose my proposals or those of my staff. I dislike confrontation, and most people feel the same way. However, on the occasions when I had the nerve to confront my adversaries, I found that it often diffused the situation. Of course, you have to do this thoughtfully and carefully. You cannot angrily confront someone, but must approach with the intention of learning more about the person's point of view. This can provide you with more information—information that could help improve your proposal.

We had a woman in our community (call her Sharon) who became extremely emotional about trees. It all started when a prominent local businessperson cut down a large, highly visible oak tree in front of his business. Sharon seized this incident and turned it into an overnight political sensation. Without getting any facts, she blamed it on us, the planners, saying we should not have let it happen, even though no regulations prevented it. The issue came before the city council and was even on regional television news programs. I specifically became her target because I was the one who had to tell the council, the press, and others what had happened and what would be done about it. The council directed staff to develop an ordinance that would prevent this kind of thing from happening again.

In the meantime, Sharon decided that she would draft an ordinance herself to present to the city because, she said, she did not have faith that we would recommend what she wanted. She began contacting people all over the country and collecting tree ordinances. I could see that her ordinance and ours were on a major collision course in the near future, so I finally got up the nerve to call her.

I could tell without her saying anything that Sharon was shocked to hear from me after all the bad things she had been saying about us. I suggested that we work together on this project, that we could both benefit by pooling our knowledge. At first, she turned me down. I finally got her to let me review a draft of her ordinance and make comments. I then recommended to the city council that we appoint a committee to help staff draft the ordinance, that Sharon be on the committee, and that we use her draft as a starting point. The council agreed.

Sharon's draft was far too radical for adoption, but it did have a number of good provisions that were incorporated into the final ordinance. More important, we avoided another public confrontation and were able to accomplish something good for the community.

Do Not Be Afraid of the Public

We planners in Oregon pride ourselves on a progressive planning program that is over twenty years old. It is based on a tradition of citizen activism that existed before the state planning legislation was passed in 1973, and this activism became a cornerstone of the program. That the program has survived three initiatives to repeal it and numerous assaults by the state legislature to overturn it testifies to its grass-roots basis.

And yet, I have been astounded since becoming a consultant to see how many of my contemporaries, including city managers and other high-level public officials, are afraid of the public. I become concerned when I receive a request for proposal that specifies "minimal public involvement program," or perhaps none at all, in a project that has obvious interest to at least some segment of the public. This is a recipe for disaster or disappointment! Either the project will be shot down when it does become public, or it will sit on the shelf for lack of support. What a waste of taxpayers' money, not to mention the time and effort that went into the planning process.

The public knows when you are afraid of them, and this instills more mistrust of government. They know when you are trying to hide something or when you are being less than honest. Over time, you lose your credibility.

Sometimes local officials avoid a public process because they know what the public wants but do not want to give it to them. However, in my observation, the public always gets what it wants eventually. People may be forced to call for resignations, use the initiative, referendum, or recall processes, or find some other avenue, but they will get what they want. As a planner, you are better off in the driver's seat than in front of the speeding bus.

Develop meaningful, effective methods of involving the public. Citizens do not expect you to invite them down to City Hall every night of the week. Most of them appreciate that you spend the time and effort to solicit their views and input when it counts and in a way that is meaningful and useful.

If you do not know how to involve the public in what you are doing, invite people in and ask them. Set up a public involvement committee to give you ideas on an ongoing basis.

Develop the Skill to Listen and Hear

Listening—and hearing—what people are saying is probably one of the most important attributes anyone can have, and with planners it is essential. Listening is giving attention to verbalization. Hearing is understanding what is being said. You have to be a good listener before you can hear and understand. Understanding requires you to put yourself in the place of the one who is speaking and see the situation from their point of view.

At one public meeting many years ago, I got this message more clearly than ever before. I had been attending this group's meetings for several months to discuss a particular issue. I listened and listened until I thought I could not stand to go to one of these meetings and take the brunt of the group's criticisms again. Then one night I *heard* what they said and things really turned around. I dropped that psychological barrier between them and me. I found myself repeating to them what they had been saying, and they were nodding their heads as if they were glad I finally understood, which I did. This was almost like receiving new information because I was able, then, to develop a proposal that got to the heart of their concerns.

Later, upon reflection, I realized what had happened. I had mentally stood back from the situation and listened to them as if I were a total stranger. When I dropped my preconceptions and biases, I heard things that I had listened to but not understood before. Things really turned around for me with this group and I went on to use this technique in other situations of conflict.

Respond and Follow Through on Commitments

Of course, you must do more than just listen and hear; you must respond. You must follow through on those things that you have come to understand. This should be obvious, but unfortunately it is not. Some planners, like some politicians, give lip service to the ideas of others and throw away opportunities to gain credibility and trust.

This came home to me in a startling experience, a real eye-opener that showed people's basic mistrust of government. Some years ago a developer proposed a shopping center in our town, something that has happened several times before and since, usually with little public demonstration of interest. Like most, this one fronted a major arterial street. However, it backed up to a single family neighborhood that has a number of local streets connecting this arterial street with another. The neighborhood organized in opposition. As the public hearing approached it promised to be ugly, and most predicted the shopping center would go down in flames. While this shopping center was no better or worse than most, there appeared to be more to this case than met the eye. I decided to see what I could do to avert a negative situation.

I contacted one of the neighborhood leaders and set up a meeting with the residents. The real issue, I quickly learned, differed from the rumors and the speculation in the press. The neighborhood didn't really mind the shopping center, but disliked the traffic that used local streets to cross between the two arterials. The situation had existed for years but the neighborhood had never been able to get it addressed; this, the residents felt, was a chance. I told them that I would see what could be done—not in exchange for dropping their opposition to the shopping center, I should add, although that turned out to be the result—and I asked for their assistance in conducting a neighborhood traffic study.

They were quite surprised when we called several days later and asked to set up a training session with the neighborhood. The training took place and the traffic study was completed. The survey showed that the amount of cut-through traffic was not as great as they had imagined, but to avoid an increase from the new shopping center, we developed a three-party agreement that called for another survey six months after the center opened and a commitment by the developer-owner to assist in mitigating this circumstance if necessary. The public hearing became an anticlimax; the shopping center was approved.

I was surprised to realize later how little faith the residents had in our process as it was occurring. Apparently they did not really believe that I would follow through because of previous experiences with or perceptions of government. But at the neighborhood meeting where we announced the results of the traffic study, the residents presented me with a certificate addressed to "the city official who keeps her word."

Do Not Be Afraid to Say You Were Wrong

As part of my planning directorship in one city, I also managed the building department. Normally, there were very few major issues that arose from administering and enforcing building codes, but one day it happened. Someone was building a house next to, and slightly downhill from, one that had been there for two years in a developing subdivision. The existing house had an excellent view of the Cascade Mountains, and this view was going to be cut off with the construction of the new house. The people in the existing house were furious, and were sure there had to be some violation of the zoning or building codes. We checked and could not find any violation. In the next several weeks a huge dispute erupted between the owners of the existing house, the owners of the new house, the builder, and everyone's attorneys, with everyone pointing fingers at everyone else and trying to find fault. It eventually ended up in front of a city council meeting. At the meeting some evidence was presented suggesting that an error had been made in calculating the height of the new building. The building official turned to me and said, "I feel I should admit the mistake. Do you agree?" I told him to admit it and agree to do whatever was necessary to resolve the problem. So he did.

Afterward, another department head came over and admonished us for admitting a mistake in public. I was astounded, said so, and discussed it for some time. There is no doubt in my mind that matters would have been far worse, and would have dragged on far longer, if the truth had not been stated publicly. Yes, the building official was criticized for making the initial mistake, but the admission of the error defused the political situation quickly.

Nothing is gained by refusing to admit you made a mistake—in public, if need be. The public may not be happy, but at least it learns you are honest and take responsibility.

Long-term survival in a planning position may mean having to admit even bigger mistakes than in the example above. You may have to admit that a policy or plan that you recommended and that was adopted based on your advice is simply not working or has become outmoded. This means swallowing some pride, but you will be better off admitting the mistake yourself than having it pointed out by others.

Do Not Personalize Events

This is my own tip, but I still find it tough to follow! We get so involved in what we are doing, we invest so much time, effort, and creativity, that it is hard not to take defeat personally. We think someone does not like us or wants to hurt us. But when I stand back and look at the many times I felt that way, I know it was not really the case. It was not me they disliked, it was something about my proposal; perhaps the issue just became too politicized by those who felt they would gain or lose.

Taking such things personally may keep you from coming up with worthwhile alternative solutions. You become helpless and ineffective. You lose power to control the situation. As with learning to listen, you have to stand back and hear the criticism as though you are an outside third party. If you can do this, you have the chance to turn what looked for a moment like a personal or professional defeat into a better, more creative approach. You become a problem solver, not part of the problem.

Be Willing to Change

We read a lot about change these days—and that will not change! There are hundreds of business and professional periodicals and books about change: how to predict it, how to manage it, and how to effect it.

Planning has always been about change, and as planners, we must become masters at managing and acting as a catalyst for change, not just at predicting it. Not change for the sake of change, but to solve existing and future problems.

Before we can manage change in our organizations or communities, we need to be willing to change ourselves. Not only should we listen to constructive criticism and understand what we must do to change bad habits, poor ideas, or outmoded thinking, but we also need to be willing to assess periodically our own strengths and weaknesses and not wait for direct, negative feedback that hits us square in the face.

Get on top of change, be ahead of it and prepare for it. If you get a new supervisor, manager, or new personality on the governing body, you can be almost sure that there will be changes in your organization. Do not wait around to hear what those are going to be and let yourself be surprised, demoralized, or put on the defensive. Try to become part of the process of change before it starts by indicating your interest in helping out and assisting with needed change. And let's face it, there are always changes that could make things better no matter how comfortable we feel with the way things are now. It's another example of being part of the solution and not part of the problem!

Know "When to Hold 'Em and When to Fold 'Em"

Every now and then, you are going to find yourself up against the wall. You have stuck your neck out to advocate a new plan or policy and you are getting chewed up by interest groups, the press, politicians, or citizens. And this may be in spite of all your best efforts to involve these groups in the process. Some things are beyond your control. What do you do, hang in or back off?

The Portland metro area has been in the throes of building a light rail transit system for the last twenty years. One line was successfully completed on the east side to the suburbs in the early 1980s. The Westside has been engaged for the past ten years in getting a line built to join the Eastside line in downtown Portland. My city, Beaverton, was at the epicenter of the Westside line. It would go through our city just seven miles from downtown Portland, but the question was how.

To consider the matter, we entered into a contemplative planning process to look at the future of our city, in particular our central area, a combination of the older downtown and newer strip suburban centers. We hired some experienced and objective consultants from out of town to help us decide the best course for the rail line to travel, based upon future development potential and intermodal connections. One route was favored by the engineers involved because it used an existing abandoned rail line and was perceived to be easy from an engineering standpoint. Our consultants recommended, and we on the planning staff embraced, another route that entered the heart of a built, suburban strip area that had strong potential for future redevelopment and promotion of transit ridership. The engineers dreaded the difficult right-of-way issues associated with this route.

The stakes were high in other respects. The rail line route traversed a large industrial campus that shunned light rail. The redevelopment route bypassed the campus but greatly affected many existing small- to medium-size businesses. There were other major issues on both routes. Sides formed, and the arguments were fierce. Those on the redevelopment route were rightly concerned about damage, takings, and other short-term issues, arguing for the clear path offered by the abandoned line. Those opposed to the rail route argued that it was in the wrong location to spur redevelopment activity and there were issues associated with wetlands, floodplain, and street crossings.

The planners reached a critical point. Should we continue on and recommend our choice for the line, facing the possibility that it would go down and take us along with it, or should we give in but make recommendations on how best to make it work? The choice was tough.

Out came the risk analysis matrix. We locked ourselves in a room for half a day and went through the agonizing, laborious process of a risk assessment. We considered not what we as planners would gain or lose, but what the community would gain or lose with each option. We came out with a compromise. We would support the rail line route on the west half and stick with the redevelopment route on the east half. On both segments we made recommendations on how to make it work best for each possible option.

Did it work? Mostly. The rail line option won out on the east segment as well, but all of our recommendations on how to make it work were accepted. It could have been worse had we gone to the mat on the whole route and not even looked at how to make the alternate work.

The lesson is obvious: know when you are fighting a losing battle. No matter what technical expertise you employ, no matter how strong and forthright your position, and no matter how actively citizens are involved, even "big guns," you may lose. Just as in poker, you have to know when to hold your hand and when to fold it. Otherwise, you will soon be out of the game entirely.

Do Not Burn Your Bridges

After the light rail experience, it was hard to face our opponents and smile. But we had to. We had to get this line built and carry through on our commitments to make it work. This is where not taking it personally comes in, and it was hard. If there was ever a time that I wanted to break down and cry, this was it. It had been an agonizing process, and we lost. But, after all, it only involved the route. We still had many years of working together to make happen what everyone wanted, light rail on the west side.

Use Humor When Possible

We sometimes take ourselves and our jobs too seriously, I think. By seeing the humor in ourselves and others and bringing it out at the right time, you can ease a tense situation. I used to work with someone who was a genius at recognizing and using humor and will always remember one time when our agency was in a very tense situation with local subdivision developers.

Historically, development had happened on the flatlands below the foothills, which created a magnificent backdrop to the urban area. But when rapid growth hit the area in the mid 1970s, the foothills became a prestigious area in which to live. One developer in particular, call him Frank Jones, saw the opportunity to make his fortune developing land that once had been grazed by cattle and sheep. The city and county were unprepared for this, and knowing the foothills were composed of fragile soils, ancient landslides, and gulches that contained flash floods every few decades, they decided to commission a consultant study to provide identification of these hazards and direction on the appropriate amount and type of growth.

The study verified the existence of these hazards, including a still-active landslide within a subdivision being developed by Jones. Not too long after the study was completed and made public, Jones called the project manager, whom we will call Mike, and asked to meet him on his site to discuss the report. I accompanied Mike because I was the one who would have to administer the proposed new regulations, if they were adopted. Jones, who was not a bit happy about the report to say the least, explained to Mike that he felt the landslide designated on the map should be removed because he had gone out there and removed all evidence of it with a bulldozer! Mike explained that it was not that simple; the landslide still existed geologically and he couldn't just remove it from the map. Jones was not happy, knowing that the map could hurt the sale of homes in his subdivision. After some more heated discussion, Mike finally said, "Well, Frank, you don't want your nice subdivision to turn into a mobile home park, do you?" After a split second of confusion, Mr. Jones burst out laughing and said "Well, I guess you're right, but I don't have to like it!"

You cannot always use this approach, but in this case Mike knew Frank had a sense of humor, so he took a chance and broke a tense, contentious situation. Jones still fought adoption of the ordinance, but without directing his anger at Mike or anyone else on staff.

Know When It Is Time to Move On

In talking about survival as a planner, I am not necessarily talking about survival in one job, year in and year out. More often, survival means moving on at the right time with your enthusiasm, integrity, and professional reputation intact.

No matter how hard you try, no matter how many right things you do to survive the political process, things can happen. Some forces are beyond your control, forces that may have nothing to do with you at all. Planners can become political pawns in high-stakes political games. Maybe you were responsible for having a developer's project denied by the planning commission years ago. Maybe that developer has been trying ever since to find a candidate for mayor who is willing to fire you, and after three tries, finally succeeds. What can you do? With dignity and grace, you pack up your office and move on to bigger and better things.

The fact is that planners are often in highly political situations that they cannot always foresee and control. Some say that you have not really been doing your job if you have not made a few enemies, and they are probably right.

Over time I learned that I would have to establish my own performance standards and seek my own rewards for a job well done. This was the best way for me to understand where I stood through the turbulent political periods, which was most of the time in the public sector.

Ultimately, satisfaction for a planner in this political world requires you to have your vision of success. Your ability to survive depends on your personal satisfaction as measured by your own values and the performance standards you have set for yourself. Furthermore, this requires a sense of vision—how you see yourself as a professional, and the difference you believe you can make in the particular positions you hold.

Chapter Nine

The Principles of Community Alignment and Empowerment

Gene Boles

My views of planning are quite different in 1995 than they were in 1966 when I committed to the planning profession as a graduate student. In many ways the changes represent my own professional growth in response to the demands of the job. In other ways the practice of planning itself has evolved. I will attempt in this chapter to offer some salient lessons from those three decades and to describe specifically a paradigm for effective planning.

Over the past few decades, planning has changed. Utopian and idealistic views have given way to much more pragmatic responses to the real problems of our society. We have moved from "urban renewal" and "model cities" to concepts of leveraging and public-private partnerships for the revitalization of declining urban areas. I have witnessed the integration of planning into the decision-making structure of government and have seen the emergence of "growth management" and, at least in some states, the rise of "environment" as an equal to economic development and growth. I have experienced the "neighborhood movement" and increasing citizen involvement. Most significantly, as a manager I have had to respond to the demand for less but more effective government. Citizens no longer leave government to the politicians and planning to the planners.

Over this same period, the level of commitment to planning has dramatically increased in those areas where true public concern and commitment exists and has declined where planning has been ineffective or subsidized. Virtually every city and urban county in the nation now makes a substantial investment in planning. In Florida, for example, where planning is mandated by law and the requirements are stringent, the annual budgets for planning are several times larger than their budgets of only a decade ago. In contrast, the artificial federal support for planning that was prevalent during the 1960s and 1970s largely disappeared with the election of Ronald Reagan in 1980. Those planning agencies that were integrated into the administrative framework of government fared well. Planning activities and agencies that relied upon federal subsidies quickly learned the public's perception of their value. Many programs and even some entire agencies disappeared in the absence of this artificial support. As a planning administrator, I have become increasingly aware that planning for the sake of planning must be avoided and that scarce resources must be directed toward activities of value within a particular community.

Planning is not an end in itself. It is not inherently good nor universally valued. In reality, our tools and techniques are only tools and techniques; there is no precise formula for their application. Effective planning requires the timely and efficient use of resources where results can be achieved.

At its core, planning is really about community building. Community building is disjointed, it resists control, it is rarely in complete harmony, and it is never finished. It is an incremental process and the planner's primary task is fitting the parts into a cohesive whole. Primarily for this reason, I believe planning must be an integral part of a community's decision-making process. It must be reflected in the administrative activity in which every governmental jurisdiction engages. From my perspective, the capacity to understand and effectively manage the increments of community building, while maintaining some vision of a desired result, is the true measure of a planner's skill.

Planning is also political. I have always found amusing the notion that planning would be a fine profession if we could take politics out of it. I do not suggest that planners should be politicians. Rather, we are active participants in a political system. The planner must function within a political structure and understand its dynamics. Political savvy—a sense of timing and of the "possible"—is synonymous with professional skill. As a case in point, during the early years of my career the rationality of planning was unassailable and I was sure that an eager public was simply awaiting a guiding hand. Reality has a way, however, of asserting itself. In the early 1970s, as staff to a South Carolina legislative task force on coastal zone management and state land policy, I confidently stated that "we must do—" (what we were to do is not relevant) only to be advised by an influential senator from the South Carolina low country: "Son, we ain't got to do nothing." And we did not. The politics for a serious commitment to the issues at hand was not right and logic did not matter.

In its broadest and highest sense, livability is the only true measure of the success of community building. If we as planners wish to measure our effectiveness, we should examine the livability of the communities we serve. But we must measure livability by the community's standards, not by our own.

A Principle-Centered Paradigm

As a practicing planner I have observed the extremes and I have attempted with experience to rely on those techniques that are effective. In recent years, largely in response to my emerging role as advisor and coach, I have sought to understand better what works, why it works, what attributes these effective techniques may share, and how they might be integrated to deliver consistent and sustainable results. Stephen Covey (1989), in *The Seven Habits of Highly Effective People*, suggests that desired results, whether produced by an organization or an individual, can only be achieved by adherence to certain immutable principles. At the community level, the guiding principle is alignment. At the implementation and management levels, empowerment is the guiding principle. This chapter examines how these two principles may be applied to the community building process and to the practice of planning. The examples from my own experience demonstrate what happens when these principles are at work and what happens when they are not.

The Principle of Alignment

Stephen Covey offers alignment as the guiding principle for planning at a community level. In its broadest context, urban planning is the alignment of vision, goals, and objectives with resources in order to achieve anticipated results. While planning is by definition visionary and future-oriented, and though it provides a public process for visualizing "the big picture," communities are also the sum of their parts. The successful blending of the parts into the whole—the capacity to see how the parts contribute to other parts and to the whole—is the fundamental challenge of planning.

Traditional comprehensive planning, the adoption of requisite plan elements, the implementation of a growth management strategy—none of these ensure alignment. They have their place, but are not sufficient and may not even be essential. A genuinely aligned planning program clearly defines regional or communitywide values, is internally consistent, produces rational results, enjoys a high degree of community acceptance, is reasonably easy to apply, and passes legal muster. The following sections include ways to test a planning program for these elements.

The Communitywide Values Test

Planning allows a community to visualize its future and to act on it—to align its resources to achieve a vision. A clear statement of what values and resources are important to the community as a whole is fundamental. Without such a benchmark, the parts cannot be consistently examined and the incremental process of community building will lack integrity.

A communitywide perspective that is focused and selective is preferable to one that is comprehensive and inclusive. Alignment is most likely to be achieved among a few key components around which there is consensus about their communitywide significance. If there is doubt regarding importance, more than likely the issue is better left to local choice.

Three fundamental criteria may be used to determine regional or communitywide importance:

- *System Integrity.* Is integrity, continuity, or connectivity of a system important to the community? Will the public interests be compromised if the system integrity is disrupted?
- *Community Resource.* Is the viability or function of a resource of community value at stake? Is the resource irreplaceable or only replaceable at great cost?
- *Community Enhancement.* Will the preservation of the resources enhance the community? Will adherence to a standard improve community quality and function?

Certain elements such as transportation, utility systems, and natural resources are of importance in every community. Other elements may be unique or simply reflect local choice. The principle of alignment does not dictate the choice but it does require that a choice be made. Environmental management provides a useful illustration of how the principle of alignment may be applied. There is a widening understanding that effective conservation and management of natural environmental systems cannot be achieved by an incremental approach. Rather, system integrity must dictate how the increments are treated. If this concept is not familiar, it is not surprising; the systems approach to the natural environment has not been commonly integrated into the urban planning framework. The norm, at all governmental levels, has been to view the natural environment as isolated components and to address environmental issues by regulating the parts. A principle-centered paradigm allows a better approach.

The Internal Consistency Test

Inconsistency and contradiction are common indictments of land-development regulation and related programs, and as the complexity of the regulatory environment increases, the potential for conflict escalates. Internal inconsistency diminishes the effectiveness of public policy and can severely undermine a community's capacity to manage incremental development.

Inconsistency often occurs between land development programs and infrastructure extension policies. The complexity of these programs is part of the reason, but a more common culprit may be the differing objectives of planners and infrastructure providers. Frequently, pricing policy is not evaluated in growth management terms, or at best the planning issues have been assigned a secondary priority. The interface of land development policy and infrastructure extension is a prime candidate for alignment.

Inconsistencies are also commonly encountered between a community's stated intent and the actual effect of policies and regulations. For example, the curtailment of urban sprawl is frequently advanced as a community goal, yet land development regulations permit estate lots on individual utility systems—essentially encouraging exurban development at its fringe. Florida's growth management law is a case in point. It requires concurrency, which means that adequate facilities must be in place before development occurs. On its surface, concurrency appears to support growth management initiatives, especially the curtailment of sprawl. In reality, the effect can be precisely the opposite. Because developers are much more likely to find adequate road facilities at a rural fringe than within urbanized areas, a leapfrog effect is actually encouraged.

The Rational Results Test

Does the planning process produce rational results or do outcomes defy common sense? Is the allocation of resources justified by the benefits realized? If nonsensical outcomes occur with regularity, misalignment may be a root cause.

In 1980, shortly after becoming planning director in Springfield, Missouri, I encountered a pervasive problem with subdivision regulation. Properties, especially within industrial and commercial areas, were routinely created by metes and bounds description and recorded without the required review and approval prescribed by the city's subdivision regulations. The legal process was simply ignored. In some instances these subdivisions presented access and dimensional problems but, once recorded, they defied any reasonable enforcement remedy.

The result was a nightmare. Literally hundreds of property owners could not sufficiently establish a legal nonconforming status or were faced with costly (often prohibitive) alternatives to achieve compliance. Relief was routinely sought through the board of adjustment either as a variance or appeal, and in the vast majority of cases was eventually granted. This procedure increased administrative costs, created delay, expense, and anxiety for a large number of property owners, inappropriately placed the board of adjustment in the role of equity judge, and considerably increased the level of citizen complaint heard by elected officials—all without any rational prospect of achieving significant public objectives or measurably enhancing the livability of the community.

The remedy involved strategic ordinance revisions to broaden administrative authority and ease the burden of proof for establishing nonconformity status. Most important, the administrative procedures were streamlined, especially for the recognition of nonconforming lots, and the requirement for full compliance as a prerequisite of permit approval was reversed. In their place, a policy was adopted granting development approval on legally recognized lots so long as existing nonconformities were not expanded. These changes effectively eliminated the backlog, providing an administrative remedy for most nonconformities. Resources, in other words, were aligned with benefits and expected results.

The Community Acceptance Test

While individual planning decisions are always subject to challenge and controversy, there is a significant and discernible difference between, for example, the isolated zoning petition opposed on incompatibility or other site-specific grounds and a persistent pattern of community disenchantment with the planning process. The former very likely represents a healthy dialogue; the latter may reflect a misalignment, indicating a need for reexamination of the relevant plans and policies.

Let me give you an example. Northwest Hillsborough County (Florida) is a semirural and environmentally sensitive area on an urban fringe; it is experiencing intense development pressure. The Future Land Use Plan for the area prescribed residential development at densities ranging from one to two dwelling units per acre. In addition, substantial public investment in infrastructure has been made or planned to support this urban expansion, and much of the land area has received zoning approval, typically in the form of cluster development in response to the extensive open space and environmental management objectives of the plan.

Despite this apparent public policy commitment to urban growth, serious misalignments emerged during the early 1990s. The area contains numerous lakes and water features and also accommodates a large wellfield system providing the major supply of drinking water to the Tampa Bay region. A five-year drought and the delayed development of alternative water supplies have raised grave environmental concerns (such as aquifer recharge, wellfield protection, and wetland depletion) and property value concerns (such as loss of amenity from lake draw-down and contamination of private wells). Simultaneously, area residents are actively resisting urbanization, advocating maintenance of the area's rural character.

In response, the government agencies at the local and regional levels sent mixed signals. Notably, and in the wake of several hotly contested development applications, the Future Land Use Plan was amended, effectively down-planning much of the area and introducing policies designed to maintain the rural or semirural character. Yet in reality, the modified development densities, combined with open space and water management requirements and "adequate facilities" provisions, continued to produce suburban development. Rather than resolve the issues, these changes created a disconnection between expectation and result, intensifying debate over growth versus no growth, development versus environment, public infrastructure investment, adequacy of facilities, and a host of other classic growth management conflicts. At the time of this writing, virtually every public decision affecting the area has been challenged and the outcomes are in doubt.

In this example, misalignment can be observed at two levels. First, the neighborhood's perspective was not reflected by the comprehensive plan; the parts were not in harmony with the whole. Second, the implementing techniques were counterproductive and did not create the expected result. Consequently, the technical solutions are mistrusted and largely discredited by neighborhood interests.

Examples like this are not hard to find. In such high-profile circumstances, change in public policy will normally occur because the situation demands it—the extreme cases tend to get attention. A more subtle but equally important task involves the routine gauging of community acceptance. The effective planner is not isolated but rather is in frequent and continuous communication with the community.

On the premise that elected officials are a barometer of the community and its values, as a planning administrator I have routinely tracked the level of agreement between staff and agency recommendations and the final outcome at the decision-making level. The target of such an exercise is not 100 percent agreement; that would very likely represent a rigid decision-making climate without the free exchange of ideas and information. Rather the focus is placed on the identification of patterns or the recurrence of a particular deficiency with technique or policy. At one level, this analysis can lead to adjustments and refinements. At another level, it may provide an early warning of serious misalignment between public policy and community values.

The Reasonableness Test

Planning, at its core, affects the use of land and design upon the land. The development process is in turn driven by market forces and occurs within an economic environment with real boundaries. Alignment has not been achieved if the requirements and exactions placed on land and the users of land are unreasonable and do not balance private restrictions against public benefit.

The concept of reasonableness carries a legal connotation: land use regulation may not deny all reasonable use of land. While this discussion encompasses these legal aspects (after all, land regulation in the United States is rooted in this legal premise), reasonableness is used here in a broader context. Affordability, fairness, consistency of application, and predictability are the more important attributes of alignment.

Severe misalignments occur when regulatory procedures do not mirror the development process itself. Development decisions are normally progressive in nature; initial investigation is preliminary and costs are kept low. As project viability increases, the level of commitment rises along with the level of investment. In the world of land development, uncertainty can be a greater impediment than absolute cost. Progressive development review, offering reliable conceptual approval based on preliminary design supported by detailed review as design proceeds, substantially reduces uncertainty while enhancing design flexibility and development quality. Is it not vastly preferable for developers to invest in infrastructure and amenities that contribute to the function and livability of communities than for them to pay legal costs, consultant fees for the management of the permit process, and capital carrying costs generated by delay?

The Legality Test

Finally, effective planning must be aligned with the constitutional, legislative, and judicial framework that governs it. In the 1990s, the legal challenges and opportunities for effective planning lie primarily within two distinct but highly interrelated arenas: the "property rights" challenge to growth management and environmental regulation, and the "rational nexus" issues associated with developer exactions and "adequate facility" requirements.

Legal challenges to land development regulation have received considerable attention in recent years, notably the Supreme Court decisions in *Nollan* v. *California Coastal Commission* (1987), *Lucas* v. *South Carolina Coastal Council* (1992), and *Dolan* v. *City of Tigard* (1994). In addition, forty-four states have considered takings bills since 1991, and property rights legislation may be introduced at the federal level in the wake of the 1994 midterm elections.

Do these legal rulings and initiatives undermine the validity of using an approach to planning based on the principle of alignment? To the contrary. Many of the legal challenges emerge from a rigid permitting concept that fails to allow for unique circumstances. The Dolan decision, in particular its emphasis on "rough proportionality," repudiates fragmented public policy and demands sound planning. The Florida Supreme Court, in *Brevard County* v. *Snyder* (1993), established "substantial competent evidence" as the fundamental test for regulatory decisions and in *Palm Beach* v. *Wright* (1993) reinforced the validity of the master plan as an element of public policy. The emerging legal climate demands alignment as a guiding principle, not the reverse.

The Principle of Empowerment

Applying Stephen Covey's empowerment principle to implementation means enabling people. As with most concepts, empowerment very likely means different things to different people and will differ with context, environment, and application.

The value of empowerment cannot be fully realized without alignment. Without a vision of the whole and how its parts may fit, empowerment is likely to be a formula for chaos. But with alignment, empowerment offers the opportunity for diversity, human-scale solutions, and synergy to a degree not otherwise possible. On the other hand, empowerment requires commitment from those who have been enabled; this capacity for response will be uneven at best. As we embrace empowerment as a guiding principle, we must recognize that uniformity and control are not its hallmarks nor its objectives.

As I reflect upon my planning career, the most rewarding experiences have involved empowerment in one form or another. Neighborhoods, community associations, and interest groups are most commonly associated with the empowerment paradigm and I will offer some representative examples. But empowerment can be much more than neighborhood planning and citizen participation.

It can be a powerful and pervasive tool influencing a broad range of community-building activity. By way of illustration, I will also discuss empowerment as an element in the land development process and how empowerment can be directed to increase the effectiveness of planning agencies.

Empowering Neighborhoods

The involvement of citizen groups in the planning process has dramatically increased in recent years, along with demands for effective participation. This trend, coupled with the recognition of the neighborhood (however it may be defined) as a critical physical, social, and political unit, offers fertile ground for fundamental change in the planning process. As with most paradigm shifts, change may be well under way before it is fully recognized and acknowledged. I believe this to be true of the neighborhood movement. The challenge for planning is to convert this immense energy from a disjointed political agenda to a positive and productive element of the community-building process.

Over the years, I have been involved with several neighborhood planning programs. In 1975, Oklahoma City initiated a major comprehensive planning effort, ultimately adopting what it called the Preservation Plan. As its key tenets, the plan attempted to balance growth with the conservation of existing neighborhoods and communities. Neighborhood stability and revitalization were highly emphasized, and a systematic program of neighborhood planning was initiated immediately following adoption of the comprehensive plan, as was an extensive overhaul of the land development codes. The revitalization of much of the city's residential core was stimulated by this process and the implementing actions. Two empowering components of the program are worthy of note.

Concurrent with the plan's preparation and the neighborhood planning process that followed, the number of organized neighborhood groups increased from four in 1974 to over a hundred in 1979. This extraordinary neighborhood movement can be attributed to two primary factors: the forum and opportunity created by the comprehensive planning process itself, and the work of a small but dedicated not-for-profit, grass-roots group called the Neighborhood Coalition. The Coalition functioned as a neighborhood advocate, assisting citizen groups with organization and providing technical assistance and education. Although the city provided some funding support, the Coalition was detached from local government. In this capacity, the group quite effectively advanced neighborhood interests while enjoying a high level of trust with its constituent neighborhoods. The Coalition also provided an important barometer for city policy makers with regard to neighborhood issues.

Oklahoma City also enacted another empowerment tool, the Urban Conservation (UC) District. This is a special zoning district designed for application within established neighborhoods (keep in mind that I define this term broadly). Prior to its enactment, the old zoning code provided only one zoning district that addressed neighborhood conservation, and it was restricted to historically significant single-family areas. The Urban Conservation District, in contrast, was not prescriptive but enabled modifications of the zoning codes specifically tailored to the neighborhood. However, the process of getting initial UC District designation was intentionally made rigorous and had to be followed by preparation of a formal neighborhood plan.

The Oklahoma City experiences above represent two forms of empowerment. City recognition and support of the Neighborhood Coalition provided effective and meaningful participation in the policy-making process by neighborhood groups while retaining identity and autonomy. The Urban Conservation District provided a few proactive neighborhoods the tools to define their own character and set their own direction, but within an intentionally rigorous process designed to ensure community commitment and support.

Most examples of successful neighborhood empowerment efforts share certain common elements. In most instances, the interest group assumes responsibility for shaping its own environment and demonstrates both the willingness and capacity to do so. The neighborhood organizations also enjoy grass-roots support and trust, attributable at least in part to their independence from government. Second, the governmental institutions involved truly share the decision-making process. They provide a public policy and procedural framework within which neighborhood interests can be focused, and they provide the implementation tools.

The degree to which empowerment produces specific benefits to participating neighborhoods is a matter of local government providing access and the neighborhoods responding with energy and determination. The degree to which the results of empowered action advance a community toward a larger vision is a measure of alignment. The Oklahoma City neighborhood program noted above exhibited this aligned empowerment.

Empowering Designers

Land development occurs within and is greatly influenced by a public policy framework of plans, policies, regulations, and infrastructure pricing. But while the elements of land development policy are remarkably similar from community to community, there can be vast differences in application and result. For example, under Florida's growth management act, all local comprehensive plans must comply with state guidelines for content and consistency, and they must be supported by regulations and capital investment programs sufficient to implement the plans. As a result, the format, content, and even language of these local plans tends to be quite similar. Yet the subtleties of construction, degree of internal consistency, interpretation, and application produce widely varying results among Florida communities.

Most land development management programs are increasing in complexity and scope. Left to evolve naturally, they may gravitate toward increased control, multiple review, expanded process, greater regulatory detail, and less tolerance for deviation. Such a system penalizes innovation, creativity, diversity, and experimentation. Unnecessary costs and delays associated with complex permit approvals diminish investment that might otherwise be applied to a better development product. The result, more often than not, is a leveling of standards. The minimum standard becomes the community standard, and the land developer is disempowered.

In contrast, performance-based programs emphasizing flexibility, reliability, clarity of expected result, and incentive are empowering. The emergence of the planned development as a zoning concept is a notable example. Flexibility in design is offered in exchange for specificity. At its best, the planned development promotes innovation, creativity, and high-quality design while reflecting community interests and responding to neighborhood concerns. The technique has been widely applauded as an effective tool for development management and can be fundamentally empowering for the developer and the community.

A variety of other regulatory devices can also promote better design. For example, the Springfield, Missouri, zoning ordinance permits (under its planned development provision) a master parking plan or a master sign plan to be substituted for the general code standards. The Hillsborough County, Florida, land development code permits a master landscaping plan to supplant the landscaping requirements for individual lots or tracts. Hillsborough County has also enacted a unified site plan provision encouraging common design of storm water and utility systems, circulation and parking areas, and open space even in cases of multiple ownership and multiple zoning classifications.

There are downsides to flexibility techniques. If not applied with discipline and consistency, they can at one extreme become a vehicle for substandard development—legislated variances, if you will—and on the other a means of imposing exactions or design detail beyond that required by conventional regulation. The former is simply bad public policy and erodes the integrity of community standards. The latter amplifies uncertainty and increases cost, precisely the opposite of what these concepts are intended to produce.

Empowering regulatory techniques generally exhibit several characteristics. They are performance-based; their controlling parameters reflect basic land development issues such as use, intensity, continuity of infrastructure, and environmental integrity but leave spatial configuration, circulation, and perimeter treatment to design; expected results are clearly articulated; they represent alternative procedures, not requirements; and plan details are largely negotiated within an administrative environment not subject to public debate or limited to only minor modification.

Regardless of the regulatory techniques used, administrative review procedures can empower or disempower. Unfortunately, bureaucracies are naturally disempowering; proactive measures are often necessary to overcome this tendency. Regulators who are told to review an application will do so, at least to the extent necessary to dispatch their responsibilities (or their perceptions thereof), especially if their performance is judged by the avoidance of error. When in doubt, they will say no.

Multiple approval authority without an expedient avenue of resolution is a formula for conflict and delay. These dynamics are subtle, but their insidious effect can sabotage any community's land development management program.

Community building within a participatory democracy presents an extraordinary challenge. The disjointed and incremental nature of this process defies precision and control; planning efforts based on them are bound for disappointment, at best, and outright failure and rejection at the extreme. In contrast, a guiding paradigm of alignment and empowerment gives values and emphasis to notions of diversity, flexibility, teamwork, networking, commitment to results, a sense of community, and collaboration.

Does the acceptance of the principle of community alignment and empowerment represent a dramatic departure from traditional practice? Are planning techniques such as comprehensive planning, zoning, subdivision regulations, and capital improvements programming obsolete? I do not believe they are. Rather I contend, and have attempted to illustrate here, that when used within a paradigm of aligned empowerment these traditional techniques become highly synergic. It is simply a more effective formula for community building.

Chapter Ten

Making a Difference with Equity Planning

Norman Krumholz

Twenty years ago in Cleveland, a small group of city planners under my direction set out to help city government to better understand and resolve some of its problems and plan for its future. After much discussion, observation, and analysis, we came to believe that the problems of the city and its people had little to do with land use, zoning, urban design, or the other elements in the city planner's traditional bag of tools. They had to do with concentrated poverty, racial discrimination, inadequate education, and other conditions. We decided to give these issues highest priority, and to emphasize the needs of Cleveland residents in all our work. Our goal was "more choices for those who have few." Did a proposal transfer money, power, or participation toward or away from those Cleveland residents who needed help? If toward, we supported and lobbied for it; if away, we tried to reframe it or opposed it. Our approach came to be called "equity planning." Here are three brief stories of our Cleveland experience and, afterward, some lessons to be learned from them.

The Cleveland Experience

In the winter of 1974, a local real estate developer approached the city with plans to construct a major downtown commercial complex called Tower City. The media, the business community, and the city's political leadership hailed the proposal as a bold step toward revitalizing downtown Cleveland.

When the planning commission staff reviewed the deal, we found several disturbing aspects. The city was asked to waive rights it held to the area and to repair some railroad bridges on the site at a cost of $15 million to $20 million. Further, the developer wanted twenty years of property tax abatement. In negotiations with the developer, we asked him to pay for the bridges himself since they were not the city's responsibility and to forego tax abatement or guarantee a percentage of jobs for unemployed city residents. He refused.

We concluded that the city had little to gain from Tower City. The bridge repairs would be expensive and our responsibility for them was unclear; the city might be forced to give away any new property tax revenue; the promise of new income tax revenue was not bright since our studies showed the market for downtown office space was not growing but simply shifting from one location to another; and the developer was not offering any permanent new jobs for the city's unemployed.

We were not opposed to new development per se. We realized new development might keep firms downtown that otherwise would leave the city completely; that development provides short-term construction jobs; and that it adds to the tax base (unless new tax revenues are abated). But we wanted new development that was of clear benefit to the city and its people. There was no give on the developer's side. So, following the staff's recommendation, the planning commission disapproved the legislation.

Very quickly, our position came under fire from the city council and newspapers. We were accused of obstructing progress and being antidevelopment. Our rebuttal was that the health and vitality of a city did not depend on the construction of new office buildings and hotels downtown, but rather on how well the city helped provide education, jobs, and services to its residents. It did not convince anyone. Eventually, the city council overrode the planning commission's disapproval and passed the legislation.

The second story has to do with negotiations that in 1975 led to the transfer of the Cleveland Transit System (CTS) to the Greater Cleveland Regional Transit Authority (RTA). Transportation problems are usually defined in terms of rush-hour congestion, auto access, or the need for more off-street parking. However, our goal of support for those with few choices led us to define Cleveland's most significant transportation problem in a different way.

It seemed clear to us that the city's highest transportation priority should be to ensure a decent level of mobility to those transit-dependent persons who were prevented by extreme poverty or a combination of low income and physical disability (including old age) from moving around our metropolitan area. We needed to improve mobility for this population, this one-third of all our families who lacked automobiles and depended entirely on public transit.

We first became involved in the transit issue through the Cleveland area's Five-County Transit Study, which began in 1970. My staff and I asked to represent Mayor Stokes and later Mayor Perk on the transit study's executive committee. The two mayors agreed. In that capacity, we argued that expanded mobility for the transit-dependent population should be the study's highest-priority objective and that adequate funding should be provided for the transit-dependent element of the study. We won on each of these points, but they were fleeting victories. The project's staff began responding to political pressures, and a wide gap developed between the goals stated in the study and the final recommendations.

The study's final recommendations placed major emphasis on the expenditure of more than a billion dollars for expanding rail facilities plus an elevated downtown people mover. Based upon a careful review of the analysis supporting these recommendations, my staff and I concluded that such a rail system was likely to provide few benefits to anyone except those involved in its management, construction, and financing. Moreover, it threatened to draw resources away from those bus service improvements offering the greatest potential benefits to transit-dependent people. So we wrote a negative critique of the Five-County Transit Plan's rail proposals, and worked to discredit the rail plan at the local, regional, and federal levels. The feds ultimately put the rail expansion on the back burner.

Ultimately, the negotiations centered around one issue—what the city would receive in return for transferring the CTS to the new regional authority. Initially, the city's political leaders simply demanded a majority of appointments to the RTA board. We felt that this was insufficient and were convinced that the city should be bargaining for fare reductions and service improvements for the city's transit-dependent population. We took the bus improvement elements of the Five-County Transit Plan, translated them into terms local decision makers could understand, and presented them to the mayor and city council. When the city's political leaders realized that abstract concepts such as "route-spacing guides," "locating coefficients," and "service headways" meant tangible improvements for their constituents, they shifted the focus of their demands.

Throughout these negotiations, my staff and I argued for fare and service guarantees while our opposition—county officials, suburban mayors, representatives of the business community, and the city's own CTS management—argued for "flexibility" (in other words, rail expansion) for RTA.

During the protracted negotiations we were forced to make a number of concessions, but when agreement was finally reached, it was clear that we had made substantial progress toward ensuring that RTA would be responsive to the needs of the transit-dependent population. In the final agreement the city was guaranteed that a twenty-five-cent fare would be maintained for at least three years; senior citizens and disabled people would ride free during non-peak periods and pay only half fare during the four peak hours; service frequencies and route coverage within the city would be improved; RTA would be prohibited from spending funds on planning or developing a downtown people mover for at least five years; and Community Responsive Transit, a door-to-door dial-a-ride service, would be initiated.

This did not encompass all of our original demands, but our transit-dependent clients got much more than they would have without us.

The third story has to do with the issue of public versus private electric power. Cleveland is served by two electrical systems, the Cleveland Electric Illuminating Company (CEI), an investor-owned regional utility company serving about 80 percent of the city, and the city's own Municipal Electric Light Plant (Muny Light), established in 1906 by the great progressive mayor Tom L. Johnson. Muny's rates were about 25 percent lower than CEI's. In the 1970s, a series of power blackouts caused us to examine Muny Light's physical needs as a routine part of our preparation of the city's annual capital improvement program. As the analysis unfolded, however, it became apparent that the issue was more complex than Muny's need for new pipes and boilers.

We found that CEI had been interested in purchasing Muny for decades, presumably to eliminate competition. We also found that, apparently to injure Muny's competitive position, CEI had steadfastly refused to allow Muny to tie into other power sources. Therein lay Muny's problem: nearly all electric power companies have tie-ins to other power systems so that they can continue service should their own facilities need repair or fail. Because it had no such tie-in, Muny was plagued with power failures. This led to numerous complaints about Muny's service, and several council members and the newspapers proposed to sell the facility to CEI.

We concluded that this might solve the blackout problem, but it would also mean that Muny's customers would experience an immediate rate hike and that the city would no longer have an effective brake on future rate increases. Thus, the issue appeared to have serious economic implications for the city's poor. Because electricity is a relatively fixed item of household consumption, any change in rates would have a definite effect on the real incomes of city residents. Moreover, a significant change in rates might influence the location of firms within the Cleveland region and thus the access of city residents to jobs.

We analyzed the fiscal and legal aspects of this question and the history of CEI's apparent long-term attempt to subvert and destroy Muny, and proposed something quite different than the sale of Muny to CEI. We proposed that Muny Light use state law to condemn and purchase CEI's transmission and generating capacity in the city. This would expand our small municipal power system into a citywide network, eliminate blackouts, and provide electricity at a much lower cost to city residents.

This proposal was greeted with derision by the news media, and did not result in the condemnation of CEI. However, it may have helped to forestall the sale of Muny Light late in the 1970s and to prevent rate increases. It also served to remind local decision makers of the original rationale for Muny's establishment. Today, Muny (now called Cleveland Public Power) is still owned by the city and is expanding. It still provides electricity for about 25 percent less than does CEI.

Lessons Learned

What can we learn from the Cleveland experience in equity planning? First, that equity planning can be done; it can produce benefits for the poor and working-class residents of the city, and planners can do it and survive, indeed prosper. Although we were involved from time to time in confrontation and controversy with powerful public and private players, we were not punished, chastised, or dismissed by any of our three mayors, one a liberal black Democrat, another a conservative white Republican, and the third an urban populist. Instead, we found we could continue to make coalitions with former adversaries on issues in which we were jointly interested, and the planning agency acquired greater influence, prestige, resources, staff, and success with the passage of time.

A corollary of the Cleveland experience is also important: equity planning is an important way for planners to attack the basic underlying problems of our urban areas. In this regard, I believe it is much more effective than traditional planning that depends on land use, zoning, urban design, and economic development. Indeed, in many cities, what now passes for planning is simply called economic development. This is a simple variation of trickle-down ideology, in which planners do not so much plan a better future for the city and its people as help package development proposals made by others. In other words, planners and other public officials shovel in all sorts of public subsidies at the top of a project with the expectation that tax increases and jobs for the city's unemployed will come out at the bottom.

Unfortunately, trickle-down does not work; it merely raises the rate of return on private investment, gets the public to underwrite the risk of new development, and costs the taxing bodies money that they might otherwise spend on services. To produce tangible benefits for the city's poor and unemployed, we do not need trickle-down, we need well-funded programs in education, training, job development, and placement, all narrowly directed toward the disadvantaged. Most of the support for such programs must come from a concerned federal government, but equity planning at the local level can help.

Another lesson of the Cleveland experience suggests that successful equity planning practice depends on the committed and cooperative efforts of many people, not just the planning director. Indeed, very little is explained by the isolated activities of the director. The staff I was fortunate to build in Cleveland was like an extended family whose members drew on each other for support. We also depended for support on a broader network of allies in other city departments and outside agencies. Some of the deals we achieved mandated cooperation among the mayor, the city council, the Ohio general assembly, and the governor. These were the big players and their agreement was essential, but the outcomes would have been far different but for the efforts of the city planning staff and our allies. Success in most of our cases was not an individual achievement, but the general accomplishment of many.

This is not to deny that my personality or the personalities of my key staff members were irrelevant; quite the contrary. But the personalities of many, many actors in the city are relevant to the quality and character of the coalitions and working relationships the planning staff can nurture and build as it works. In every city, every day, planners across the country have opportunities to build coalitions and to initiate and pursue a professionally effective, politically astute, equity-oriented planning practice. If planners want to work toward more equitable outcomes, the opportunities are everywhere.

One of the reasons interested planners can work on an equity agenda is because planners have a certain freedom to broadly define their functions. Planners do not follow rigorous procedures as do such line agencies as police, firefighters, or waste collectors. To some extent, planners are free to define their own agendas. My staff, for example, at one time or another worked on highways and public transit, public versus private electric power, neighborhood revitalization and housing, regionalization, changing state law on the ownership of tax-delinquent private property, and negotiating leases on Cleveland's port, stadium, and waterfront parks. The reason we were able to involve ourselves in such diverse functions had little to do with the definition of planning in the Cleveland city charter, which was essentially based on land use and zoning; it had to do with our interest in these areas because of their equity implications, and because no one else in local government was deeply involved in them.

It should be clear that few people in local government understand just what it is that city planners are supposed to do. That confusion seems to extend to practitioners and to the university as well. What APA conference has been without at least one panel agonizing over the question, "What is planning?" There is a reason for the agony and the confusion. Beyond the narrowly defined powers and responsibilities mandated to planners by their city

charters, the scope of the planning function is not usually specified by law, nor is it uniform from city to city by practice. You don't
believe it? Try comparing your work program with those in San
Antonio, Pittsburgh, Chicago, New York, or San Diego. You'll find
little similarity. So we have some freedom to define our own roles.

We must, of course, be visible to decision makers. The mayor
and other powerful players will not instinctively turn to their planners when seeking wisdom. Neither law nor custom nor their own
political instincts will suggest that they do so. Mayors Stokes, Perk,
and Kucinich did not naturally turn to their planners; we went to
them. Nor, contrary to the expectations of many planners, will
political decision makers spell everything out for them. Politicians
usually say nothing on an issue until they are confident of the
extent of political support. They assiduously avoid stating clear
goals or objectives. As a result, planners themselves must expect to
define problems, look for equity angles, and shape directions.

So the ball is in our court. If we want to be effective, we must
seize the initiative, develop the kinds of work programs and equity-
based analyses that are relevant to political decision making, bring
our work to the attention of decision makers, and convince them
of its worth.

I am not saying that planners should act like the proverbial bull
in a china shop, arbitrarily doing whatever they want to do. But by
broadening the definition of the planning function and taking a
more equity-oriented activist posture, city planners can broaden
their responsibilities. They can do what is important: help poor
and working people, protect public resources, negotiate for public benefits, and save valuable city assets.

Strategies, Tactics, and Techniques

Perhaps this section should be called "How to Do It." Planners
interested in introducing more equity in their work must operate
on two levels of engagement. First, planners should understand
the ramifications of proposals made by themselves or by others.
They must be responsible to the goal of equity in their analysis of
these proposals. They must ask whether the clear benefits of these
proposed programs go to those in need or to those not in need,
and ask whether those who are called upon to pay for these pro-

grams are those most able to pay or those least able to pay. Then they must make the results of these analyses available to the planning commission, the media, the public at large, and local decision makers. Simply raising the question of the impact of these programs on the city's poor and working classes and on their future is an incredibly useful function. It may be castigated as being "divisive," but it can never be wrong.

The second level of engagement requires some competence in economics, cost-benefit analysis, and political finesse. Once planners understand that given proposals lead away from equitable outcomes, they must design alternatives where the clear benefits go to those in need, and where those most able to pay do, in fact, pay most of the costs. Then, they should use their institutional role in the community to argue for these programs. In this model, the equity planner's function is not to seek consensus—that is a politician's job—but to articulate the interests at stake and the impact of alternative choices on residents, and then to advocate decisions consistent with the interests of poor and working-class residents.

A related point: the best way to get information to the public is not through a planning report, but through the news media. As a result, it is important for planners to establish good, respectful relations with the press and television people. Be friendly and open with them; do not try to snow them. Write your own press releases, especially on controversial actions. Take the time to make sure reporters understand the reasons for your decisions. Try to make them like and respect you; they can make the planning agency look good or terrible. When writing, keep in mind the importance of selection of details, evocation of tone, arrangement, and emphasis. Remember that you're trying to influence policy.

Another important part of public visibility may be viewed as petty and mundane, but I believe it is important. It has to do with how one speaks and dresses. In Cleveland, our public posture was to present ourselves in a cordial but professional way, and to never compromise the facts or our integrity. We wanted to be seen as professional, apolitical, and neutral but competent advisors. We found that a good way to do this was to wear conservative suits, dark ties, and button-down shirts. As for speaking, we strictly avoided taboo words and concepts. Some words and concepts in our society are so weighted down with negative meaning that they can keep otherwise reasonable ideas from ever being discussed. Consider the fate of "central economic planning" or "socialized medicine." Yet controversial ideas can reach the table if couched in acceptable language.

Let me offer as an example our controversial proposal to condemn and expropriate Cleveland's investor-owned electric utility CEI in favor of expanding the city-owned municipal light plant. I could have made the proposal to the planning commission while wearing striped bell-bottomed pants and a tie-dyed T-shirt, and might have said: "We propose to expand public power by smashing the greed of the private sector. All power to the people!" That would have been indiscreet; we chose not to describe it that way. Instead, dressed like serious businesspeople, we described it as "a sound business venture," "a good deal for the city"; one that "would lower electric costs" and "make Cleveland a more attractive location for new investment." I think our low-key presentation helped reassure people who might have been stunned by the creative nature of the proposals, helped capture some support, and reminded people why Muny Light was built in the first place.

Based on our experience, then, a planner can publicly advance equity interests most effectively by posing the issues in a sober, faintly skeptical, professional way while looking businesslike. So, avoid being seen as ideological or political; be professional, but focus attention on the equity aspects that are inherently a part of many of the local issues that come before you.

There are two other elements would-be equity planners should consider: time and persistence. To be accorded a place at the public bargaining table, planners, like other players, must be prepared to invest time and energy in developing a position and achieving the respect of others. Many of the Cleveland cases above evolved over very long periods. The transit issue took five years, but at the end the poor won more service and lower fares. The Muny Light issue took ten years and is still not over. If my staff and I had not participated in those issues over the long pull, it is doubtful we would have been able to influence the outcome. You have to pay your dues in time and participation to sit at the table when the key decisions are made.

Persistence is also invaluable. Planners should be prepared to bring up over and over again good ideas that have been shot down earlier. The cast of local characters is always changing, as are the times and circumstances, and good ideas rejected at one time may be adopted when the time is ripe. Nobody in local government but planners is likely to perform this important function of repackaging and reselling old but good ideas.

Like all good pastors, I have tried to make three main points in this sermon. First, equity planning works. It is clear that a planning practice that focuses on equity considerations can be accomplished and can provide important benefits to the poor and working-class people of the city.

Second, opportunities to do equity planning exist every day in every city in America. Opportunities to pursue a professionally effective, politically astute, progressive planning practice need only be seized. Indeed, there is plenty of evidence from many cities that such efforts are under way. Consider Ray Flynn's Boston and the work of Peter Dreier and the people at the Boston Redevelopment Authority, Rob Mier's work in linking downtown development to the poor residents of Harold Washington's Chicago, Rick Cohen negotiating low-income set-asides in new market-rate housing developments in Jersey City, and the lessons from Santa Monica and Berkeley that Pierre Clavel has reported in *The Progressive City*. We need to be visible and public, professional and persistent, and educate our political superiors and the public at large.

Practicing equity planning may be less ideological than simply practical. Sadly, the problems addressed by equity planning are not going away. In many cities, the number of poor and near-poor residents is growing to the point where they make up a substantial portion of the population. More and more black and Hispanic mayors will be coming out of that population. These minority mayors will not all see the world in the same way. There will be differences among them: Coleman Young is not like Harold Washington any more than Tom Bradley is like Carl Stokes. But while some minority mayors may not mandate equity planning any more than their white predecessors, still they will want to do more for their constituents. For planners in these and other cities, anxious to explore their own models of redistributive justice, the Cleveland experience might be a good place to start.

Chapter Eleven

A New Vision of Collaborative Public Service

Elizabeth L. Hollander

"What is your vision of the public servant?" David Rosenbloom, editor of the *Public Administration Review,* asked me almost two years ago. I was in Washington, D.C., at the time to report on the work of the Illinois Commission on the future of public service.

I did not have a ready answer for Rosenbloom. As someone who has spent a lot of time as a planner, I am aware of the power of visions; over the ensuing months, the question nagged me. We need a vision of public service that fits our times—hard times, with limited budgets and unlimited demands. I sketch here an emerging vision that is rooted in our uniquely American democratic traditions of a government that is "us," not "them." In it, the public servant is an active partner with the public, linking citizens with resources. This vision is profoundly influenced by my service as planning director for the City of Chicago from 1983 to 1989. This was a time of enormous change in the city, with the election of its first African American mayor, Harold Washington. It was a time when we sought the active engagement of many Chicagoans who had felt excluded from decision making.

Historical Trends

How have we thought about public servants in the past? Patricia W. Ingraham and Rosenbloom, in a seminal 1990 article, provided a history that I will drastically abbreviate here. In the 1930s, we thought of the public servant as a social engineer who both formulated and implemented policy. This idea was replaced in the 1950s with a vision of the public servant as an apolitical technocrat. In the 1960s, when we discovered the power of citizen involvement and the limits of expertise, the technician lost credibility.

In the 1970s, there was no new vision, but we began to believe that public servants should reflect the diversity of the public that they serve. In the 1980s, the dominant motif was one that had always been lurking in the background: the public servant as scapegoat for all that was not working. Starting with President Jimmy Carter, and reaching a zenith under President Ronald Reagan, bureaucrat bashing became a way of life. At the same time, however, many cities, such as Chicago, were rediscovering the power of working with neighborhood groups on designing and implementing strategies for community improvement.

The bashing of the bureaucrat is happening as the role of government is rapidly shifting. During the 1980s and early 1990s we experienced shrinkage in public budgets and a shift of responsibilities to state and local governments, often in the form of unfunded mandates. At the same time, the citizenry feels increasingly isolated from public life as a result of the growth of political action committees, information overload, and the complexity of issues such as the deficit and the global economy. Major scandals in the government sector add to disaffection.

A New Vision

The good news is that a new vision of public service is being crafted in response to all of the criticism. It is a vision unique to American democracy because it borrows heavily from our traditions of individualism, localism, respect for citizen involvement, admiration for the entrepreneur, and impatience with bureaucratic structure. It is a vision for changing times, which celebrates quality and insists on responsiveness to citizens. It is a vision for an America that does not "have it made" anymore, but must fight for its position in the global economy and invent new means of upward mobility.

If I were to try to capture the new vision of the public servant in one word, it would be as collaborator, the link between citizens and resources. Government workers are not social engineers. They cannot solve the problems of society but at their best can use limited resources for maximum effect. Using resources does not mean simply money but people, including the frontline worker and the citizen. For many who lived through World War II, the word *collaborator* carries a negative connotation. However, in this context it reflects the word's more positive primary definition: to work jointly with others toward a common goal.

For example, when Mayor Washington sought to address the problem of homelessness in Chicago, he asked me to organize a task force that included all affected city departments, state and federal agencies, shelter providers, and nonprofit activists. At that time we did not even have ordinances governing homeless shelters. Working together, this group devised a city policy, wrote ordinances governing shelters, allocated limited dollars to providers, and sought additional resources. "Together" was the key concept. While I was convener, nongovernmental participants provided key leadership. Instead of simply lobbying for resources from the outside, they joined in the hard decisions about allocating existing resources and balancing interests. When the fire department called for strict and expensive fire protection measures for shelters in church basements on the basis that clients might die in fires, shelter providers argued that excessive cost could shut shelters and their clients would die of the cold. When the agreed-upon package came before the city council, the nonprofit groups were as important a lobby as the government officials. In fact, it was the nonprofits that found a Polish priest running a shelter who turned around a key alderman opposed to the package.

Linking citizens with resources also includes thinking creatively about the use of private and nonprofit resources as providers or partners. In my current work running the nonprofit Government Assistance Program to improve government, we brought local health administrators together with community organizations to devise an immunization plan. One remarked afterward, "I did not realize that all these people also own the problem of immunizing children. This is not just my problem."

This new vision of the public servant requires a perspective of deep respect for the citizen. In a democracy, the citizen is both the government's customer and a major stakeholder in the government. As a stakeholder, the citizen must take some responsibility for government's success or failure. In return, public servants must share hard choices and responsibility with those they serve.

For instance, to involve downtown Chicago civic groups in devising planning strategies for the Central Area, the planning department organized a Downtown Advisory Committee that included everyone from the landmark and land preservationists to the advocates for State Street, North Michigan Avenue, and central city neighborhoods. This provided an accessibility to the planning department that was unprecedented in Chicago. Essential to the working of this group was a shared agenda. They could raise issues, as could the planning department. The other key is that groups that had lobbied the department separately on single issues had to confront the variety of perspectives faced by the public servants. Another interesting dynamic was that the planning department could lay out issues on which it would have liked to move but faced severe political constraints. We would then leave the room and often the citizen groups would devise a strategy to move an agenda on which we were stuck.

Rather than pretending that government can fix everything, public servants should heed the words of Alexis de Tocqueville: "The duties of private citizens are not supposed to have lapsed because the state has come into action; but every one is ready, on the contrary, to guide and support it. This action of individuals, joined to that of the public authorities, frequently accomplishes what the most energetic centralized administration would be unable to do" ([1835] 1956, p. 70).

Also required is a government that frees the frontline worker to provide services more flexibly, and to feed back his or her ideas for improving service. We need governments that celebrate the entrepreneur, defined by French economist J. B. Say as one who "shifts economic resources out of an area of lower and into an area of higher productivity and greater yield" (Drucker, 1973, p. 22).

We need government agencies that have a clear vision of what they want to accomplish and are focused on outputs, goals, and performance, not tasks and process for its own sake. We need an ethic that says it's more important to get something done and possibly take some heat for it than to do nothing and stay out of trouble. And to support government workers trying to deliver services, we need modern technology and regular investments in training of staff.

When I first came to the Chicago planning department in 1983 I held a staff meeting for every employee and discovered it was the first meeting of the entire staff since 1968! Following that meeting I went around to talk with people and would ask them, for whom they were writing a report? Who wanted it? What difference was it going to make? People looked at me as if I were crazy and would tell me things like "I was just told to do it, I have no idea who wants it or why."

Imagine spending your day preparing a report without knowing what impact it might have. The Government Assistance Program that I now run works with agencies to devise strategic plans and then engage every level of staff in their implementation by providing hands-on, just-in-time training in techniques for government reinvention.

A Realistic Vision?

Are there significant barriers to such a vision of public service? You bet. When resources are inadequate to known need, public servants have a natural tendency to become defensive. Instead of sharing hard decisions, they hide. It's all very well to empower the frontline worker and encourage risk, but what about all the negative press when a mistake is made? Collaboration is time-consuming, complicated, and sometimes messy, like the rest of democracy. And what about all the rules built into legislation because of real concerns about fairness and equity? Aren't they a real barrier to flexible decision making? Besides, in hard budgetary times who is going to come up with the funds for training and information systems necessitated by the new approach?

You do not have to be a Pollyanna about the tough challenges of public service to hold out this new vision. Everywhere there is evidence of a willingness to try new ways of doing business. When we organized the Government Assistance Program in 1989, reinventing government was like a summer storm on the horizon: we could see lightning but did not know if the drought would be broken. Now there is a virtual hurricane of interest at every level of government, as documented by David Osborne and Ted Gaebler (1992), the National Commission on the State and Local Public Service (1993), and the National Performance Review (1993).

Cook County Hospital, one of the most resource-scarce local agencies, has found the resources to work with the Government Assistance Program to engage its leadership in strategic planning and its frontline workers in quality improvement teams. What has been the payoff? The hospital was reaccredited on the first try for the first time in its history. Teams of doctors, nurses, and technicians have significantly reduced the wait for surgical procedures. One twenty-year employee reported he "cannot wait to get to work because somebody is listening to my ideas."

Can we honestly say that government is dominated by collaborators—that is, by government workers who are citizen-responsive, entrepreneurial, risk takers, enablers, reflective of the diversity of their constituents? Vision, according to Webster, is "the ability to perceive something not actually visible." In order to change, we need first to imagine a new future.

From my perspective, the Empowerment Zone legislation is a national vision for addressing community building in poor communities that reflects the strategies evolved in many cities and towns under the leadership of collaborative public planners and policy makers. St. Paul, Cleveland, Baltimore, and Atlanta were among the leaders. In Chicago the Harold Washington administration made collaboration with our extensive and effective community-based organizations a conscious policy. The 1984 Chicago Development Plan, better known as the Chicago Works Together plan, laid out this approach. We did not try to write a traditional comprehensive land use plan; we didn't have the resources, and it was not clear what impact it would have had even if we could have done it. Instead, a policy plan articulated the need to balance development in the downtown and neighborhoods and celebrated strategies to engage citizens and community groups in joint approaches to community development. It was also significant that this plan was a joint effort of all of the development departments (planning, economic development, housing, employment and training, cultural affairs) as well as citizen activists.

This policy plan built an important framework for departments to devise specific strategies to use public resources to strengthen the power of community organizations. It led to such projects as the regular publication of lists of buildings in housing court showing when cases would be heard, what violations were at stake, and building addresses. This simple list was a powerful tool for community activists. (It was, in fact, not such a simple list to prepare; it took a year of work with three departments to get it up and running.)

Other examples of plans that followed were The Boulevard Plan and the industrial development planning process. The Boulevard Plan, a strategy for neighborhood reinvestment, addresses the need to improve Chicago's historic boulevard system, an "emerald necklace" designed by Frederick Law Olmsted that runs through black, white, and Hispanic neighborhoods. The plan details a series of boulevard improvements that will catalyze other investment in the surrounding neighborhoods. One of many concrete outcomes is that Neighborhood Housing Services, a nonprofit housing developer, in collaboration with local banks is achieving major housing rehabilitation investments along boulevard segments.

The industrial development planning process is another example of a strategy that recognizes the power of collaborative approaches in a resource-constrained environment. There was a desire for a comprehensive industrial land use plan. Lacking the money to undertake such a plan, the city planning and economic development departments, industrial brokers, the economic development commission, and local nonprofit development groups devised a staged strategy to address the city in segments (North, South, and West sides). In each segment an effort was made to identify areas of opportunity for industrial development. The city then committed limited moneys for necessary infrastructure, and industrial brokers marketed these targeted area. Started before I left city government in 1989, the plan has recently been completed for all three segments and, meanwhile, new industrial parks are under way.

Einstein once said, "The significant problems we face cannot be solved at the same level of thinking we were at when we created them." The rigors of delivering public services in a time of diminished resources and increased expectations require us to move to a new level of thinking. Let's seize the opportunity to paint a vision that will inspire or reinspire the many in and out of public service who want to reinvent government.

Lessons on Effectiveness

Here we look at several principles that can be learned to achieve effectiveness in planning. Clearly, planning must go beyond theory and method, beyond politics and economics; it must be implemented to be effective. To be good, planning must have results.

The five chapters in Part Three look at principles from several points of view. Chapter Twelve deals with principles that are based on planning's core values; the next chapter stresses achieving results through a commonly held vision of the future. After a discussion of principles for planning effectiveness within an emerging participatory democracy, Chapter Fifteen urges a look into the planner's toolbox to make sure it is well stocked with the necessities to succeed. Finally, Chapter Sixteen takes a forthright look at, among other things, women in planning, success through working with emerging citizens' groups, and the role (for good or evil) of architects, engineers, and politicians in the planning process.

Chapter Twelve

Core Values and Principles of Effective Planning

Robert W. Becker

My career in planning has taken a variety of turns through the years. I've worked in the public sector as a city planner and eventually as planning director of one of America's most interesting cities, New Orleans. I've worked in a quasi-public capacity with a downtown improvement district. And I've worked in the private sector where, among other tasks, I currently manage a modern zoo on a day-to-day basis.

I've gone from believing government could do no wrong in my early career to wondering if it can do anything right. I've prepared large capital budgets, revised central business district zoning ordinances, and been responsible for the public planning side of a mega-event, the 1984 World's Fair. Through all of this, I've often been amazed at what I did not know. Despite every effort to convince my employers, the mayor, the city council, and many citizens that I knew everything and had every situation under control, I have developed a healthy respect for the vast body of knowledge in our profession with which I am only slightly familiar.

My challenge is to concisely impart what planning knowledge I may have gained in twenty-five years of practicing in the public and private sectors without putting the reader to sleep in mid-chapter. And I've hit upon a novel approach. I'm just going to tell it to you directly, beginning with a set of basic values for planners.

Core Values

My years of observing developers, politicians, citizens, interest groups, bureaucrats, and the rest of the universe of people who play some role in planning have reinforced in my mind something that should have been obvious in the first place: certain principles and ideas are of overriding importance for effective planning. Here they are.

Planning Is a People-Oriented Profession

The central focus of our work should be helping people solve problems and achieve a better quality of life for themselves and their families. If you do not like people, or do not believe that people are basically capable of making informed choices about their problems and their futures, then I suggest you might be better off in another profession. Window washing, perhaps, or theoretical mathematics.

Power Comes from Enduring Values

Qualities such as professionalism, honesty, integrity, compassion, commitment, and leadership still have real meaning and value in today's world. Planners will never have real political power, probably will not have monetary power, and usually do not have charismatic personal power. So what do we have that makes a difference or is of value to our fellow citizens? It seems to me that what sets us apart is our technical training, professional opinions, reputation for honest analysis of problems, willingness to sympathetically hear the views of all parties, and ability to facilitate solutions. These are qualities to which we must adhere.

Planning Works Best Within Common Social Boundaries

Stay within the lines. We must recognize that we do not practice our profession in a vacuum free of the broad beliefs and values that characterize American society. In general, to be effective, we must practice within these boundaries: rule by the majority, protection of the rights of the minority, commitment to elective democracy, individual rights, basic commitment to a managed free enterprise economic structure, and recognition of diversity.

The recognition of these principles and their impact on planning is often frustrating. During my own career, the political process has led to actions that I felt were not in the city's best interest, and I was frustrated and angry. On the other hand, I have come to appreciate that the process works, disputes are resolved, and action is taken. It's best to accept that planning operates in this environment of beliefs unless, of course, one's hopes follow in the footsteps of Lenin or Che Guevara.

Even Short-Term Plans Need a Long-Term Context

The most important value of planning lies in helping to direct the future and in accommodating change. Much has been written recently about the value of strategic planning, incrementalism, immediate problem solving, giving customers what they want, and so forth. And I think those things do have value and importance. However, I also believe that when planners give up the role of visionary and abandon the process of looking at short-term issues in the context of their long-range implications, we are shortchanging our clients and failing to provide effective leadership. Our role is not only to serve our customers and their immediate concerns. It is also to provide effective leadership in helping to construct a brighter future. Therefore, plan for the long-range future, not just the immediate future!

Practicing Principles

Here are seven principles of practice that I have come to rely upon.

Practice Horizontal Management

Or: it's okay if you don't know who heads your division. In 1981 the City of New Orleans was awarded the right to hold the 1984 World's Fair. To ensure a successful event, the mayor designed his office, and particularly the planning commission where I worked, to be the principal liaison to the private fair management team. My immediate reaction was that we should instead assign the project to our own World's Fair Planning Division, with its skilled chief, planners, and staff.

Except, of course, that we had no such thing. So we had to improvise. Basically we put together various teams from across the commission's responsibilities—transportation, zoning, urban design, and others—to deal with the many issues generated. On some issues the chief of the transportation division was project leader; on others, the responsibility was assigned to a Planner II. The distinction between vertical hierarchies was broken down, and teams were put together to utilize the skills of anyone who could participate and contribute in a meaningful way. As issues were resolved, teams were broken apart and then reformed to address the next crisis. Professionals from other departments were brought together with our planners to ensure that everyone who could contribute did contribute. This horizontal structure was very effective, allowing everyone from the lowest planner to the director to have a say in problem solving. The fair was extremely successful from a planning perspective, and how we approached these issues was a major factor in that success.

Provide Leadership

Much has been written about the quality of leadership, so I won't elaborate too much here. If you are the planning director or team leader, your staff and your commission will look to you for leadership. Pull people together, motivate them, inspire them, set ground rules, assign responsibilities, and outline expected results. Never hesitate to step in and provide guidance. Encourage people to be creative, to involve other contributors, to ask questions, and to question answers. You cannot be shy and retiring. Leadership also means that you support your people. You stand with them when their work is criticized, as well as when it is praised.

Conserve Your Personal Political Capital

In any position of authority, you have to confront many controversies. A typical planning department will have 500 to 1,500 items appearing on its agenda annually. Many of these are routine and ordinary, but many others are very divisive and controversial.

Let's say that during the course of any given year, you have to make recommendations on 100 controversial issues. Of these, perhaps 25 have some real significance to the future of the city or one of its neighborhoods. These are important issues, and you probably feel strongly about each one. Yet you know that the mayor, or city council as the case may be, will disagree with you on a number of them for any variety of reasons. You must decide how much you want to press your views with the decision makers. In doing so, remember an important principle: everybody has only so much personal political capital. In other words, you can only go a limited number of times to the mayor or council members and ask them to go with you on an issue they ordinarily would oppose.

If you are respected and your opinion is valued, many times a personal appeal will shift the decision in your favor. But if you go this route too often, you will use up your bargaining chips and eventually be ignored. How often to put your personal prestige on the line is a skill not taught in graduate school. Yet developing and utilizing this personal capital is extremely important in being an effective planner.

When I was in charge of developing a new zoning ordinance for our central business district, I came to realize the importance of this skill. As usual, there were many issues relating to the ordinance and many special interest groups who had strong views on the issues. Business groups, preservation groups, developers, and politicians all had positions, seemingly on each element of the ordinance. Parking regulations, sign controls, and building setbacks were among the concerns. The mayor and council were briefed on many of these issues, and generally I had a good feel for how far the political leadership would go to support the regulations.

I would argue aggressively on each regulation about which I felt strongly. One day, when I went down to brief the council president and to argue for his support on a particular issue, he said, "Bob, just tell me the three most important regulations you think are necessary to ensure the effectiveness of this ordinance." So I told him, and he said, "I'll stick with you on these, but don't bug me if I go a different way on some of the others." He remained true to his word and helped pass radical new floor area ratio regulations, historic building controls, and strict height controls. He went against me on sign controls and a few other things, but I did not press the points. He taught me a valuable lesson. Use your capital for the things that count rather than exhausting your personal capital on every item.

Practice the Politics of Inclusion

It seems a foregone conclusion that everyone should have a say in matters that affect them. Yet every practicing planner knows this is easier said than done. In fact, the more people involved in any decision or issue, the messier it becomes and the longer it drags out. Face it, planning is a very sloppy business. It takes time and patience to try to give everyone a voice, and the process is exhausting and frustrating. It's also the only way. I used to tell my planners that if a new issue was raised at a public hearing over a certain controversy, and they had not heard it before, then they had not done their jobs; they should have gotten this input early in the process.

People will not accept any conclusion to a controversy unless they have had a chance to meaningfully make their views heard. The worst thing that can happen at a public hearing is to have a citizen stand up and say, "I did not know anything about this!" or "No one bothered to talk to me about this and I live in the neighborhood!" or "I know the planning staff talked to the developer but not to us average Joes!"

Take time, involve everyone, make sure all views are known and all issues are put on the table. Then try to resolve the problem.

Perception Is Reality

The perception of reality is as important as reality itself. How many times have you witnessed it? You go before the planning board or city council or school board to testify on something very important to you. But you find that only a few board members are paying attention. Others are holding side conversations, eating a sandwich, talking on the phone, or, worst of all, huddling with your opponent in a corner of the room. I believe few things undermine citizens' faith in their government more than these types of experiences.

As a planner you must continually remind your staff and commission or decision-making board about the importance of acting professionally at these public meetings. People must perceive they are getting a fair shake when they appear before a decision-making body; of course, one hopes the perception and reality are the same. They must come away from the proceedings with the feeling that they were heard and their views considered. Otherwise, their faith and commitment to the entire process of planning as a tool to resolve problems and create a brighter future will be lost.

Not All Developers Are Evil

Let's be clear about what we as planners do and what we do not do. We do write rules and regulations to guide development. We do try to resolve quality-of-life disputes and controversies over various development issues. We do provide leadership and direction in considering future possibilities for our community.

We do not build homes, install infrastructure, take market economy risks, or borrow large sums of money. These are things developers do. I've known many planners who view developers through a jaundiced eye as pillagers of the environment, suppressors of neighborhoods, ruthless capitalists, political insiders, and general nogoodniks.

While certainly I have met a number of these types, my general experience with developers is that they are honest, hard-working, bright, forceful, and goal-oriented. For the most part, they make things happen, and in that role, they have a very difficult job. Our job as planners is to provide an environment where good development can flourish, bad development can improve, and really bad development does not happen. To achieve that type of environment, we have to work with developers. Learn to recognize the bad from the good, and always, and I mean always, be professional in your relations with them. Remember: today's developer could be tomorrow's planning commissioner and your boss!

Play the Game

If not all developers are evil, perhaps the same can be said of politicians. We live in a representative democracy and although its roles shift, it is unlikely to be transformed dramatically. So for the foreseeable future, public policy will be enacted by elected political leaders. If you want to be effective, you must interact with this political process, not stay aloof from it. Does this mean you have to like all politicians or prostitute yourself to politically objectionable acts? No. It does mean you have to work with politicians, influence them, teach them, learn from them, and cooperate with them as much as you can. They are players, important players, and if you refuse to play with them they will play the game without you.

More Words of Advice

These didn't fit in the other categories, but they are worth thinking about.

Lighten Up

Planning can be a very tough business with a lot at stake. However, if you allow yourself to be consumed by the job day and night, always seeing only the negative, you'll be of little good to yourself, your family, or eventually your job.

As a young planner I was called upon to make what I felt was an important presentation to the city council on a development issue in our French Quarter historic district. It was a lengthy spiel, designed to let the council see the entire rationale for our position. The longer I spoke the more impressed I became with the compelling nature of my presentation.

About two-thirds of the way through I noticed that the district council member who represented the French Quarter (whose position was crucial in influencing the rest of the council), could barely be seen. In fact, he was leaning way back in his chair so that just his face was visible above the podium. Even more infuriating was that he had his eyes closed! In fact, it seemed as though the more I spoke the less of his face I could see.

The more I went on the angrier I became. Finally I could take it no more. I departed from my prepared text. Speaking forcefully and with all the might of righteous indignation, I called the councilman by name. "Councilman!" I yelled. "I am making an important presentation about a matter that affects your district and not only are you not paying attention, but you are sleeping!" There was quiet in the chambers. This was a senior council member who was very influential and certainly not used to being addressed in this manner. I was feeling pretty smug about myself for demanding the attention I felt was due an important subject.

Slowly the councilman raised his eyes. Without moving from his chair he took the microphone and, with crystal clarity, said, "Son, I may be sleeping from the neck down, but I'm listening from the neck up!" The entire audience erupted in howls of laughter. At first I was angry, but as the laughter went on I realized that what was so important to me simply was not to the councilman. The gravity with which I viewed my presentation was not shared by him. Pretty soon I just laughed along, finished my presentation, and sat back to contemplate the experience. By the way, he agreed with our position and eventually voted to support our recommendations.

Go to Other Professions' Conferences

Hey, all knowledge is not transferred at the annual American Planning Association conference! Go to other conferences and seminars that bear upon your responsibilities. Learn what other professions are thinking. Attend Urban Land Institute offerings. Visit the Council of Shopping Center Developers Conference. Sit in on land use seminars offered by the American Bar Association. You'll come away with a broadened view of the issues—and the ability to talk to other professionals in their terminology.

Compromise

Not only should you be willing to compromise, but you should be a facilitator for compromise. Most issues and controversies will not be settled in a way that makes someone a 100 percent winner or a 100 percent loser; usually they'll fall someplace in between. Be a part of the process, and you can achieve successes impossible to achieve if you are outside that process. The art of effectuating compromises and negotiating arguments can be learned. Make sure you do!

Make the World Your Oyster

There are many careers in which a planner's training will prove useful. Do not hesitate to take jobs in nontraditional fields where your training will be of use. Expect to change jobs on a regular basis. Get a broad experience and always be open to new opportunities that may not lie in traditional fields. I know planners working in real estate, labor organizations, chambers of commerce, charities, and, yes, even zoos. Your training is useful and good preparation for a variety of jobs if you keep an open mind.

Be Results-Oriented

This seems simple enough, and everyone assumes they are so oriented. Yet we can all list fellow workers who are driven to write lengthy reports, engage in endless debate, forever pursue additional alternatives, and otherwise skirt the final goal. Get rid of this baggage. When writing reports, less is generally more. Be concerned with making something happen, and fight against the natural inertia of the bureaucracy. Always pretend you are pregnant and must produce the best possible product. Then push it out and get on with life.

Chapter Thirteen

Visioning for Tangible Results

John A. Lewis

My perspective on visioning and goals-setting began to take shape when I was hired as the executive director of Goals for Corpus Christi in 1974. Among all the candidates, I was chosen for two reasons. First, I was perceived as the most neutral. I was knowledgeable about many community organizations without being closely identified with any of them. Second, I had no personal agenda. There were no issues that I personally wished to advance, and I had no interest in using the job as a stepping stone to a position with another organization. Neutrality and no agenda got me hired (later I was told they liked my sense of humor, too); knowing that was my first awareness that there are some very important principles to follow for effective visioning and goals-setting, the most important being to maintain neutrality for the sake of a credible process.

With that one principle as a basis, I set about identifying others in order to ensure the success of Goals for Corpus Christi. I found some of them in the Goals for Dallas program, which was started in 1965 and soon became a model for other communities. I quickly saw that community leaders needed to do more than lend their names to the program. They needed to devote their time and effort to ensure its success. It also became clear to me that conclusions needed to be reached by consensus; unanimity was not expected. And widespread citizen participation not only needed to be encouraged, but vigorously sought.

A list of principles was beginning to emerge, and I added another based on my training and experience as an economist:

having too many goals is as bad as having no goals at all, and goals without priorities yield few results. A basic tenet of economics is that scarce resources must be allocated. This is certainly the case for community resources and the time and talent of citizens, which must be allocated among many deserving programs and projects. To reach toward goals, trade-offs must be considered, choices made, and priorities determined.

The basic principles that guided me through Goals for Corpus Christi resulted, by most accounts, in a successful program. But mistakes were made. For example, I feel that there were so many opportunities for citizen involvement that the actual extent of such involvement turned out to be less than it could have been. I have noticed over the years that most persons who organize and lead community visioning and goals-setting programs make similar mistakes. The sad thing is that they, and the communities they serve, never get a chance to learn from the mistakes. Most community visioning and goals-setting programs run at intervals at best, and their executive directors and leaders move on after their first experience.

After Goals for Corpus Christi, I too moved on, becoming executive director of the Community Association at The Woodlands, Texas, one of the most successful new town developments in the country. I was responsible for the planning, construction, and management of community facilities. I was charged with implementation—achieving the goals that had been developed with much community involvement. From then on, in all future visioning and goals-setting efforts I was involved with, visualizing how goals would be achieved became an important aspect of the goals-setting process itself.

In 1979, a devastating tornado ripped through Wichita Falls, Texas, and community leaders felt that a communitywide goals-setting process was important to the rebuilding process. I accepted an invitation to serve as the program's executive director. I could not resist the opportunity to apply what I had learned in Corpus Christi. We really got results! In just over a year, almost 10,000 people participated in the Goals for Wichita Falls program. By any measure, this was phenomenal in a community with a population of 97,000.

After Wichita Falls, I served as coordinator or consultant for many visioning and goals-setting efforts across the United States, in large cities and small towns: Memphis, Tucson, Rochester (New

York), Pensacola, Fort Worth, San Diego, Jacksonville and Graham (both in Texas), and many other communities. I served as executive director of the Goals for Dallas program from 1981 to 1993.

Twenty years of experience in the area of visioning and goals-setting has led me to develop a list of sixteen fundamental principles for success. Many evolved as I worked in so many communities large and small; others I adapted from business leaders who were involved in the programs I was associated with.

I have had the pleasure of working with many such leaders, ranging from Erik Jonsson, cofounder of Texas Instruments, to Carl Sewell, the country's top luxury car dealer and author of the best-seller *Customers for Life*. They instilled in me the importance of producing results and adhering to principles that produce results. Many persons involved with community visioning and goals-setting programs believe that "the process is the product." While there are benefits from the process, only tangible results give it lasting value. In fact, they are necessary for the process itself to last its course.

I've learned that the techniques and procedures of visioning and goals-setting can (and should) vary among communities, and, from time to time, should vary within a community. However, the sixteen principles for success are always the same. Here, I have grouped them into six categories to make them easier to discuss: getting started, visioning, goals-setting, developing plans, getting results, and the most important principle.

Principles for Getting Started

The most common excuses when a visioning and goals-setting program fails is that it wasn't a good idea in the first place, the timing wasn't right, or it just wasn't needed. In reality, a program usually fails because of a lack of thoughtful start-up planning, no understanding of the overall decision-making and community environment, or serious mistakes by individuals. It is not uncommon to find programs where, six months in, people are still trying to figure out what they're doing at the same time they're doing it—a certain prescription for disaster!

But disaster can be avoided. Here are the three most important principles to rely on when starting any visioning and goals-setting program.

Have a Plan and Follow It

This should be obvious, but it's amazing how often a plan is an afterthought. Sometimes it purposely is overlooked. When Goals for Tucson was started in 1982, a general organizational meeting of volunteers for "issue committees" was called before a plan for the program was developed. Leaders wanted a public meeting quickly in order to keep interest strong after the program's initial announcement. However, without a plan to follow, committees started setting their own agendas and heading in different directions. Fortunately, a committed leadership was able to backstep quickly, develop a work plan, and get the program back on track.

In a large Southwestern city, the mayor developed lengthy background and position papers on community issues. When they were presented for public consideration, it became obvious that they would have a better reception if they were considered in the context of an overall community visioning and goals-setting program. After needless delay, an action plan was developed and successfully implemented. However, the effort would have been more successful if a plan had been developed before background papers were prepared.

At the kickoff meeting for a visioning and goals-setting program in a small community in Washington state, volunteers for various committees such as transportation and the environment essentially were told: "You are the experts. You are the citizens with a real interest in these areas. This is an informal and unstructured process. You've got lots of freedom. You know what to do. Now go do it." Not much happened. The truth is that participants in visioning and goals-setting programs like to see a plan or a road map of what they are going to do and how it will get done, preferably written down and with time lines, responsibilities, and expectations in place. When they see this, they get excited and get down to work because they know they are not at just another meeting.

For the Goals for Dallas program that ran from 1983 to 1989, at least 150 people were involved in developing a plan to follow. Over a period of weeks, they first met in small groups to consider alternative approaches. Then, they all came together to reach a consensus on a final plan.

I have observed and helped with programs in Memphis, Rochester, San Diego, and many other communities that demonstrated good planning at the beginning of visioning and goals-setting programs. Before kickoff, these communities developed conceptual plans, operational plans, budgets, and initial funding. A conceptual plan outlines the basic approach, and is grounded in an evaluation of the relative importance of various criteria; for example, the need to involve all segments of the community, the importance of dealing with all aspects of the community, and the desire to be useful to existing organizations. Having and following a plan that participants have bought into enhances the program's viability; it is absolutely essential to the success of a community visioning and goals-setting program.

No Plan Is Right for Every Community

A plan that is right for one may be wrong for another. There are many ways to arrive at a vision and goals, each with its own internal integrity. When matched to a particular community and a particular time, however, one process almost always stands out as preferable.

For example, in deciding which approach to follow during the 1983 cycle of Goals for Dallas, a singular view of the community seemed to captivate planning committee members: "There are hundreds of organizations in Dallas, each with its own agenda and priorities. There needs to be a way of getting each of these organizations to evaluate its own interests in the context of its suggestions for communitywide goals. Then there needs to be a way of reaching an overall consensus." This community view dictated the visioning and goals-setting process that was adopted. Over 300 meetings involving more than 4,000 persons were held with organizations ranging from chambers of commerce and junior leagues to school classes and activist organizations. After each group discussed community needs and how it could deal with them, it suggested five communitywide priorities. One hundred final goals and priorities were determined at a goals-setting conference that included all participants in the smaller meetings.

In deciding upon an approach for a new cycle of goals-setting in 1989, a new view of the community prevailed. The economy was down in Dallas, racial tensions were up, and businesses themselves could not see very far into the future. The question was: What do we need to be focusing on in the next couple of years in order to turn Dallas around? There was no time for hundreds of meetings and a communitywide goals-setting conference. There was not enough patience to deal with 100 goals. So a new process took the place of the old one. It called for a series of focus group meetings to determine possible solutions to problems, a Goals Poll of citizens to determine preferences, and a decision by Goals for Dallas trustees on eleven goals.

Interestingly, at the very same time this new process made sense in Dallas, it did not make sense in Fort Worth, just twenty-eight miles away. There, two members of the city council joined together to form Goals for East Fort Worth. They knew from first-hand experience that the people they represented, and the organizations to which these people belonged, did not feel listened to at city hall. The process that Dallas had used starting in 1983, therefore, made perfect sense to Fort Worth in 1989.

In contrast, neither of these approaches made sense in Wichita Falls in 1979. After the tornado, more was at stake than mere opportunities for citizen participation in rebuilding; it was critical to the spirit of the community that as many citizens as possible actually get involved. Therefore, the goals-setting process included hundreds of persons on committees that defined the issues and choices facing the community, and almost 10,000 people made the choices through a special newspaper tabloid and ballot. The tabloid not only laid out the choices, it also included background information and pros and cons on each choice. At different times, and for different places, different visioning and goals-setting processes are required for a successful effort.

Effective Programs Have Four Phases

Every effective visioning and goals-setting program has four parts or phases: visioning, goals-setting, development of action plans, and follow-up. These are like the legs on a chair; take one away, and what remains is far less stable. When the Goals for Corpus Christi program was first organized in 1974, developing action plans and following them was not seen as the role of the Goals program. It was felt that a neutral effort was needed to determine the goals, though all the good people at city hall, the chamber of commerce, the school district, and so forth would know what to do with them once they were determined. Two years later, when concern developed about what actually was getting accomplished, a retreat was held to evaluate progress. If goals are to be achieved, a concerted and coordinated effort to follow through on them is needed immediately after they are set. Communities, however, sometimes act as many people do. They assume that once they know what they want, everything somehow will fall into place.

Principles for Visioning

In 1993, I served as consultant to a planning process that was seeking the best approach to a goals-setting program for San Diego County. At one meeting, when I asked what the best approach was for incorporating vision into the process, one woman angrily threw her pencil down and yelled, "I've been involved in so many visioning processes over the past twenty years I'm starting to hallucinate! Let's get something done!"

Keep Visioning in Perspective

In *Built to Last: Successful Habits of Visionary Companies,* James Collins and Jerry Porras (1994) define visionary companies as those that "prosper over long periods of time, through multiple product life cycles and multiple generations of active leaders." Their opinion is that these companies did not rise to greatness because they wrote one of the "vision, values, purpose, mission, or aspiration statements that have become popular in management today. . . . Creating a statement can be a helpful *step* in building a visionary company, but it is only one of thousands of steps in a never-ending process of expressing the fundamental characteristics we identified across visionary companies" (p. 201).

My opinion is that the same is true for communities. It is a myth that communities become visionary by having vision statements. Communities become visionary through a never-ending process of reinventing themselves—including everyone in the process, continually redefining goals, and working together to achieve results. Vision statements can be helpful as a starting point. However, an inordinate amount of time should not be devoted to the visioning process, especially nowadays when the focus is on results.

When 112 people in various San Diego planning meetings were asked about their preferred approach to incorporating vision into their program, only 38 percent opted for a lengthy visioning process that already had been proposed for the community. The rest favored other approaches such as using existing vision statements as the starting place (for example, from the chambers of commerce, the City of San Diego, or other organizations).

One approach I have found productive is to ask each individual to write down a vision for the community at the start of the goals-setting session, and I encourage some discussion of these views. Then, during the goals-setting process, I ask that each person use his or her vision statement as a guide for suggesting goals. At the end of the meeting, after a consensus on goals is reached, I ask each person for a revised vision statement. In most cases, participants report that the goals-setting process broadened their view—their vision—of what was needed in the community. They didn't want to spend a lot of time talking about vision statements, though they appreciated seeing how their vision had broadened as a result of goals-setting. Individual vision statements can be edited into one statement with a consensus of approval, which can be helpful especially in making the whole process look complete on paper. However, having a vision statement is not as important as following a well-thought-out process to become a visionary community.

A Vision Statement Is Not Essential

In fact, the word *visioning* itself is not needed in a visioning and goals-setting process where the objective is to create a visionary community. Goals for Dallas, started in 1965, is the nation's longest-running community goals program, and truly helped Dallas become a visionary community. However, the program never produced a vision statement. It did produce goals, many of which were achieved. The same is true for many other communities.

Erik Jonsson, cofounder of Texas Instruments and four-term mayor of Dallas, started the Goals for Dallas program after the Kennedy assassination. He said it was the best way he knew for getting people talking again after this tragic event, and the best way he knew of to build a city of excellence. He challenged every citizen to care deeply about Dallas and become involved in its affairs because, after all, it was the collective character of everyone that would determine the future of the community. His vision of Dallas as a city of excellence and as a caring community galvanized thousands into action. His own action in creating Goals for Dallas instilled this vision in others. He did not begin the Goals for Dallas program by calling for a visioning process or a vision statement. Nor did President Kennedy say, "I believe this country should have a vision of landing a man on the moon." He said, "I believe this country should commit itself to the goal of landing a man on the moon and returning him safely back to the earth by the end of this decade." Perhaps this is the best example of how a powerful goal can lead to a visionary community.

Principles of Goals-Setting

Often, there is a great effort to distinguish between goals, aims, strategies, objectives, tactics, and so forth. It's one reason many goals-setting efforts bog down. One of the keys to successful goals-setting and results, especially when many people are involved, is to keep the process simple. I do this simply by speaking in terms of things that need to be established, and in what order. The most important things are the goals themselves. Next are the basic steps that need to be taken to achieve the goals. How is a basic step accomplished? It is accomplished by taking a series of first steps. Goals, basic steps, and first steps. Dividing all the "things to do" into these categories is at the heart of the goals-setting and achievement process. Knowing how to differentiate between goals and action steps, and knowing how to set priorities, means adhering to four fundamental principles of goals-setting.

Goals Are the Ends; Plans Are the Means

This is one of the most important of all visioning and goals-setting principles. Following it is the best way to separate goals from action steps, and one of the best ways to avoid bogging down. It also goes against what is found in much of the writing about goals-setting; for example, that goals should begin with an action verb or the word *to*.

Suppose I ask someone at a meeting to suggest a goal. The person responds: "To build Town Lake." What happens? Someone else is sure to say something like: "I'm getting tired of building all these things and not providing the funds to maintain them." So, as a good facilitator, I go to the butcher block paper, make an insertion, and the goal becomes: "To build and maintain Town Lake."

A half hour later, after much discussion, I might end up with a goal such as the following: "To build Town Lake, including a source of funds for maintenance, financed partially by user fees, using local contractors. . . ."

The problem is that "To build" is part of the process of achieving the goal. Once the door is open, everything else that has to do with the plan for building Town Lake enters in. And it's not so much that it enters the discussion. What matters is that everything must be worded in such a way as to engender a consensus of support. The actual goal here is simply "Town Lake."

Too Many Goals Is as Bad as No Goals

In 1977, the Goals for Dallas program published 205 goals. Each was assigned a priority: high, higher, or highest. No one wanted to assign a goal that was set by citizens a low priority! Many goals were achieved. However, many participants felt that more could have been accomplished if the effort was more focused, as happened in 1984 when only 100 goals were developed. There were about ten goals in each of ten major subject areas such as transportation and housing. It was felt that since different people and organizations were working in each area, this was a reasonable number of goals to have. Still, many people believed the program lacked focus.

In the last cycle of Goals for Dallas, started in 1989, just eleven goals were adopted. Finally, after twenty-four years, the Goals for Dallas program provided a clear focus for getting things done. Other communities also have learned this lesson. Goals for East Fort Worth resulted in six top goals. Goals for Graham, Texas, resulted in twenty-seven goals, including an overall top ten list and a top five list with the City of Graham as implementor. Goals for Jacksonville, Texas, culminated in fifteen goals. The Goals for Memphis program is taking on only several goals at a time, and then adopting others as these are achieved. Making choices is difficult, although nowadays more and more communities are making these difficult choices through formal goals-setting programs.

Only Some Ideas Can Become Goals

Ideas should meet strict criteria to be given consideration as goals or priorities. Sooner or later, the question becomes: which ideas become goals, and which goals become priorities? In examining ideas to decide if they should become goals, and in deciding what priority to give goals once they have been chosen, see if they meet most of these criteria:

- *A single outcome.* Include only one idea in a goal statement. Usually, when more than one idea is included in a goal statement, it is a sure sign that the lesson of making choices has not yet been learned.
- *Communitywide.* It affects a great number of citizens, or calls for a communitywide effort to assist citizens with special needs.
- *Achievable with local action.* It is important to count on local action for achieving goals. Nothing can be done locally, for example, about mortgage rates or inflation.
- *Precise.* A goal should be stated in broad enough language so that a consensus to adopt it can be reached, yet worded precisely enough so that it is meaningful. For example, the goal of an improved transportation system is too general. A goal for a stop sign at a particular intersection is too specific. The goal of a bypass loop around a community meets the preciseness criterion.
- *Concise.* The KISS ("keep it simple, stupid") principle applies here so that everyone will understand the goal. A committee, or the person who suggested it, may not always be around to explain the goal.
- *Commitment.* Behind each goal there should be a commitment of the time, money, and enthusiasm required to achieve it. If individuals suggesting a goal cannot visualize this commitment, and therefore achievement of the goal, it should not be adopted.
- *Important.* Of all the goals on a list, achievement of which goals would do most to further the achievement of other goals? These should be given consideration as priorities.
- *Balance.* In most communities, it would not be desired that all goals be in one area of community concern (such as crime and drugs), or that all goals dealing with one area of concern deal with the same subject (such as all goals dealing with crime and drugs aimed at strengthening the police department).

The level of priority for a goal in any community will depend on the extent that it has dealt with the issue in the past. In Dallas, for example, a goal in the 1960s was to establish a regional transit authority. Once that was achieved, a goal in the 1970s and 1980s was accelerated implementation of the transit authority's plan.

Velleities Are Not Goals

A velleity is a wish unaccompanied by an effort to attain it. A goal that is set without establishing the means to attain it isn't a goal, it's a velleity. The criterion of commitment in goals-setting is so important that it needs to be underscored as a separate principle. Often after a goals-setting process is completed, people voice great hope: "I've never before seen such a great diversity of people come together in our community." "I can't believe we've reached agreement on a common set of goals from the long list we started with. It's amazing." "The process was so exciting, I don't see how we can fail." I've heard comments like these one year, only to hear the people who uttered them complain the next year that nothing much has happened. Many of them had never been part of a deliberate communitywide planning process before and they enjoyed the process, thought it good that the number of goals was limited, and agreed with those goals that made the list. But they may never have had a burning desire to see to it that any of the goals were achieved. And achievement requires burning desire, by communities as well as individuals. Former Dallas Cowboys quarterback Don Meredith once said that the best football players have a lot of "want to." From the beginning of any visioning and goals-setting program, participants should constantly be reminded that the purpose of the program is to arrive at goals, not velleities.

Principles for Developing Plans

To reach goals, plans must be made. Good plans can help save time in achieving goals, help coordinate achievement activities, and provide performance standards so that we know if we are making progress. Plans help communicate our intentions to ourselves and others more thoroughly than can the list of goals itself; goals with plans attached are taken more seriously. The next four principles help to develop effective plans.

Make No Big Plans

In the 1960s, Goals for Dallas produced several hundred pages of proposals for plans to achieve goals. After community review, a final book of plans, also several hundred pages long, was published. The same process was followed in many other communities. Nowadays, with information in abundance and perspiration often in short supply, big plans often are out of date before they are published.

Today, when I present alternative approaches for developing plans to groups designing visioning and goals-setting processes, big, lengthy, detailed plans are rarely chosen as the path to follow. Plan outlines are popular. Almost in spreadsheet format, basic steps for achieving a goal are identified, first steps to take are mapped out, assignments of responsibilities and leadership are listed, completion dates for each step are anticipated, and work in progress is noted. They often are kept on a computer so that changes can be made quickly. The process is fast, simple, and gets the achievement process under way fast. Plans provide the starting place for getting something done, and continually change until a goal is achieved.

A recent goal of one community was "Jobs and college scholarships for high school graduates with good grades and attendance records." One of the basic steps identified for achieving this goal was to establish an endowment fund to fill the scholarship gap. At the time this was a popular objective in several large cities, so a plan was quickly developed based on the experience of these other communities, and the legwork toward achievement began. As the achievement process began, it eventually became apparent that an endowment fund wasn't the greatest necessity to achieve the goal, but rather a better system of matching students with existing scholarships. The plan was quickly changed, and a computer matching system was introduced into the high schools. If a thorough and detailed plan for a scholarship endowment fund had been developed before the achievement process began, enthusiasm and momentum probably would have waned before results were accomplished.

Achieving Goals Is Not Part of Visioning and Goals-Setting

It is tempting for committees of a visioning and goals-setting program to take on projects themselves, to actually list themselves as responsible for goal achievement. It's not a good idea, because it's an inefficient use of the program. Organizations probably already exist that can assume responsibility for achieving goals. The unique role of a visioning and goals-setting program is to serve as catalyst for getting things done. With follow-up committees to the goals-setting process, it can serve a unique function and not duplicate what other organizations should be doing.

In chemistry, a catalyst is something that causes a reaction without being consumed itself. That is very close to the proper role of a visioning and goals-setting program: it should spur the achievement of goals without having to do the work itself. This also helps preserve neutrality, that important principle underlying almost all other principles. Ways of serving as a catalyst include coordination of plan development (especially when many parties are involved), presentation of goals and plans to implementing organizations for action, maintaining the visibility of goals within the community, and establishing a tracking procedure for keeping track of progress.

Enlist Existing Organizations to Achieve Goals

As task forces and committees gather to develop plans for achieving goals, an interesting phenomenon sometimes occurs. Suddenly, new organizations are needed to get things done! Often, the purpose of these new organizations is to "coordinate." It has always been interesting to me that, even in large cities with hundreds of existing organizations, a new one is needed to ensure the achievement of a particular goal. Although this happens less often now than in the preceding three decades when funding for new organizations was more plentiful, it still happens too often. In determining responsibilities for taking the action steps needed to achieve goals, the first thought that should come to the minds of task force members is: What organization is already doing something in this area, and does it make sense to enlist its support for the achievement of this goal? Courageous task force members might ask: In the process of achieving this goal, can two organizations with activities in this area be combined into one to save community resources?

"Ongoing" Is Not a Date; Neither Is "ASAP"

In *Steps to Goals,* published by Citizens' Goals for the Colorado Springs Community in 1978, 54 percent of all major goal achievement steps had anticipated completion dates of *ongoing, continuing, as soon as possible,* and *immediately.* Completion dates for many other steps were *to be determined, six months,* and so forth. I still see these terms listed in many plans today. But these are not dates, and they usually indicate that plans are not clear, individuals writing the plans do not want to be held accountable, or that the would-be planners simply do not understand what developing a plan means.

Suppose that a step for achieving a goal is *Support of local governments for X.* A planner might honestly assign *ongoing* as a completion date, feeling that it is a continual job to develop support among local governments for X. But it would be better to change the plan step to, say, *Resolutions passed by all local governments supporting X.* And then put a real date on it.

Or perhaps a plan step calls for *Annual inspections of X.* If it happens every year, it seems natural to call it *ongoing.* But remember: the reason annual inspections are listed as a step toward a goal is that they aren't being done now. Once the inspection program has been established, the plan step is complete even if annual inspections continue forever. As visioning and goals-setting people, you'll no longer be concerned about it as of the date the program is established. So that's the completion date you write down for that plan step.

Anticipated completion dates can and should be assigned to each step in an action plan. Otherwise, how can anyone know when something should be finished? How is progress measured?

Principles for Getting Results

The principle that achieving goals is not the responsibility of a visioning and goals-setting program, described above, also applies as a principle for getting results. Two others apply here as well.

Expect Results Immediately, and Expect the Unexpected

Some people think community visioning and goals-setting programs cannot offer a quick fix, that lasting results take a long time to achieve. Some get tired of hearing that there are no quick fixes. I have good news for them: in my experience, some results can be expected immediately from a goals program. I even believe that the possibility should be announced publicly at the beginning of any such process.

My earliest observation of the beginning of a goals program, in Corpus Christi in 1974, was that results from such a program start flowing as soon as people start getting together and talking about what needed to be done. At the first meeting of the Public Safety Committee, someone mentioned that there was no matron at the city jail to search female prisoners. A matron was hired shortly thereafter. In Jacksonville, Texas, a nonprofit Education Foundation to coordinate community education projects was formed even before this community-determined goal could be announced. In Goals for Memphis, the board of Memphis Light, Gas, & Water Division acted on two recommendations from the Goals for Memphis Housing Committee before the ink on the plans was dry. The policy changes added up to an estimated $1,500 cut in utility-related costs that low-income home buyers needed to pay when buying a home.

Also, expect the unexpected. One of the questions I am often asked by community groups considering a visioning and goals-setting program is this: "We don't lack for ideas or goals. We've got a lot of them. We've had them for years, and nothing has happened. Why should we believe that anything will happen now just because we have a visioning and goals-setting program?" I explain that a deliberate and well-thought-out community goals program can lead to quick action over ideas that may indeed have been talked about for many years. Often, a formal goals program is the first time that priorities in a community become established, and sometimes that's all it takes to create action. When the Rotary Club in Graham, Texas, contributed $20,000 to establish a crisis center in the community, the *Graham Leader* reported: "Though such a center has been a concern of local ministers and others directly involved with crisis situations for a long time, the idea of a 24-hour crisis program first got widespread recognition when it was identified as one of the Health and Human Service goals in Graham's Goals for the 80s Program" (Monk, 1982).

Record and Celebrate Incremental Gains

Many community goals of the 1960s through the 1980s were matters of bricks and mortar for airports, libraries, road systems, city halls, and the like. You knew when these goals were met. You could see the results and they were big. They were glamorous projects with which to be associated. Many goals nowadays are less glitzy but no less important: managing growth, reducing pollution, ending domestic violence. Unfortunately, achieving some goals today isn't as eventful as the opening of an airport, mainly because they tend to happen in increments, which is much less exciting. As a result, the gains from visioning and goals-setting programs often are not recognized, and support for them wanes. This can be especially true in the business community, where many people want to see, touch, and taste a goal before they will believe it has been achieved; they may be pleased with a 10 percent gain in profits, but not with 10 percent progress toward a community goal. This is a very difficult obstacle for visioning and goals programs in the 1990s to overcome. The only way to do it, I believe, is to continually track incremental gains toward many goals and report them together. Sometimes people then realize that quite a lot is getting accomplished.

The Most Important Principle

My first fifteen principles are helpful for getting started, visioning, goals-setting, developing plans, and getting results. The sixteenth, if taken to heart, should help with them all.

Achievement Comes Before Work Only in the Dictionary

Everybody has to get into the trenches and get the work done if a visioning and goals-setting process is to be successful. Having an interest in a goal and volunteering to serve on a task force or achievement committee is not good enough. I learned this first-hand early in my career, working with a task force with four members. Their names were Anybody, Everybody, Somebody, and Nobody. Anybody could have gotten the work done. Everybody thought Somebody would do it. So Nobody did it.

At a Goals for Dallas conference in 1983, various community leaders were asked to share their perspective on what it takes to actually achieve particular community goals. Philip Montgomery, volunteer coordinator for the development of a plan for the Dallas Arts District, prefaced his comments with these words: "I am pleased that our former mayor, Mr. Jonsson, is here, because more than anyone he taught us to dream. More than teaching us to dream, he taught us to work. And more than teaching us to work, he taught us to work with patience and good sense, and with courage. In many ways the Arts District is a legacy from Erik Jonsson."

A visioning and goals-setting program with leadership such as Erik Jonsson's can teach a community how to dream and how to work together toward common goals. A continual process of dreaming and working together is how a community becomes visionary—one that prospers over long periods of time, through multiple identities and multiple generations of active leaders. In setting out the challenge and promise of the Goals for Dallas program, Mayor Jonsson told the citizens of Dallas: "We can do it. All we have to do is care enough."

Every community can become a visionary community—if we all care enough.

Chapter Fourteen

The Five Principles of Effective Practice in a Participatory Democracy

V. Gail Easley

Planning is a second career for me. Once upon a time I went to college with the idea that I would become a teacher of science. For several reasons I did not stay in college; my first career was as a secretary–administrative assistant, work I did for ten years in the College of Agriculture at the University of Florida (UF). When I returned to college, I studied public administration. At the same time I served on the first Citizens' Advisory Committee for Community Development (CACCD) in Gainesville, Florida. At UF I worked in the Poultry Science Department, where one of the faculty spent an increasing amount of time testifying at hearings where the subject was the incompatibility of poultry farms and nearby subdivisions. In public administration I studied a range of subject matter, including planning. On the CACCD I met real planners, who insisted on the need for data collection, analysis, and formulation of plans followed by action to improve housing and infrastructure in the neighborhood. Though I did not realize it until later, these were all working on me and shaping my ideas about how things ought to be.

After obtaining a master's degree in planning from the University of Tennessee, I began work at the Metropolitan Planning Commission (MPC) in Knoxville. Planning was exactly what I expected: data collection, special studies, analysis, formulation of plans. I did not stay long enough to see the action that followed, though it did. In graduate school and at MPC (which we all thought of as postgraduate study), I learned early on about the importance of citizen participation. There were not a lot of surprises for me in my first two years as a planner. As a beginning planner, I was involved in citizen meetings of all types, including one where I was threatened with bodily harm. But I was not very close to the decision making, which was frustrating. At any rate, I began to understand the importance of meaningful citizen participation, early and often, and the need for a high degree of credibility for the planner.

It's hard to say whether the principles discussed in this chapter came from being a planner, or whether I became a planner because it is a field where I can put these principles to work. Either way, my ideas did evolve during the next seven years at the City of Largo in Florida, where my interest in ethics in planning solidified.

Most of the evolution came about from a project I carried out to create a unified land development code using innovative performance zoning concepts. Because the concept was so new, it required intense citizen education and participation. This caused me to focus on the issues of participation and to develop some of the principles that served me well then and have continued to do so since.

This interest continues today. Much of my recent work has been in visioning, and my research interest for a doctoral degree is on visioning as a form of citizen participation. It has always been important to me to be credible to those I work with and for, and I think all planners should place value in their credibility with the public. Some of the important principles that contribute to credibility are not particularly hard to follow. But they will make or break your career.

Participatory Democracy

My most basic planning value is simple: I believe in the right and the responsibility of citizens to be informed about and involved in planning for the communities they live in. Many of the practices I feel are important to effective planning derive from the need to ensure the opportunity for citizens to exercise this right.

Over the years I have observed that many practicing planners merely endure citizen participation; it is not central to their programs, though they may grudgingly acknowledge that there must be committees and meetings and hearings. The implication is that we, the knowledgeable, the experts, the professionals, could do a much better job if we did not have to devote so much time and effort to providing meaningful participation. Yet the participation of citizens in government processes is as old as this nation. Although the mandate for affected citizens to participate in planning decisions is fairly recent in our history, the idea is time-honored and, I believe, it is just plain right. I am a planner today because I once served on a citizen's advisory committee, found the issues intriguing and important, and chose graduate school in planning as a result. As a citizen participant, I simply wanted to get things done and was often frustrated by the jargon, the lack of action, and the need to follow a process. Though I am on "the other side" now, I still experience those same frustrations. It has colored my outlook as a planner.

I believe we are beginning to recognize that the future of our cities and countryside rests in the actions of ordinary citizens, not in the creation of ever-better, technically correct plans. In a recent event in Citrus County, Florida, called Vision Fest, an address by Carl Moore highlighted this trend. He noted that in this country we are finally realizing that we cannot turn our problems and our futures over to the experts. We must not only take responsibility, he said, but must invest personal effort into problem solving and shaping the future. Another Vision Fest speaker quoted Margaret Mead: "Never doubt that a small group of thoughtful, committed citizens can change the world. Indeed it is the only thing that ever has."

Principles and Practices

Within the framework of participatory democracy in planning, I have shaped my practice. I see my role as helper, facilitator, sometimes leader, and as someone who has experience and knowledge to share. A planning problem in a community requires a team effort. I see myself, the planner, as part of that team. To carry out these roles, I follow five principles and practices.

Aim Before You Shoot

It seems obvious that you should be knowledgeable about your subject. But what is your subject? Certainly many of the basics come from formal training—university or college training in planning and often in various planning specialties. Given how interwoven planning is with daily city life, however, you should realize that two years of study are but a survey of the field. When I earned a master's degree at the Graduate School of Planning at the University of Tennessee, we were drilled on the planning process. We had to learn general problem-solving skills, because the variety of problems encountered during a planning career would be so great that learning to solve each one in advance was impossible. That was one of the most useful messages I got from graduate school, and it has served me well. That, and an embarrassment during my first planning project in my first planning job.

In conducting a small area planning study, I researched, surveyed, analyzed, and organized. There were maps and tables and documents to depict all that I had learned. During the first citizen's meeting in the area, a question was raised about a major industrial project planned for the area. Although it was probably the biggest thing going on, amazingly enough I did not know about it (but I could quote population projections and environmental inventories at length). The next day I was quoted in the newspaper as saying, "I only know what I've been told." Rest assured that never since have I waited to be told; I aggressively learn about an area before I try to become a participant in its planning. By learning aggressively, I mean finding out more than what usually appears in report data—population, inventories of features, numbers of things, trends calculated by analyzing the data, and so on. Read the newspaper. Talk to elected and appointed officials outside the planning department. Convene a meeting of citizens and ask them what is going on, what is important to them. Usually we call this issue identification, and it is incredibly important.

It is at least as important to know the rumors, the politics, and the personalities of an area as it is to know the facts about land use, road systems, and population growth. One is not worth much without the other. The planner's real job is to know about planning that has been tried elsewhere and why those plans worked or didn't work. Applying such knowledge locally is a matter of learning not only about places and things in the area, but also the aspirations of its people. The ability of a planner to effectively serve as helper, facilitator, or planning expert is tied to knowing the facts, the aspirations, the politics, and the personalities. Otherwise, when you take aim at a problem, not only will you miss, you are likely to shoot yourself in the foot.

Stake Your Claim

Part of the effectiveness of a planner is knowing what you know and what you do not know. I have said that it's important to acquire broad knowledge about the area in which you practice, but I acknowledge that you cannot know all there is to know. There are two reasons. First, while you may not consider yourself a specialist, you probably are not a generalist either. Your experience and training have led to a deeper interest in, and more knowledge about, some aspects of planning than others. While you are focusing on these more personally interesting aspects, you are not able to stay abreast in all the other areas. This is okay; you work harder at what interests you, so you will be more knowledgeable and more effective as a result.

Second, when beginning to study a community, it takes a long time to really know what is important. It takes a long time to gain a historical perspective as well as identify aspirations for the future. It takes a long time to sift the facts, analyze them, and develop a working knowledge of the area. In the meantime, how can you effectively perform as a planner?

Decide where your strengths lie, what your areas of expertise are, and then seek the assistance you need to fill in the gaps. This does not mean you need additional planning staff, or experts in a variety of subjects, although these may be important parts of the solution. The community will be full of ordinary citizens with expertise or experience to supplement and complement your own. Make the best of what you know, admit what you do not, and build a team to address the situation. The participation of citizens can be the difference between planning success and failure.

Small towns and rural areas often have too little money for planning. Creating a team of citizens and planners may be the only way to get the job done. I have created work programs in which the citizen committee took responsibility for tasks or groups of tasks— collecting data from agency sources and printed documents, for example, or surveying land use. Sit down with the citizens at the very beginning, explain what is needed, ask for volunteers, make assignments, and function as a team. It works.

An important part of staking a claim to your own area of expertise is the ability to admit that you do not know all the answers, that
there are issues about which you are not fully informed. I have
never gotten in trouble for saying clearly, "I don't know the answer
to that question, but I will make a point of finding out." Of course,
you must follow through. Citizens (and bosses) have long memo-
ries. You will not fail for not knowing, but you will lose your credibility if you fail to follow up on your commitments.

Effective planning requires credibility, and credibility comes in
part from following through. It also comes from ethical behavior.
By ethical behavior, I mean not only what is called for by the American Planning Association/American Institute of Certified Planners (APA/AICP) Code of Ethics, but what is demanded by your
personal code of ethics. I see professional planners as members of
teams, and team members must be credible and reliable.

Tell the Truth

When I worked in the City of Largo, the community development
department encompassed long-range planning, development control, and building. My staff and I interacted with citizens on everything: construction, code enforcement, complaints, planning,
housing, and more. My consistent message to citizens across the
counter, in public meetings, and to commissioners was: "You don't
have to like what I say, but you can count on it being true." The developers came to understand that I was not playing games, that I
would tell them the truth as clearly as possible about requirements.
My staff came to understand that I would back them up completely
under the same conditions: fully explaining requirements, helping citizens accomplish what they wanted within the law, and giving accurate and complete information. The planner's relationship
with the public demands the credibility that only comes with full,
complete, and accurate information.

I also believe it important to acknowledge that the most accurate answer may not be what the other person wants to hear, especially if it is "no." There are many ways to approach such situations.
Part of telling the truth is to recognize that the person across the
counter may be asking the wrong question, may need guidance in
identifying the exact problem. The planner's job is to help articulate the problem and then impart full, complete, and accurate

information. Having done all that, the answer may still be "no." After spending some time practicing this approach, I began to spend less time in the mayor's office explaining why a developer could not do project X. Both the mayor and the developers began to rely on us planners for clear, accurate information. In other words, they knew we were telling the truth.

Once the citizens and elected officials feel they can trust your word, however unpopular it may be, you can work together to craft plans and programs which represent the community's aspirations. I especially noted this when working with small towns and rural communities to implement comprehensive planning under the Florida growth management laws. The rules were unpopular and, in the opinion of many communities, a costly burden. The only way to be an effective planner in those circumstances was to be a member of the team, sharing information and seeking mutually acceptable solutions.

If you've read the APA/AICP Code of Ethics, and surely you have, you know that the planner has many responsibilities—to serve the public interest, to consider long-term consequences of current decisions, to consider the interrelatedness of issues, to competently perform work for clients, and to accept responsibility to the profession, among many others. But sometimes, planners must negotiate a compromise to solve a planning problem. How can ethics be balanced with compromise? This leads to another principle.

Know When to Hold 'Em and When to Fold 'Em

Too often planners are seen only as naysayers and predictors of crisis. In our zeal to point out the long-term effects of a particularly boneheaded decision, we engage in battle with the elected body, with boards and committees, with other government departments. First, you must realize that no matter how great your training, how prestigious your degree, how knowledgeable you are about the disastrous potential of the decision before you, there is another side to the story. Just as you must learn to acknowledge that you cannot answer every question, you must accept that you are not the keeper of all knowledge about what is right and good and moral and just. You are a professional planner, with skills and knowledge and training and experience. But there is always another point of view besides yours, and it may also be right and good and moral and just.

If you are to be effective, you must know when to seek compromise. Conversely, you must know when to take a position and stand your ground. As a planning director, I regularly faced a planning staff full of frustration because of the bad or wrong or political decisions made by the elected body. These planners were sure that their analyses clearly pointed to a single proper decision. And from their point of view, they were right. However, my director's role was to identify other valid points of view and seek ways to accommodate them. This didn't mean failing to present and press for the "proper decision," just trying to understand other viewpoints and the goals of the decision makers. If we professional planners couldn't have our way, I had the duty to present ways of conditioning the final decision to mitigate the problems it might cause.

On the other hand, when the time comes—and it will—you must take a stand and remain unwavering. In discussions with my staff, I characterized these times as the ones I would stake my job on. If faced with the choice of giving in or losing my job, I would lose the job. Seldom was this necessary, but when it was, remarkable things usually happened. Because I had stuck with the principles described above, I had credibility with the elected officials. If I took a stand and refused to budge, they knew I had good reason and they took my advice.

But be very careful. So few things in life, including planning decisions, are so one-sided that all actions but one are unthinkable. If you believe this and behave accordingly, you will be effective.

Walk the Talk

In planning as in any other aspect of life, it is easy to talk about how to behave. But to be effective, only your actions count. We know you can talk the talk, but can you walk the talk? Do you actually behave in the ways you say are important and appropriate? To be an effective planner, you must walk the talk. I believe this is done by following some simple guidelines. Listen before you act or speak. Except when you need to shout "Fire!" in a burning building, listening first is always important, but rarely more so than in engaging citizens in planning. As I pointed out earlier, you must learn about an area before you undertake to plan for it. One of the ways to learn is to listen. There is little to be gained by demonstrating how much you know. Instead, demonstrate your willingness to listen and hear the concerns of the citizens with whom and for whom you are planning. The same goes for the other members of your team, your boss, and the elected body. Trust me; they know things you need to know, and you can only learn by listening. There is always time to talk and act. Once you fail to listen, it will be very hard to recover the opportunity.

Another aspect of walking the talk relates to timeliness. Much of what you do involves deadlines: project deadlines, filing deadlines, agenda deadlines. You expect others to be prepared, submit on time, provide complete documentation, attend meetings on time, and so on. You must do these things too, and do them first. I hear too many planners lament that they should be better at planning ahead, usually as part of apologies for being late or ill-prepared. We're human. Things happen. Traffic congests. Mail gets lost. Cars stall. The copier jams. The computer crashes. That these things happen is no surprise. That they happen to you (and always at the last minute) seems to be the surprise. Well, as a friend of mine says, "Get over it." Actually, I think some people secretly pray for the jam or the crash so they can use it as an excuse to cover their lack of planning. Get over it. Act like a planner and be ready on time. It enhances your credibility and that enhances your effectiveness.

One thing we planners learn, and I hope we believe, is that everything is attached to everything else. The five principles and practices I have discussed here are not discrete. They all revolve around my goal of being effective by working through a highly participatory planning process. That is because I believe in participatory democracy, the right and responsibility of citizens to influence decisions affecting the future of their communities. Even if I had a different central theme, these would be good principles for effective planning. They are not the only principles you need; they are not the only ones I use. But they are really important to me. I hope they are important to you.

Chapter Fifteen

Tooling Up for Effective Planning

Angela N. Harper

In the late 1950s and early 1960s, my family took our loaded-down station wagon on several vacations in the eastern United States. Before we'd start out, my mother did a lot of planning. She saved money from her check every week; she contacted chambers of commerce for information; she listed all the educational opportunities between Nashville and the destination city. The plans for each day included meals, sights, relatives to be visited, and lodging. Just as Mom was the "planner," Dad was the "implementer." He made sure we accomplished all her plans. My brother and I had other roles: we experienced the landscape and history, took naps, and asked "How much further is it?" a lot.

Frequent stops at service stations gave me an opportunity to begin my collection of road maps. When I was about nine, I started using the maps to find out where we were and to help Dad get us where we were going. As the years went by I became the navigator for our trips. Thus began my love of maps and travel. I can still remember how stimulating these trips were. Besides the impressive views of the cities and the countryside, the Burma Shave signs, billboards, and barn roofs caught my attention.

In the 1960s friends from church became candidates for the U.S. Congress and the state legislature. In Nashville, there were lots of opportunities to be involved in the election campaigns. After untold volunteer hours of campaigning for several eventual winners, I realized I had an interest in government service. I began college thinking that a political science major would give me a career in a foreign embassy. But each year I changed focus, going from federal to state to local government.

In search of an elective for my last semester, I discovered a new course in the geography department titled "city planning." I wish I had saved the course description. It sounded like something that would combine all of my interests, even my minors in sociology and public speaking. After graduation I was fortunate to become a planning assistant for the Metropolitan Nashville–Davidson County Planning Commission. During my year there I was exposed to all types of comprehensive planning projects and an occasional zoning case. From the beginning I was committed to getting a master's degree. The question was whether to study city planning or city management. Visits to various universities convinced me that city planning best fit my interests and skills, so off to the University of Virginia I went.

Why there? First, it had a recognized graduate degree program in planning. But more important, on one family vacation I had fallen in love with the campus. Since the school had an all-male undergraduate admission policy, my first opportunity to attend Mr. Jefferson's University was for graduate school.

Several years later, equipped with a master's degree in planning and some experience in the field, I began my professional planning career in Henrico County, Virginia. Twenty-four years later, I am still there. Why? Probably because of William F. La Vecchia. La Vecchia, as director of planning, hired me, and his knowledge, management style, and friendship have kept me in planning. I am but one of many planners and managers that he mentored. When he retired in 1992 as county manager after thirty-three years, he was recognized by the International City Manager's Association with the L. P. Cookingham Award for Career Development for being an outstanding mentor throughout his career.

Packing the Planner's Toolbox

I have found that one of the biggest challenges of being a planner is telling other people what a planner does. Some people think I have said "planter" or "plumber," and it's true that certain aspects of those professions come into play when you are a planner. "Facilitator of the planning process for community development" is not a job description that is so easily understood.

Every year I am asked to talk with elementary, high school, and college students about the career of planning and to suggest to them what education and experience they need to apply for a job as a planner. As I seldom can remember jokes, I use analogies to help convey my points. I suggest that packing a toolbox with skills and knowledge is critical to being effective as a planner. The tools necessary may vary depending on a particular planner's role.

Through education it is possible to learn the writing and public speaking skills necessary to communicate your ideas and those of others. The personal computer has made communication easier because it makes graphics available to highlight or demonstrate our written points. But packing these tools in the box isn't a one-time act; they must be continuously updated to stay effective.

Being organized is essential in preparing reports, scheduling, involving citizens, and gaining support for your plans. Many aids, such as pocket scheduling calendars and time management guides, are available to help you organize. As I tell my teenage daughter Allison, always do an outline before you do the paper.

Understand maps and scaled plans. You need not be a drafting technician or urban designer to be a planner, but it is crucial to know how to find the location of a proposed project and to perceive its scale. The ability to visualize a plan and convey that information to your listener is invaluable.

I have served on national awards committees for the American Planning Association (APA) and the American Institute of Certified Planners (AICP), and have been impressed by visioning projects that illustrate how a community will look if various scenarios are selected for implementation. These pretty pictures showing the proposed change of appearance of an aging downtown or an abandoned industrialized riverfront can excite the community and result in the public-private partnerships that can be the catalyst for action.

It takes information to prepare plans, so knowledge of ways to obtain information must also be in the toolbox. Early in your planning career, most of your working hours are devoted to gathering and analyzing data and then evaluating alternatives. The data must be accurate and complete, or the planning recommendations you make based on them will be flawed. As you progress as a planner to positions with more administrative responsibility, you may be responsible for presenting plans based on information that you did not accumulate yourself. This takes trust; fortunately I have been blessed with a staff that has earned my trust with thorough and accurate work. My staff, in turn, trusts me to make the best recommendations possible based on their work as I present it to others.

People skills are vital to being prepared. A planning education usually does not provide courses on listening, caring, persuading, supervising, counseling, negotiating, facilitating, leading, following, customer service, and team building. Such training is available from many employers, especially local governments, and also from junior colleges, chapters of the APA, and consultants. Any of these can provide courses and workshops with "how to" instructions, but you have to use them to be able to put them in the toolbox. Without strength in these skills, promotion to more responsible positions is very unlikely.

Special expertise in one or more aspects of planning should be added to the toolbox as soon as possible. The most popular areas are comprehensive planning, land use regulations, transportation, urban design, environmental quality, housing, historical preservation, and open space. Students have the opportunity when selecting projects and paper topics to choose real (rather than theoretical) planning problems; doing so can build a resume that will help get that first job. The larger the public planning department or consulting firm, the more likely that some planners work full time on projects within a specialized aspect of planning. The more areas of expertise in your toolbox, the more flexibility you have in employment opportunities.

The Code of Ethics of the AICP needs to be in the toolbox. The challenge to professional planners is to behave ethically so that the planning process will be fair to all involved. There are resources available from the AICP for training and for advice on the application of the Code to a wide variety of situations.

Principles of Effective Planning

The planner's toolbox contains not just tools but principles. Here are the ones I consider most vital.

Use the Entire Planning Process

Planning Made Easy (Toner, Gil, and Lucchesi, 1994), published by the APA, is a manual for planning commissioners, members of zoning boards of appeals, and elected officials. In it, planning is defined as "the process through which we reach well-considered decisions." When I was in graduate school I remember being surprised to learn that the planning process is almost identical to the scientific method of research I had already studied.

I emphasize using the entire process because I have noticed that failed planning processes usually skip or give too little attention to a needed process step. Most frequently the problem is using a disproportionate amount of time for data collection. More effort usually needs to be made to involve the right mix of people to generate and evaluate plan alternatives. If the people directly affected by a plan are involved in drawing it up, it is much more likely to be implemented.

Implementation tools need to be approved at the same time as the plan itself. Failure to complete this step has caused more problems in my community's comprehensive planning than failure of any other step. If land use plan classifications provide different land development opportunities, the zoning ordinance needs to be amended and in effect when the plan itself becomes official.

Provide Sufficient Qualified Staff to Administer the Plan

The quality of the planning staff must be high if decision makers and citizens are to accept the importance of planning. Administration is more effective too if staff members are empowered at all levels to make decisions and if they are extensively cross-trained so they can respond to peak demand. In addition to staff, today's planning department needs computer hardware and software to accommodate the numerous data storage and research needs.

The most difficult aspect of planning administration is being consistent yet flexible in the application of requirements and policies. Each interpretation may set a precedent. The authors of plans, codes, and policies cannot anticipate the creativity of the business community, the engineers, the home builders, and the developers. Creative genius and changing technology may mean that what was a chimney now handles a gas fireplace and what was a bay window now holds a hot tub. Who would have predicted Foosball parlors and tanning salons? What about cold-air balloons as attention-getting devices?

Involve the Community Throughout the Planning Process

For effective planning, citizens must realize that the community *is* their backyard and not embrace the "not in my backyard" theme that has become synonymous with opposition to development. Sometimes appointed and elected officials want to plan based on the mandate they believe they received at the polls or simply on their sense of what is best for the community. While officials have terms of office, the voters are the strength of the community and need to be invited to participate from the beginning and through-out the process. In Virginia, legislation requires a public hearing before the planning commission and the board of supervisors be-fore the board adopts any plan or ordinance. This is a minimum requirement. Citizens should have many more opportunities to participate in the making of plans; they then have "ownership" and the plans are more likely to be successful.

The four most important elements of a citizen participation program are a well-organized educational program that includes readable written materials, good speakers, and attractive graphics customized to the neighborhood or community; a marketing approach that cheerleads the selling of good planning; timely solic-itation of public involvement after the educational program; and an attitude among appointed and elected officials that citizen par-ticipation is meaningful and valuable.

Persuade Decision Makers to Stand Up for Good Planning

To persuade even one decision maker of the value of planning takes an educational process that emphasizes the benefits to the community of planning and the consequences of not planning. This may be accomplished through the citizen participation pro-gram, but decision makers will be more effective if they have lead-ership roles in the educational program. In my community, one elected official is a voting member of the planning commission. The appointment, usually rotating among the five supervisors, pro-vides the board a liaison with the planning commission and lets staff form an alliance with an elected official that can be critical in persuading the other supervisors and the community at large of the importance of planning.

Provide a Visioning Process for Your Community

Every decade there needs to be an opportunity for the community to participate in a visioning process. A cross section of citizens should work together to assess the community's "prouds" and "sor-ries," identifying which problems and projects should be tackled in which order. Recently, the Richmond Regional Planning District Commission sponsored a process titled "Focus Forward." The kick-off meeting was on a beautiful March Saturday morning. More than 500 people preregistered; by the end of the day, 651 had signed in. At 4:00 P.M. the assembly room was packed with more people than there had been at 8:30 A.M. Participating as just another citizen, I found the experience really exciting.

While the goal is to identify community priorities, the self-identification of citizens willing and able to help is a wonderful benefit. The key is to mobilize the volunteers to work on the priority items. The visioning process may also result in guidance for the comprehensive plan goals and objectives. If there is a community vision, the plan can become an implementation tool.

Emphasize Plan Implementation

I mentioned above that implementation is a step in the planning process. As a plan is adopted, the implementation tools must be made available, and their use must be encouraged at the right times and places.

Monitoring implementation is the only way to know if a plan is becoming effective. One technique we have used is a "State of the Land Use Plan" report. Its purpose is to evaluate whether zoning application approvals, subdivisions, and site plans have been made in compliance with the adopted plan. We found that the rate of compliance is usually very high during the first three years, and then falls. The election of new supervisors may alter commitment to plans, or rezonings may be granted that vary slightly from the plan and influence other rezonings as time passes.

I suggest that when a trend of land use decisions in conflict with the plan is recognized, the staff should alert the planning commission and present analysis and alternatives so that the credibility and effectiveness of the plan is not lost. It is better to change the plan rather than allow it to deteriorate into irrelevance.

Consult Other Jurisdictions

In Virginia, cities and counties are completely separate. Each has its own taxing authority and the authority to plan and regulate land uses. With each comprehensive planning update, we consult the six jurisdictions that border our county. We share information and request comments on plan proposals. In 1994, the General Assembly passed legislation requiring that surrounding jurisdictions be notified of rezoning applications that might affect them. We have all agreed to exchange zoning agendas.

For special planning projects such as ordinance amendments, fee increases, policy guidelines, and special topic reports, we always provide comparative information for jurisdictions in the Richmond region. If we need to go outside the Richmond area, we strive to find comparable suburban counties with over 200,000 population.

What I Have Learned in the Planning Trenches

In almost twenty-five years of planning experience, I have learned a lot.

I know I must market good planning to my staff, to appointed and elected officials, and to the community. I know I have to be the advocate for my staff to obtain the resources we need through the county budgeting process. I know that cheerleaders for good planning can be found among community organizations, developers, appointed and elected officials, and in the staff.

I have learned that making your boss look good is good for the organization, that the acceptance of your role as an advisor is the only way to achieve credibility, and that being thorough and timely are two virtues that lead to planning success.

I understand the need to always be alert for opportunities to educate officials, staff, and citizens; that implementing a plan incrementally is often the best way to save a recommendation; and that being active in professional organizations is worthwhile because of the educational and networking benefits it brings.

I have observed that a director of planning who acts as a team leader will maximize the staff's effectiveness and enhance morale, and that volunteering time to assist students of planning and their universities will reap benefits to the profession in the form of better-trained new planners who start out with real-world exposure.

I have come to believe that writing about planning successes is very important so that the information can be used by other communities; that you should try hard to implement a plan after it has been decided upon, even if you disagree with it; and that it is important to seek a balance of land uses to maintain a healthy tax base, provide sufficient services, and create a quality living environment.

My professional journey is not over. I have many more miles to travel, and as a lifelong learner I am looking forward to the future. Perhaps the road map I have laid open here will help you decide what you need in your toolbox to make your own journey more enjoyable.

Chapter Sixteen

It Seemed Like a Good Idea at the Time

Marjorie W. Macris

Women entering the field of planning today probably do not understand fully how things have changed since I started out in the 1950s. As my daughter, also a planner, says at times when we are discussing women's issues, "What's the big deal, Mom?" Now, women are prominent in all fields and at all levels of planning, and our profession and the communities we serve are much richer for it. I believe women bring a balanced, holistic view to planning and have management and consensus-building skills that may come partly from their experience as mothers. And, of course, we do represent more than half the population.

Four decades ago, women did not have the opportunities they have today. I originally wanted to be a newspaper reporter, and I received my undergraduate degree in journalism from the University of Illinois. When I was in my junior year, I inquired about job possibilities at various Chicago newspapers. My potential employers were quite direct: "We don't hire girls." This was before nondiscrimination laws and affirmative action programs.

I discovered the field of planning during a field trip to Chicago for an urban sociology class I was taking. We visited, among other places, the offices of the American Society of Planning Officials and met with the executive director, Dennis O'Harrow. I asked him about career opportunities, and he replied, "Yes, we need planners so desperately that cities are actually hiring women."

The head of the planning school was reluctant to have me sign up, even though my grades were excellent (fourth in my graduating class). However, I persisted. One statistics professor told me early in the year that I could not possibly have an analytic mind because I was a female. I got an A. In my real estate class, which consisted of 150 students, I was unanimously elected Queen of the Class. I was the only woman.

My first job for the Chicago planning department provided a wide range of experience in research, writing, public speaking, and working on the city's comprehensive plan. Mayor Daley took pride in the fact that the planning department was politically pure. Occasionally when he was accused of filling city hall with patronage employees, he would observe, "Just look at the planning department. They're so unpolitical, they practically don't even vote." The elevator operators, all precinct captains, recognized the planners when they entered the building by their tweed jackets instead of shiny navy blue suits, their absence of white-on-white shirts and pinkie rings, and possibly their vague facial expressions. "Tenth floor?" the operators would ask tolerantly.

Chicago had access to a great deal of federal money because of Mayor Daley's close ties to the Kennedy and Johnson administrations. This enabled the staff to develop extensive community improvement programs. However, it was all top-down planning. The Chicago political organization was not good at recognizing the importance of citizen involvement and dissent, as witnessed by the tragic events at the 1968 Democratic National Convention.

Mayor Daley was, surprisingly, good on women's issues. His mother had been a suffragist, and her son held her views in the highest respect. I married one of the planners on the staff, whom I met at the University of Illinois at Urbana. When I had our two children, I was able to arrange with the city to return to work soon afterwards. This was not a generally accepted thing to do in conservative Chicago during the early 1960s. There were no child care centers, and none of my friends returned to work after having children. However, thanks to a supportive husband, a wonderful baby-sitter, and my high energy level, things worked out. The reaction of the payroll clerk when I told her I was returning to work was typical: "I could understand it if you were an unwed mother, but you have no excuse."

We moved to California in 1968, right before the ill-fated convention. As I looked for planning jobs there, I found that many older planners who were very liberal on social and economic issues were not supportive of professional women. Typical comments were: "I can't send you on this business trip because the other planner's wife would get mad." "You can't represent us at this Model Cities meeting because the Latino community wouldn't understand." "It wouldn't be safe for you at attend this meeting in a black neighborhood at night." (I went anyway.)

I began working in the Marin County Planning Department in 1970. I moved up in the ranks by working hard and being better than my competition. In some ways, being a woman had advantages. Developers at the counter would sometimes be caught off-guard by having to deal with a competent professional woman. Some probably considered it a surprising oddity, like a dancing bear. They were probably less argumentative with me when I told them things they did not want to hear than they would have been with a male planner.

When the planning director position came open in 1978, I was nominated to fill the vacancy by then Supervisor, now Senator, Barbara Boxer. At the time, I was the only woman county planning director in the fifty-eight counties of California. The emergence of women elected officials like Barbara Boxer as respected leaders has helped immensely to pave the way for female staff members.

By the time I went to Berkeley as planning director in 1984, things had really changed. At a meeting held soon after I arrived, someone noted that the planning director, community development director, city attorney, assistant city manager, and mayor were women. Opportunities for women have opened up across the board—half the students in planning schools and about 40 percent of American Planning Association (APA) members are women. This is not to say there are no problems. Advancement to the highest management levels is still difficult.

Are women better planners than men? Probably not, although as I noted earlier they may have certain advantages in consensus-building. It is more likely that many of the best women planners became planners in the first place because other fields historically offered them fewer opportunities to achieve.

My experience in planning has spanned five decades and a wide variety of political settings—from the first Mayor Daley's Chicago, where citizen participation consisted of voting early and often, to Berkeley, where the conservative elected officials were liberal Democrats. I have been a consultant since 1989. It has been a gratifying career, and I have never regretted choosing to be a planner even during the difficult times, which have been many. To me, the most rewarding aspect has been helping to enable the people of a community to shape its future.

I hope my observations help other planners retain their perspective and possibly their sanity. There are seven of them, and they are personal, involving no research or regression analysis.

Most important, always remember two rules:

1. There are no universal right answers; every situation is different.
2. People often cannot or will not do what planners think they should do.

Bearing those in mind, here are the seven observations, each with accompanying suggestions for increasing your effectiveness as a planner.

Many Things That Seemed Like Good Ideas at the Time Probably Weren't

It is important for individual planners, as well as the profession as a whole, to examine and evaluate what they have done, acknowledging mistakes while pointing out victories. The nature of our work usually means we can't tell for a long time if a given program has succeeded, but the exercise is still worthwhile.

For example, one judgment I helped make that turned out to be incorrect involved the 1973 Marin Countywide Plan, which sought to increase new jobs and decrease new housing in the area to encourage more people to both live and work in the county. To accomplish this, the county and the cities reduced residential densities and increased the amount of land designated for commercial and office development.

When we revised the plan in the early 1980s we found that the numbers were on target; the number of jobs had increased and the number of housing units had decreased at about the level advocated in the plan. But most of the people holding the jobs lived north of Marin, where housing is less expensive, and most of the people living in the housing continued to commute to San Francisco. Traffic congestion, consequently, was much worse than what we had anticipated. The problem was that we had not taken other variables into account. Housing costs, multiple-worker households, and the desire of some people to choose their place of residence for reasons other than proximity to work—all these and other factors we didn't consider. In other words, we had ignored Rule Two above: people may very well not do what planners think they should. And still planners continue to propose the elusive goal of a job and housing balance. Housing advocates push programs to play catch-up after the shopping center has been built, but questioning where its employees will live should be done before the center is developed.

Other common planning mistakes have involved redevelopment programs that destroy interesting neighborhoods and leave vast tracts of land vacant for years. I think the APA should have, in addition to its achievement awards, an annual "It Seemed Like a Good Idea at the Time" award to help us acknowledge and learn from our mistakes.

If Engineers Have Their Way with Cities, They Will Mess Things Up

Most of the mistakes that the "new urbanists" complain about resulted from engineering standards, not the malevolence of planners. Obvious examples are the freeway that cuts off downtown Seattle from its waterfront, and streets in suburban communities so wide that you have to pack a lunch to cross them.

I believe that one of the main responsibilities of the planning director in any jurisdiction is to stand up to the public works director, almost always a male with more power and money at his disposal than the planning director. But public opinion is more likely to support the planning director. Sometimes the public takes things into its own hands. In San Francisco, for example, public opinion halted extension of the Embarcadero Freeway, which would have gotten cars from the Bay Bridge to the Golden Gate Bridge quickly but at the cost of separating the city from its waterfront; eventually even the existing portion of the freeway was demolished. Sometimes planners can work creatively with citizens' groups to stop bad projects, but this must not be done in an insubordinate way unless the project is so bad you are willing for it to be the "big one" over which you will be fired. Often, if you just make sure information gets to the right activists, they can take it from there.

If Architects Have Their Way with Cities, They Too Will Mess Things Up

Most architects think in end-state product terms. Unlike planners, they tend to have an aversion to considering the processes that determine how cities evolve. Process involves public opinion and politics, and is often long and boring. Architects prefer one-shot charrettes that produce pretty pictures but usually not links to the citizens and decision makers who determine what actually happens. Architects also tend to be good at drawing, which depicts an end state, and poor at writing, which requires following a process.

Architects like to build monuments to themselves, and they often exhibit a disdain for the context of their buildings. I call this the Howard Roark school of architecture, in honor of the hero of Ayn Rand's novel *The Fountainhead;* he destroyed one of his buildings because it did not turn out exactly as he wanted it. The Roark character was patterned after Frank Lloyd Wright, who overtly hated cities. Examples are his proposed mile-high building, which would have destroyed any city where it was built, and Broadacre City, his proposed utopia where everyone would live and raise food on one-acre lots—an early version of urban sprawl. Fortunately, neither of these schemes was realized; unfortunately, Wright's Marin County Civic Center was. It is a beautiful monument built to arch over hills (one of which is fake) out in the country. Its construction moved the center of government out of downtown San Rafael, seriously impairing the vitality of that city. People who wish to visit the Civic Center, which contains the main library, have no choice other than to make a single-purpose trip by automobile. Moreover, the roof leaks and the building's orientation to the sun requires the use of air conditioning even in the wintertime.

Ludwig Mies van der Rohe, the other great architect of our times, was the father of modernism, which led to the form of freestanding boxes in windswept plains, an unfortunate characteristic of some failed redevelopment projects, as mentioned above.

Now we have the new urbanists, who claim that their architecture will save the cities from the planners, ignoring the sorry results of the work of leading architects in the past. The new urbanists' cute houses with front porches out in the hinterlands (Seaside, Laguna West), sometimes designed to be friendly to transit if it ever arrives, have nothing to do with urbanism, which is the revitalization of our cities. Rather, what we have here are sentimental subdivisions.

We need architects, of course, but they need to operate within the rules that respect the character of a community and the goals of its citizens. Planners help to devise these rules, which determine how a community evolves over time, not all at once.

When architects say, "This city needs a vision," they are probably talking about bricks and mortar, and they want to be paid for putting them into place. Usually the vision involves selling architectural ideas to a presumably ignorant public with the help of the planner. Often, though, a community's vision for its future consists of goals that cannot be achieved through building developments— for example, preservation of population diversity, small-town character, and environmental resources.

If You Can't Do the Right Thing, Find Someone Who Can

When you are a public official or a consultant working for a public agency, you are constrained by the policies of your jurisdiction. Sometimes, there may be an issue about which, in your professional judgment, the wrong decision is about to be made, but you cannot confront it directly. It may be possible for you to work creatively with other entities that can raise the issue effectively with elected officials. Sometimes this involves a cooperative relationship with forces that are beginning to attain political effectiveness and can benefit from technical information and support.

An example was the emergence of the environmental movement in Marin County in the late 1960s and early 1970s. The various citizens' groups concerned about overdevelopment and environmental degradation were dedicated and committed, but lacked technical expertise and a clear focus. The county planning department was able to work with these groups in the preparation of the 1973 Marin Countywide Plan by providing information, assisting in organization, and giving access to the planning process. The resulting plan established the environmental ethic for county planning, and its principles have guided development in Marin in the ensuing years.

Reaching out to citizens' groups can be dangerous if you want to keep your job, and often it does not work. For example, soon after I became Marin County planning director I met with a group of citizens who supported the Countywide Plan. We discussed the problems associated with the proliferation of shopping centers being promoted by the cities as revenue sources in the wake of Proposition 13, the property tax-limiting measure passed by California voters in 1978. Some of the city managers learned of this meeting and complained to the county administrator that I should stop meddling in the cities' business. The administrator directed me to lay off if I wanted to keep my job. I did so, largely because I realized that my efforts and those of the citizen activists would be futile in the face of the cities' determination to do fiscal planning. Also, I did want to keep my job. Unfortunately, three regional shopping centers have been built since then. The existing downtowns have been badly decimated by the closing of traditional department stores and high vacancy rates. However, it is likely that fighting this trend would have been jousting with windmills.

It is important to be aware of the risks when you seek to influence decisions in your jurisdiction by indirect means. You also need to assess carefully your chances of effectiveness. Choose your "big one" carefully. You may be out of a job without having accomplished anything. However, remember that your values and professional judgment are important, and you must respect them if you are to respect yourself. As one of my favorite planning professors once said, "A good planning director's job is on the line once a year."

Politics Is as Much a Part of Planning as Curbs, Gutters, and Sidewalks

Elected officials are responsible for making decisions. Often they disagree with the planners. This is just part of the game. I am tired of hearing planners whine about how politicians do what they do, which is to act politically.

Politicians have their job; planners have theirs. The planner needs to be aware of political pitfalls, but not try to second-guess the politicians. Your job is to give your best professional advice while addressing the political issues you know exist. For example, you may be handling a proposal for an affordable housing development that you support but that has encountered opposition because of fears of adverse effects on property values. Your staff report could include findings from studies that show how attractively designed, below-market-rate projects elsewhere have not had adverse effects. You could also see if a housing advocacy group might elicit the support of residents near the project site who would speak at public hearings. These approaches are likely to be more effective in swaying the opinion of elected officials than arguments that the project is necessary to provide our numerical fair share of affordable housing and if we don't approve it we will probably be sued.

You are paid for giving your best professional advice, regardless of the political consequences. If you do not do so, you are not doing your job, and your employers will eventually figure this out. If you want to make political decisions, run for office. If you lose, expect to be fired from your planning job. If you are doing a general plan for a city where there is a change in the planning philosophy of the city council, expect to deal with The Project from Hell. If the Catholics are right, you may be entitled to time and a half off in Purgatory for the time you spend in the effort.

We Have Our Own Heroes and Heroines

Planners do make a difference, and we should not be defensive about our role. We also should not latch onto every fashionable buzzword that comes along. *Paradigm* usually means "a way of looking at life." *Sustainable* usually means that a developer has included a few environmental features to help sell a project. *User-friendly* documents are those that are easy to understand. We should not be afraid to say what we mean in simple language.

Also, we should remember that we are not acolytes for developers; our client is the public, whether we work for a public agency or a private client. If the free market worked perfectly by itself, we would not be needed.

Obviously, public agency planners must be helpful and supportive to all members of the public, including developers who are proposing something not allowed under the city's rules. We should strive to simplify rules, write and speak clearly, and make systems work as efficiently and quickly as possible. Most bureaucratic procedures are unnecessarily complicated, and we should strive to streamline them. Nevertheless, we must remember that we serve the public interests. Often this involves telling people things they do not wish to hear. This can be especially difficult for a consultant working for a private client who must be told that a proposal has to be changed to comply with local standards.

The most important role of the planner is to work with the public to identify a community's goals, then help to marshal resources—community organizations, developers, and elected officials—to accomplish them. Central to the planner's work is respect for the inherent character of a community. There is an analogy to the sculptor's work, described by one as discovering the true nature of the stone and bringing it out.

Our real heroes and heroines are the planners who want to make a difference in their communities and manage to produce remarkable results over the long term. There are many examples:

• The planners who are establishing reuse plans to revitalize communities where military bases have closed.
• The community development director in Burbank, California, who worked with developers and the community to create a real "beautiful downtown" in that maligned city.
• The San Francisco planning director who guided the preparation of the plan that reshaped the appearance of the downtown by establishing requirements for contextual architectural design, to ensure that buildings respect their neighbors. He incurred the wrath of the architectural critic of one of the local newspapers, an apostle of Modernism über alles.
• The Denver planning director who introduced a social dimension into the city's general plan and involved the schools and social service providers in developing programs that were incorporated into the plan.
• The planning director of a medium-size city in Illinois who is helping local environmentalists and farmers organize to protect prime agricultural land from urbanization by providing them with planning expertise and helping them get in contact with each other.

There are many more, some working quietly and inconspicuously. Our profession should give them support, credit, and praise.

You Never Really Know Anything for Sure

Self-righteousness can get you through many difficult times. If you know you are right, you can sit through an acrimonious public hearing and view the proceedings as urban theater.

Usually, you do not know you are right. There is always another piece of needed information. However, planners tend to suffer from "paralysis by analysis." It is important to make decisions in a timely manner, based on the best information available, if you are to maintain your professional usefulness and credibility. Even if you do get that additional piece of information, there could still be consequences that will affect the course of events in a way you did not anticipate. The essential reason for planning is to apply rationality to decisions, with the understanding that decisions made in the light of reason, albeit sometimes imperfect and incomplete, are better than decisions made in the absence of that light.

Because what we do is imperfect, it is all the more important to evaluate what we have done and acknowledge and learn from our mistakes. By evaluating and revising our professional perspective, it should be possible for us to assert that the decisions made with our influence are better than those made without it.

And if the APA ever does establish an "It Seemed Like a Good Idea at the Time" award, I would be pleased to be a recipient.

Part Four

Lessons on Customers

In this final part of the book, we look at a new orientation for government in general and planning in particular. Planners today must consider citizens as customers who have needs and wants that should be met. Businesses have known this for years; now, perhaps, it is time for planning to be more businesslike. The new orientation is that the customer should be served rather than regulated; satisfied rather than given orders; and educated rather than made dependent.

This line of thinking is consistent with ongoing work of reinventing government. It is clearly related to concepts of empowerment in political thought, yet it is innovative because it relies more on business practices than government regulations.

All six chapters in Part Four have to do with citizens as the customers of planners. Among the topics covered are the use of customer service principles to provide a consumer base of action; how the customer service approach can lead to planning success; and the follow-up premise that if citizens are customers, then planners must be entrepreneurs. The final chapter in this part and in this book argues that in addition to traditional planning skills, planners must also learn the fine arts of production management and negotiating.

Chapter Seventeen

Gaining Credibility and Trust Through Teaching, Patience, and Timing

Robert W. Marriott Jr.

A product of the late 1960s campuses, I came to the planning profession full of the motivation to change things, make the world a better place, and add a people- and environment-centered ethic to the way the world worked. My views were very significantly modified by two years working as a planner in Iran, where I came to realize that understanding the local culture is necessary in order to be effective. They were further tempered by graduate school in Scotland, where the United Kingdom's rich planning tradition and more centralized form of government control were very much in evidence. The Scotland experience provided me with an opportunity to watch the extraordinary steps that British planners took to gain political permission to implement their plans. And an early project I worked on in Baltimore County, Maryland, involving a proposed hiking trail through a wealthy area, also helped me to realize that a plan, whatever its environmental and social merits, stands no chance of implementation without general acceptance by the population. This was an easy lesson to learn when the citizens involved had enormous political and financial clout and were obviously in a position to control the destiny of land in their area.

In the twenty-five years since then, I have watched America chew up its land resources. I have designed and presided over large, sophisticated systems for making sprawl acceptable and have accepted responsibility for providing a politically viable climate for elected officials. The organizations I worked for, and I as a manager, have proved more effective when we are able to weave together a system of values and tactics that move our original 1960s-based agenda forward. Not being the Shah of Iran, I have instead been a part of a democratic process that has allowed me to watch the physical pattern and social fabric of America twist itself into an increasingly complex and inefficient series of knots. But it is, after all, how America works, and I guess it's better than the other systems. It's certainly better in terms of personal freedom and motivation for productivity than the others I've worked in. Effectiveness as a planner is difficult to measure in a society that does not place high value on long-term thinking but instead glorifies the bottom line in the annual report or the home run on one swing. There have been, however, many programs that I have watched, contributed to, and in a few cases led that made a difference. This chapter is about what it takes to make that difference.

Teaching, Teamwork, and Staff Empowerment

Most of the political and planning systems with which I have worked have been large and sophisticated (read: complicated). They usually spurned individual leadership in favor of group participation, consensus, or informed consent, and they were so complex that each took me a long time to learn before I felt I was able to make a significant contribution. Like many of today's managers, I have come to view flat structure, empowerment, and participatory democracy as important organizational features. But there are other things I believe critical to the success of planning as a profession and planners as professionals. One is being a teacher. I spend a quarter of my time explaining what I'm doing and why to junior staff, college interns, senior staff, other departments, and elected officials (and perhaps also to myself). I do not differentiate this teaching from selling, and I believe it is one of the best ways I have of getting others to accept my thinking on a subject.

Most successful professionals are promoted through the ranks because of their energy and interest in taking responsibility for the delivery of product. I have frequently seen staff with five to ten years of experience successfully charging up the career ladder, speaking eloquently, writing beautifully, and driving their projects to completion. No details overlooked, thirty-minute turnarounds on revisions, and relentless pursuit of a win. But as one ascends (or descends, depending on how you look at it) into management, the qualities that led to early success can become a handicap. It rapidly becomes impossible to control all aspects of all the projects within a large area of responsibility. If you reach that stage, it is critical to develop teams that can bring the necessary talents to bear without requiring your direct intervention. Among the benefits of a team approach, of course, is the joint feeling of success generated by team members as their work progresses. When the work is not directly controlled, rewritten, or steered by the manager, these individuals are truly the reason for the team's success; they are "empowered," in the current lexicon.

Customer Service

Personal drive and team-building skills are valuable and necessary for planners striving for the top of the profession, but more is required. Though most planners bring a philosophy or agenda to the table, pushing it through requires a strong ethic of customer service.

Customer service is critical because it establishes your credibility among the broad range of important people who tell others what they think of your abilities and personality; it leads them to trust you. It also establishes a relationship between you and your customers so that when the issues you care about come up for consideration, they will listen and, usually, try to help you win the day.

For the same reasons, it is very helpful to develop sound working relationships with other government agencies and private entities. Focus in particular on the individuals within those agencies who, because they have technical knowledge or for other reasons, may be called upon to speak to the issues raised by your planning agenda. For example, if you were to propose a change in the policies affecting rural roads, you would be best prepared if you already knew, had worked in the past with, and have negotiated agreements with the people or groups bound to be interested in your proposal: movers of farm equipment, the local department of public works, the state transportation department, local Automobile Association of America (AAA) officials, sand and gravel hauling companies, and any others from whom you might get support or opposition.

Actually, part of the planner's job is to manage special interest groups so that the position of any one of them does not create an unnecessarily extreme reaction from others. For example, if historic preservation groups take an extreme position on the rural road issue, you may encounter backlash from AAA or other auto safety groups. The holistic approach some planners use to incorporate all concerns and points of view within a plan may not prevent all conflict, but it is a defense against the paralysis that may otherwise result from actions taken by groups with opposing points of view.

Recognition of successes large and small within your organization and on the part of your customers has many things to recommend it. It rewards positive behavior in a profession that has few rewards. I try to recognize every good thing that the planners around me do, but I'm especially pleased to see loyalty, the building of new relationships, and strategic timing.

Recognizing outstanding performance in the planning office is great for morale, of course, and it may even help build trust with customers when the recognition is done publicly. It can be fun, too, even while it's inexpensive. A performance award can be a hat, shirt, mug, or even a broom sprayed gold to signify this week's "clean sweep." I've generated frenzied efforts to get reports in early by encouraging the staff member responsible for compiling our commission agenda to post, in a highly visible location for a week, the name of the author of the first completed report. It's nothing but a sign written in magic marker, and only the staff knows what it means, but people run down the hall trying to be first. All these recognize excellent service; we are all each other's customers.

Timing

Timing may not be everything, but it still is an important something. It is vital to wait for the proper time to ask that your issues be considered. It is vital that the proper groundwork be laid in terms of education, explanation of the issues, and illustration of the problems. Want to revise the fire code for public buildings? Wait until just after a major fire. Of course, planners should not actually wait for (let alone allow, encourage, or facilitate) a disaster in order for people to understand the importance of what we do. But taking advantage of lesser opportunities (and disasters too, if they occur) is important; you and your staff should be prepared for opportunities every time they arise.

Keep in mind that it can take decades to bring major elements of a plan to fruition. In the late 1970s I worked on plans for two new growth areas in Baltimore County: Owings Mills and White Marsh. It has been more than fifteen years since those plans were adopted, but many of the elements called for in the plans are still only partially constructed, partially protected, and partially completed. Another twenty years may pass before anyone can judge whether we made the right decisions for the two areas. By then, I wouldn't be surprised if computers, women in the work force, and other technological and social changes make our old decisions look bad. Planning is a continuing, never-ending process that evolves as society and its structures evolve. There are few right answers in the long run.

Getting the White Marsh and Owings Mills plans accepted required a considerable commitment on the government's part for new facilities and services that would support new schools, millions of square feet of retail space, and other employment. In today's era of severely limited government resources, such plans probably would be difficult to recommend, let alone to get approved.

Much relies on shifts in the political and economic climates. At times since the early 1970s, it has been possible to recommend increasingly sophisticated measures of environmental protection and get them approved. At other times within the same period, political agendas have precluded such recommendations; they would never be approved.

Constituent Development

Politics and economics notwithstanding, the success of any planning agenda also requires building a constituency for it. By working closely with the local farm bureau and the Future Farmers of America chapter, two planners in the Baltimore County planning department got effective testimony from farmers to support an agricultural preservation zone. The farmers supported it because they were convinced that farming would have a future in the area only if speculative pressures were stopped; speculators had made land values too high to support agriculturally and too lucrative for some farmers to resist selling out. So, to reduce the value of the land to speculators, the new zone reduced the development potential on farmland from one unit in three acres to one unit in fifty acres.

As this went on, nearby counties were also at work on agricultural preservation strategies, including counties with much stronger farming communities and much weaker real estate development forces. But these counties were unsuccessful, mainly because they were unable to get their farmers to understand and support their programs. I should not imply that Baltimore County won the hearts and minds of every farmer, but the eight or ten who testified certainly turned the tide in favor of the preservation program; it passed the county council unanimously.

Patience

Timing and the development of constituencies are certainly crucial in promoting a planning agenda. Patience may be the most critical element of all if it is properly married to the others. You have to keep your agenda clearly in mind, and you must constantly rethink how to get there, how to get it done, how to achieve it. Quality service and strong personal and professional relationships take patience to build and patience to maintain.

I counsel planners to be patient, to wait for the right combination of national and local economies, politics, and constituencies to develop before they press their most vital programs. I think most of us have a pretty good idea of twenty or thirty important things that we could do in our careers to make life in the United States better by improving how cities function, protecting natural resources, increasing safety, and adding to the quality of communities. Yet it is tempting to merely tackle the daily in-basket and work on that project with the specific schedule and budget already in place. But in my experience, that is not where the real victories lie. They lie in preparing for issues that we know are important so that when the confluence of economics and politics occurs, the constituency is available to us and the technical reports can rapidly be prepared.

Learning and Developing Relationships

What do the strategies, skills, and efforts I've discussed here have to do with the curriculum of planning, architecture, engineering, and social services most planners learn in college? Very little. Which means that in most planning organizations, especially sizable ones, there will be multiple projects under way that require training, teaching, encouragement, and work demonstrations so that your peers and employees can learn on the job. At the same time, it is important that your staff have enough technical credibility to be able to work with other technical agencies whose respect you must earn. And so a working knowledge of public finance, traffic engineering, computer systems, and other subjects is also mandatory.

Part of what makes working in planning both fun and challenging is that we have the opportunity to learn so much about other professions. It is, however, not just an opportunity but an obligation. True, I have worked for large agencies that had traffic engineers with master's degrees in planning, landscape architects with planning degrees, and other registered professionals with planning backgrounds. But in my experience it is possible to have a planning organization that functions at the highest level without them. Bright people with much less formidable backgrounds can establish relationships with the finance department and learn how municipal finance works, or with engineers and learn how big a sewage pipe needs to be in a downtown block. When it comes time to talk about the specifications and financing for a new sewage treatment plant, they will be able to carry on a credible conversation on the subject.

If you have the proper emphasis on customer service, it should be fairly easy for your staff to establish these relationships. Someone on the planning staff probably provides the finance department, for example, with population and demographic projections that it uses in annual statements, school enrollment projections, and the like. That person, then, already has a noncompetitive, even supportive relationship with the financial people: the two departments have a link. That is a place to start and a relationship on which you can build.

Worry About Winning the War, Not the Battle

There is no shortage of pitfalls in planning; most of us have the scars to prove it. I do believe, however, that becoming involved in a crisis over a single development proposal, wetland, bridge, or other decision is a trap. It's very easy to fall into, and I've done it myself.

Avoid it. In the long run, small, single-issue decisions must not be allowed to undermine your overall effectiveness. Your ability to win one battle isn't the issue. Don't let a skirmish exact such a huge cost in trust and working relationships that you can't win the war.

Chapter Eighteen

The Six Operating Principles of Effective Customer Service

Bruce W. McClendon

First as a high school student and then while going to college in the 1960s, I worked for planning agencies by coloring maps, performing calculations, collecting data, and conducting basic initial research. At that time, planning was the embodiment of the public service attitude and spirit that was so popular with my generation. I was mesmerized by the potential and excitement of the profession and the many dedicated planners I met who were certain that they could change the world and make it a better place for everyone. There is no doubt in my mind that planners were here to help.

Today, I often use the statement "I'm from the government and I'm here to help" as the punchline of my opening remarks at public meetings. Invariably it gets a laugh and the meeting starts with a lighthearted, humorous tone. Unfortunately, though people accept that I am from the government, many of them reject the basic notion that I am there to help. Over the years, too many planners have created problems for themselves because of an inability to render basic, useful, and valued services to their customers. The public believes that planners are part of the problem, not the solution, and that government causes more problems than it solves.

As a young planner struggling alternately between survival and career advancement in such places as Lawrence, Kansas; Butte, Montana; Bethany, Oklahoma; and Corpus Christi, Galveston, Beaumont, and Arlington, Texas, I learned the hard way, one decision at a time, how to be effective. There were many uncertain and stressful times in my life because many of the traditional principles, theories, and practices that I had been taught in graduate school did not often produce the results I was seeking. Fortunately, I was able to channel my youth, energy, rebelliousness, and natural inquisitiveness into a positive search for effectiveness. Eventually I was able to settle upon a number of pragmatic principles and practices that increased my effectiveness and produced the results I was looking for. The one principle that has consistently produced results for me is the concept of customer service and customer empowerment.

Customer Service: It Works for Me

I have found that effective planning is achieved by providing needed, valued, and useful products and services to customers and clients. And make no mistake about it, planners in local government are in the business of customer service. Many planners show a disturbing reluctance to regard the people they are planning with, or for, as customers. Some resist even using the words *customer* and *client*. Why? One public agency planner told me that to refer to people as customers would cheapen and demean the practice of planning. He told me, "We're not Wal-Mart," and he was right. Wal-Mart is much more successful and much more effective at serving its customers than are most planners.

A client, according to the dictionary, is someone who engages the professional services of another, and a customer is someone who purchases a commodity or service systematically or frequently. Karl Albrecht, coauthor of the best-selling book *The Service Advantage* (Albrecht and Bradford, 1990), wrote in a follow-up book, *At America's Service* (Albrecht, 1992), that in virtually all Western nations, citizens basically consider government to be a service. However, he notes that many government people, consciously or unconsciously, perceive themselves to be in positions of bureaucratic influence over the public rather than at the disposal of the public.

Historically, the public sector in this country has not had a commitment to public service for the simple reason that it has not needed to. Lacking competition for customers, what government employees had the incentive to develop an orientation that would put the needs of customers ahead of their own? While increased competition has begun to reach the public sector, Albrecht (1992) contends that for government to become really service oriented, someone in charge has to become so obsessed with the idea that he or she takes the concerted, aggressive, long-term action needed to transform its culture.

As evidenced by my own book, *Customer Service in Local Government* (1992), I am one of those managers obsessed with the concept of customer service both in theory and practice. Often there has been both internal and external disagreement with my desire to instill a customer service orientation in the practice of planning. As recently as the 1993 annual conference of the Association of Collegiate Schools of Planning, Donald Krueckeberg (1993), professor of urban planning at Rutgers University, warned that "the paradigm of 'customer service' is packed with consumer sovereignty, and who believes that?" However, sovereignty is the highest level of power, especially in government. To borrow the words of Dennis Hopper in a memorable Nike commercial, I have found that "baaaaad things" happen to people in both the public and private sectors who don't believe the customer is sovereign.

In addressing the 1990 annual conference of the International City Management Association, held in Fort Worth, Texas, Costis Toregas, president of Public Technology, Inc., advised that "customers are the dominant driving force in the private sector and the customer must become the primary focus and dominant driving force in government." I share this view and contend that the goal of every planner should be to treat everyone like a customer and to provide each with effective planning services. To me, effective planning is a remarkably simple concept. It is planning that makes a difference, produces measurable results, and, most of all, is reliable and satisfying to our customers. According to the authors of *Delivering Quality Service*, extensive surveys of customer perceptions reveal that the most important attribute a service company can exhibit is reliability—that is, the ability to perform the service dependably and accurately on the first attempt (Zeithaml, Parasuraman, and Berry, 1990).

Reliability for planners is both simple and challenging. It can be simple in that planners should be able to consistently fulfill routine but essential bureaucratic functions without making mistakes. The public should be able to rely on planners to provide consistent interpretations of plans and ordinances and to process applications. Yet it is not uncommon for planners to provide inaccurate answers or fail to properly prepare or distribute legal notices.

There is often one fundamental reason why planning departments do not always provide the error-free reliability that is essential for the development of respect and trust: they put their youngest and least experienced planners at the front counter or in other positions that have frequent contact with citizens seeking information. What brilliant form of management causes the least qualified, least trained, and least experienced people to be placed in the front lines of public interaction? Anyone who understands the concept of customer service and the importance of reliability during each and every individual service experience would not follow this practice.

In my experience, developing a customer orientation is a demanding but essential first step in positioning a planning organization to participate fully in, and benefit from, the potential demand for planning services. In making the transition, planners should model their behavior after that of other successful service providers. After conducting a comprehensive review of the business literature on customer service, reviewing customer service programs in a number of local governments, and considering my own experiences, I have concluded that successful customer service demands that an organization adopt six practices, as follows.

Listen to Customers

One planner told me that his community must be satisfied with the job he was doing because nobody was complaining. I replied with a story about Carl Sandburg, who once fell asleep during a dress rehearsal he had been invited to attend by an aspiring young playwright. The playwright was disappointed and angry and complained that, as Sandburg had dozed during much it, he would not be able to give his opinion of the play. "There is no need for you to be disappointed," responded Sandburg. "Sleep *is* an opinion."

The first essential characteristic of superior customer service is listening to your customers and hearing what they are saying. If they are not talking to you, it is cause for concern. The most valuable form of communication is face-to-face, one-on-one dialogue. In *The Service Advantage* (Albrecht and Bradford, 1990), the authors point out that the whole menu of human response is accessible in the one-on-one interview because, unlike the telephone or written survey, the interview allows you to watch the respondent's reactions to your questions. You can see the furrowed brow, the frowning face, and the intensity of the customer's feelings and assess them in a way that pencil-and-paper surveys do not allow. Also, you come to see your customers as individuals who bring specific preferences and expectations to your business.

There are liabilities to the face-to-face technique: it limits the number of customers you can survey and it calls for a method to verify what you learn. Above all, it is dangerous to generalize the feelings and experiences of just a few customers. You will need to supplement personal interviews with quantitative surveys that reach a broader customer base. The combination, however, gives you a real-world report card on your organization that can be an important step toward providing better service.

Who are your customers? If you are going to interview or survey them, you have to find them. As everyone is a planner's potential customer, you first need to bring some sense of order, structure, and priority to the market. Start by listing your major customer groups, first in order of their importance to you and your organization and then in order of the actual amount of staff time and resources currently committed to serving them. At the top of the first list should be the individuals, organizations, and entities upon whom you depend to conduct your business. This may lead to a startling discovery: some planners find that, for much of what they do, they are their own best client and they either do not need customers or do not really have any. That should make it easy to understand why the public is upset when it discovers that tax dollars are being used mainly to serve and fulfill the planner's own values, needs, and priorities.

The second category of customers should be those with whom you have a mutual dependency. This could include other city or county departments and various government entities. The third category comprises customers with whom you do not do business directly but who are important to your success—local news media, for example.

Another way to identify customers is to make a list of all your current products, programs, and services and find out who is using them. Then determine if others could or should be availing themselves of these existing services. Finally, look at the markets that you are not currently serving. If you are networking with other planners—going to conferences and workshops, reading professional literature—you may also be able to improve your competitive performance by copying or improving upon their strategies.

Define Superior Service and Establish a Service Strategy

What is planning? What business are you in? What services do you deliver and what products do you produce that demonstrate visible results and are really important to your community? How do you want your customers to perceive you? These are the fundamental questions all planning organizations must answer if they are to be effective. Recently I taught a graduate class and as an initial assignment I asked each student to review the available planning literature and bring a definition of planning to class. From seventeen students I received seventeen definitions. There were overlaps and similarities but they were, in fact, all different. The definition of planning that I have come to value and to appreciate more with each passing year was articulated almost forty years ago by Harvey Perloff (1957): "Planning refers broadly to the ways in which men and women, through organized entities, endeavor to guide development so as to solve pressing problems around them and approximate the vision of the future which they hold" (p. 3).

There are a number of interesting and appealing aspects to this definition. Long before political correctness came into vogue, Perloff referred to both men and women. And he stated that men and women, not planners, were doing planning *through* organized entities, not *within* organized entities. Next he suggested that planning should involve guiding, not imposing or dictating, and that this guidance should be intended to solve pressing problems. Solving implies reaching results, and the emphasis on pressing problems denotes limiting, prioritizing, and focusing, not attempting to do everything for everyone. Finally he mentions vision—an approximate vision, not a singular, fixed, end-state one—as something that belongs to the people with the problems. The community's vision is important, then, not that of the planners.

You can start to answer the four questions I asked in the beginning of this section by finding out what you are uniquely qualified to do, and what it is that your customers want that you can do well. Most organizations have an essential product, service, or specified area of expertise that is the heart and soul of their existence. It is rarely static; it will probably evolve over time. Every organization I have worked in has had a different focus. In Beaumont it was economic development and grantsmanship; in Arlington, strategic comprehensive planning; in Fort Worth, citizen participation and neighborhood problem-solving services; and in Orange County, Florida, growth management and neighborhood assistance.

Most customers want satisfactory solutions to current pressing problems, and planners, in theory, are well trained in helping people solve their problems through the planning process. But planners and government in general are not seen as effective problem solvers. And if Howell Baum, author of *Planners and Public Expectations* (1983), is right that "the future of planning practice depends on our efforts to find ways to restore faith in government as a problem-solving instrument" (p. 247), then planners have an important responsibility to learn how to become more effective problem solvers and to do a better job of satisfying their customers.

One way for planners to increase their ability to help people solve their problems is simply to remember that government should not tell people what to do or attempt to take on their responsibilities for them. Government should assume the role of facilitator and consensus builder; it should offer to be part, but only part, of the solution and not an independent, autonomous solver of the problem. Individuals and groups own the problem and must be expected and allowed to assume the bulk of problem-solving responsibilities. A do-it-yourself approach produces results and as new skills are learned and confidence is built, it strengthens the capabilities of the community and prepares people to tackle even tougher problems. Nothing is better in the long run than bringing people together to solve their problems and create a true sense of community.

James Heskett, author of *Managing in the Service Economy* (1986), recommends that every organization develop its own strategic service vision. This is a four-part blueprint for service managers that involves targeting a market segment, conceptualizing how the service will be perceived by consumers, focusing on an operating strategy, and finally designing an efficient delivery system that transforms vision into action. To put it simply: first decide what to do and then decide how to do it well.

It has been suggested that local government in general and planning in particular are not growth industries. Is there a market for more planning products and services? Theodore Levitt pointed out in his classic article "Marketing Myopia" (1975) that there is no such thing as a growth industry, only "companies organized and operated to capitalize on growth opportunities" (p. 47). For the alert, responsive, entrepreneurial, and innovative planner, there are an amazing number of opportunities to develop new customized planning products and services. Success in this environment depends primarily on a marketing commitment to meet these opportunities rather than on attempting to impose or sell traditional, standard products and services to disgruntled citizens.

Planners are usually better at selling than at marketing, and there is an essential difference between the two. Selling focuses on the needs of the seller while marketing attempts to identify the customers and satisfy their needs. Market-oriented planners create products and services that consumers need and want. When marketing is done properly, customers will demand and pay for these products.

With a market-oriented approach, products and services are determined by empowered customers, not by planners. Production and delivery become a consequence of the marketing effort, not the other way around. The marketing effort determines the form of the product or service, how it is to be created, how and when it is to be delivered, and under what conditions it will be made available to clients. It involves a conscious movement from production orientation to customer orientation. It means using existing technical knowledge and specialized expertise to create and deliver new customer-satisfying products and services. It also means developing new technologies, processes, and products in direct response to customer needs. If you are truly market-oriented you are driven by the needs of your customers, not by technology.

The choice between becoming a master of technology or a master of markets is easy if you are committed to effective public service. Care must be taken to develop products that are tailored to the comfort level and capabilities of your customers. A product that is too complex and too sophisticated for intended users is of limited value to customers and damaging to the producer. Customers want products they can use and value, not user-hostile monuments to some planner's technical expertise. Unfortunately, many practicing planners and academic researchers have concentrated on developing more sophisticated models, techniques, and products to correct a system that does not work the way they believe it should.

Look critically at everything you do and use these questions to help analyze your products and services: What things can we get others to do? What do our customers want that we can do more efficiently? What should we stop doing? Peter Drucker (1989) contends that government rarely abandons a service or practice even if it is ineffective. Lacking the discipline imposed by the marketplace, and subject to the sometimes excessive influences of special interest groups, local government clearly has trouble reducing or eliminating services. When reductions do take place, they can more often than not be traced to budget concerns rather than the recognition that some services are ineffective or no longer needed. This explains why cutback management can be the innovator's best friend. If planning organizations are going to be able to develop and fund new customized services, the planners who work for them will need the courage and political skill to reduce or eliminate some existing products and services. While the period of expansive government is over, the opportunities for effective service are growing—for the entrepreneurial risk taker.

Developing new products and services does not require that you expand your organization or find access to more resources. In fact, I have learned that if you don't know what you are, bigger will not make you better, only poorer and even less effective. An important key is how quickly you act. Planners can gain a noticeable perception of improved services by shortening the period between the observed demand and the actual delivery of the product. The goal should be immediate service, not promises of a better tomorrow.

Set Quality Standards and Measure Performance

"Scorekeeping is the heart of athletics, and it must be the heart of every successful business," asserts Charles Coonradt in *The Game of Work* (1985, p. 26). Coonradt believes that the manager's primary responsibility is to set the rules, create the scorecards, and manage by measurement. Indeed, it is a recognized management adage that what gets measured gets done and that, when performance is measured, performance improves. Conversely, good performance that goes unrecognized and unrewarded will deteriorate and areas for which there are no specific measurable objectives will be neglected. Keeping score is an incredible motivator. If you do not believe it, just ask any planning director who is required to set departmental goals as part of an annual budgeting or performance evaluation process.

It is increasingly rare to find a planning department that does not have an annual work program. Salem, Oregon, has been cited as having successfully implemented an employee work-planning process based on management by objectives. The Lafayette Area-wide Planning Commission in Lafayette, Louisiana, is another excellent model. In Lafayette, the planning staff meets with the planning commissioners in an annual retreat, where they jointly develop the next year's goals and objectives for the organization. These goals and objectives are measurable, very specific, and highly publicized. Objectives must be readily translatable into work with clear, measurable results, deadlines, and accountability.

To return to a recurring theme, planners must ask whose quality standards they are trying to meet. Quality should be a direct function of the customer's needs, not dictated by staff. Furthermore, quality should not be used as an excuse for ineffectiveness. Customers are becoming increasingly critical of planning that does not meet their expectations and produce results. Hence, customer participation should be an integral part of any performance measurement process.

Planners need to provide products and services that are timely and of high quality in the eyes of the public. Production standards should be based on customer needs. Balance is crucial to an effective program. To these ends, planners should constantly monitor and evaluate performance in the eyes of their clients. They should strive to deliver the highest level of quality that can be achieved under the resources and time constraints. Their primary objective should be to maximize effectiveness; quality should be a strategy, not the ultimate goal of their performance.

Select, Train, and Empower Employees to Work for the Customer
It has been said that people do not care about how much you know, until they know how much you care. Unconcerned service employ-

ees account for most of the dissatisfaction with service establishments. Almost 70 percent of nonrepeat customers are responding to employee indifference.

It is much easier to hire planners who are naturally service-oriented than it is to try to change someone's personality and attitude after the fact. Unfortunately, if the organization does not already have commitment to customer service, no effort will be made to select people with a natural service attitude. Effective planning organizations include a commitment to customer service in their mission statements, and they recruit and select employees who believe in the importance of service. Many organizations are conveying a service philosophy to employees and customers by using the word "service" after the traditional title of the planning organization. For example, the planning department in Richardson, Texas, is now part of the Development Services Department, just as it is in Fort Collins, Colorado; Glendale, Arizona; and Danville, California. One particularly effective way to recruit responsive people is to include a service orientation requirement in all job descriptions and in any advertisements for employment.

If you are looking for planners who have a natural predisposition toward service, then you want people with pleasant personalities, a relative lack of ego, a calm, unflappable interpersonal style, a caring attitude, a positive outlook on life, and an ability to work with people. James Heskett (1986) noted that "employee attributes of success in high-contact service situations include flexibility, tolerance for ambiguity, the ability to monitor and change behavior during the service encounter, and empathy with customers" (p. 123).

Most agencies administer some type of test to determine the adequacy of the applicant's technical knowledge, but few test for interpersonal skills. There are benefits to using a personality assessment test to see if prospective employees have the service traits you are seeking. You should know if your applicants consider people's feelings, are positive and optimistic, are easy to work with, and have a sense of humor. Unfortunately a significant amount of public contact in the typical planning organization is handled by entry-level planners. Hence, much of the public opinion about your organization is going to be shaped by contact at this level. Both you and the people you hire need to be aware that they are representing your organization every time they have direct contact with a customer.

In addition to hiring people with the right kind of attitude and outlook, organizations have to constantly train people to give superior service. Formal training programs are superior to informal socialization processes. Ultimately, superior customer service is going to depend on delegating authority, autonomy, and responsibility to competent frontline employees who have direct public contact.

The call for superior customer service demands a brave new world where accountable frontline professional planners with specialized expertise are free to operate without general supervision. Devolution of authority is critical. Workers at the lowest levels must be empowered and expected to act responsively and quickly to provide effective service to their customers. Frontline planners must stand behind or underneath their work, so to speak. The ancient Romans had a unique practice for assuming personal responsibility and accountability. Upon completion of an arch, the engineer in charge was expected to stand beneath it while the scaffolding was removed. He was the first to know if the arch did not hold. Not surprisingly, many of these arches are still standing.

People, the actual service providers, are the strength of any service organization. The latest equipment and technology, the best physical plant, and superior knowledge are of little value if you are not able to deliver personalized products and services that meet the specific needs of your customers. Select people whose philosophy fits that of your organization, and then train and empower them to become winning service providers. Create a work environment where people feel motivated and committed to giving their best to their customers and their organization. Encourage each of your employees to put forth their best efforts, and to strive for the biggest possible satisfaction from helping others.

Empower Customers

The ultimate expression of customer service is to empower your customers by involving them in all aspects of the development and delivery of products and services. Charles Murray, in his book *In Pursuit of Happiness and Good Government* (1988), says that "the satisfaction one takes from any activity is a complicated product of the degree of effort one puts into it, the degree of responsibility one has for an outcome, and the function it serves" (p. 265). This suggests that people with problems should be empowered to solve them themselves. Planners do not own people's problems nor do they own the solutions.

Successful planners are using volunteerism, self-help, and co-production techniques to ensure that their customers are given actual authority and shared responsibility for solving problems. These planners are empathic advocates for their customers. They are substituting passion and emotion for rationality and objectivity. They are helping their customers by empowering them to become their own planners through teaching them about networking, conflict resolution, consensus building, and the realities of the political decision-making process. Conditions are being created in which people can act to fill their own unique environmental needs and can make distinctions and choices among the experts' technical and personal judgments. Intermediaries between the people with problems and those with the power to help solve them are gradually being eliminated from the process. Eliminating intermediation and giving people joint responsibility through coproduction processes is one of the key ways in which many service organizations are reducing cost and becoming more effective service providers.

Coproduction describes what happens when you integrate customers into the process for developing and delivering service. In government, the most common coproduction activities involve citizens either volunteering their time to aid public sector agencies in providing services or citizens providing private goods and services that substitute for those publicly provided.

When I was a youngster living in San Antonio my mother would put our garbage in trash cans in the backyard. The next morning municipal garbage collectors would stop their truck in front of our house, go into our backyard, carry the trash cans to the truck, empty them, and then return the containers to the backyard. Sometimes they would abuse our trash cans, leave a trail of garbage strewn across our lawn, or fail to shut the gate so the dog could get out. Today, I sort and separate my garbage into customized containers and place them adjacent to the street. I now provide some of the same services for myself that were formerly provided for me. And my experience and satisfaction as a coproducer is consistent with most other people who help themselves. I like it and it is better and more satisfying than it was before.

Multiple benefits have been reported from the use of coproduction. From a customer service perspective, the best benefit is that surveys consistently show that coproduction produces higher levels of consumer satisfaction. When the customer has partial ownership and responsibility, the whole service experience is perceived in a better light. Other significant benefits include reduced costs, increased productivity, and product and service improvements.

Many of the examples of coproduction that I know of, including most of my own experiences, came about as the result of budget pressures. Coproduction is one of the most effective ways to maintain or even improve performance at the same time operating budgets are being reduced. In Fort Worth, we went from a dozen neighborhood planners to four and at the same time were able to significantly increase the number and the quality of the neighborhood plans we produced. The program, known as Targeted Area Planning (TAP), was able to increase production and neighborhood satisfaction by changing the staff's primary responsibility from preparing plans to teaching, training, and facilitating the development of plans by the people living, working, and operating businesses in each neighborhood. People were given training on how to do land use and structural condition surveys and how to organize and conduct meetings. They were taught techniques on how to work together to reach a consensus on goals and priorities and how to form coalitions to increase their influence and effectiveness in the political decision-making process. One of the unexpected benefits from coproduction occurred when I had to delay printing documents until the beginning of the new budget year. Excited about the results of their work and unwilling to wait, the residents raised the necessary funds to print the plan and even arranged for a neighborhood publishing business to give them a significant discount. This and many other examples of community self-help were the basis for Fort Worth receiving the City Livability Award from the U.S. Conference of Mayors. Later, I was surprised to learn of the similarities between the Fort Worth program and the private-sector-driven Atlanta Project, sponsored by former President Carter in Atlanta, Georgia.

Examples of coproduction abound. Community-based policing programs have been and continue to be tried in hundreds of communities all across the country. Signs for adopt-a-park, adopt-a-road, adopt-a-school, and adopt-almost-anything-else-you-can-think-of programs are everywhere. In Orange County, we have an adopt-a-lake program, which recently received an award from the National Association of Counties. This program provides training and water quality monitoring kits to selected residents so they can assist the county's efforts to protect water quality.

I particularly like the adopt-a-park programs that are very popular and highly effective. Involving local residents in designing, constructing, maintaining, and policing neighborhood parks guarantees that you will increase both the frequency of park usage and the personal satisfaction level of the user. The total integration of the user in every aspect of the development and delivery of services, as in these adoption programs, is a model that should be applied to almost all local government services.

The regulatory part of planning is also a prime candidate for coproduction. I have found that by involving representatives from the industry that will be affected by revising or developing a new ordinance, a better product is produced. For example, recently we had an unsightly nuisance problem with small advertising signs being attached to utility poles. Because it was so difficult and expensive for our inspectors to remove these signs repeatedly, we decided to develop a citation ordinance and also to seek to fine the utility companies for these violations. We did develop the citation ordinance so that we could treat zoning violations in a manner similar to traffic violations, but by working with local utility companies, we jointly came up with a better solution. They voluntarily agreed to develop an aggressive program to remove and keep signs from their utility poles and the problem has been solved.

Empowering Vision

In the future, the primary function of most planners will be visioning and hands-on problem solving. Visioning can be defined as having a long-term, long-range perspective that sees the future and tries to manage it. It means having an awareness of the big picture, the various critical interrelationships and linkages between essential activities and, above all, a sense of priorities. It is not a fixed, inflexible, and narrow end-state view but rather consists of multiple, evolving, approximate visions.

An effective planner must be aware of the possibility of the unexpected and have a kaleidoscopic view of many possible futures. In examining possible futures, it is necessary to constantly ask, "What would happen if . . . ?" Effective vision is collective and community-based and most of the time it is already there. It is just waiting for the planner to help the community find it. And never forget whose vision it is. In Witold Rybczynski's newest book, *City Life* (1995), he takes delight in the forces and often idiosyncratic decisions that have shaped American cities. He points out: "The American city has been a stage for the ideas of ordinary people: the small business man on Main Street, the franchisee along the commercial strip, the family in the suburbs. It all adds up to a disparate vision of the city" (p. 33).

The people who live and work in our communities have a sense of community and place. Their traditions, values and beliefs are important and should be respected and built upon. They do not want to react to some planner's proposals but rather to be involved and participate in creating their own destiny. The future is severely limited for planners who want to create and impose a vision on the community. Remember, it is much more challenging and even more rewarding for planners to help a community find or create its own vision of tomorrow.

The key to making vision relevant is connecting it to the present, and making it possible to make decisions today on today's problems with an awareness of the impact on the future. Planners are uniquely trained and qualified to provide the important linkage between today's decisions and tomorrow's consequences. If the planning profession will position itself to take advantage of its unique strengths and deliver reliable and satisfying products and services, then each of us will be able to say with pride, "I'm from the government, and I'm here to help."

Chapter Nineteen

Helping Customers Solve Their Problems

Ray Quay

Trying to reflect on your career and then bundle up some sage advice for your peers is not an easy task. It requires you to look not just at your successes but also at your failures. And who likes to relive their failures? Besides, isn't it your parents' job to tell you in hindsight when you left the straight and narrow path and doomed yourself to failure? My parents have a hundred such stories that they like to torture me with in front of their friends and total strangers. Actually, one of these stories summarizes my career well. The story goes that when I was little, my mother had a ritual she would use at nap time. She would wind up an old alarm clock and use it to show me when I could get up from my nap. I think the real idea was that the ticking would lull me to sleep. One day my father came home and found me in my room with the alarm clock spread out in pieces on the floor. I was sitting there earnestly but unsuccessfully trying to put it back together. My father, in one of those stern get-to-the-facts voices, asked "Young man, just what are you doing?" As innocently as possible, I replied, "I just wanted to figure out how it ticks, so I could make it tick faster."

This urge to explore, understand, and manipulate my environment has pretty much been the driving force in my life and career. It is at the heart of my successes and my failures. It made me a computer brat by the time I was eighteen. It made me change my major in college a dozen times and kept me in school for five years before I was able to accumulate enough hours in any one field to get an undergraduate degree. It drove my graduate professors crazy when I insisted on creating my own graduate course tract. It drives my family crazy because I start a hundred projects and am lucky if I finish two. Ironically it has also made me very successful.

Until about ten years ago, I was happily careening through life having a good time and not having the slightest idea when I was succeeding or failing let alone understanding why. Then I read *In Search of Excellence* by Peters and Waterman (1982). If it were a movie, I would say that a great light engulfed me and I discovered the meaning of life. Though not quite as dramatic or as quick, the actual effect was just as meaningful. Over the next year, Bruce McClendon and I began to reflect on the ideas of excellence and effectiveness and just why we had succeeded and failed in the past. We began to share these thoughts with others and eventually wrote our own book, *Mastering Change* (1988). Since then I have made it a habit to slow down and reflect about events that have just passed. What worked? What didn't? Why? This reflection has given me some concepts and techniques that I now consciously (rather than unconsciously) utilize on a regular basis. Here are a few I hope you will find at least stimulating if not insightful.

A Customer Service Philosophy

I believe in a customer service philosophy of planning. I define planners' work as what planners do to help others help themselves. This definition is short and to the point, but loaded with meaning.

What do planners do? I recall that the question came up often in graduate school; the profession was having internal discussions about it, and we wondered how to embody it so as to meet the American Institute of Certified Planners' entrance requirements. Now, after almost twenty years, I realize we had missed the point entirely. We were so focused on the details of our specialties, and trying to fight to have those included within the definition, that we missed the big picture. What planners do is everything and anything that relates to solving problems in the human environment. In my career I have done environmental planning, social planning, economic planning, neighborhood planning, transportation planning, historical preservation, urban design, and growth management, to name just a few; there are many other kinds of planning, and I bet you can add to this list.

The hard part of the customer service philosophy is the one about helping others help themselves. It embodies three concepts.

First, people—your customers, not you—have problems they want solved. This implies ownership; the problems are theirs, not yours.

Second, you can help people solve a problem through a process that includes understanding goals, identifying and analyzing the problem, identifying alternative solutions, making a decision, taking action, and performing an evaluation to see if the problem is solved.

Third, people want to help themselves if at all possible. They want to feel as if they are in control of their environment and lives. Otherwise they become frustrated and eventually angry. Since it is their problem, they want to be the ones to decide how it will be solved. And since it is their problem, they want to decide when it has been solved.

What you as a planner are doing, then, is solving problems, and the reason you are doing it is because people have asked you to help. These are your customers and your service is problem solving. Actually, this is the basis of any service-related business. McDonald's serves hamburgers because people have a problem. They are hungry. McDonald's helps solve that problem by giving them something to eat. Note that McDonald's does not actually solve the problem; the problem is solved when a person eats, thus people visiting McDonald's solve their own problems. McDonald's simply helps each one understand the alternatives, make a decision, and obtain the resources needed to take action. McDonald's facilitates problem solving, the customer does the rest. This is the essence of customer service.

This philosophy is at the heart of most views I have toward planning. It provides me with a framework in which I can adapt my approach to planning to meet new challenges and environments.

The Pentium Principle

Even if you really know best, you have to let people make their own decisions. Obviously, they might make what you believe is the wrong decision. But my experience has been that if I give people the same information and knowledge about an issue that I have, they usually will come to the same conclusion that I reached.

When they do not, I was wrong anyway. Experience has also taught me that when you do not let people make their own decisions, the backlash can be worse than if they make the wrong decision. I call this concept the Pentium rule because there is probably no better example of this backlash principle than Intel's 1994 fiasco with its Pentium computer chip.

Intel's problem began with Thomas Nicely, a coal miner's son in Virginia who was pursuing rather obscure mathematical research at Lynchburg College. Professor Nicely had a program he used in his research that computed the prime quadruplets for all positive integers up to very, very large numbers. His program had been running on a half dozen computer systems for over a year, one of them a Pentium system. His program would periodically check its values with known published primes to ensure the accuracy of the computations. On June 13, 1994, his program found a discrepancy between its computation and a published value, which in his field was quite serious and brought into question a year's worth of work. After four months of investigation, Nicely found that the Pentium Floating Point Unit, which can do very precise numeric calculations, was returning erroneous values for very specific calculations.

Professor Nicely contacted Intel's technical support staff in an attempt to find a solution to this apparent flaw in his Pentium chip. After a week Intel still had not provided him an answer. The company had actually found the flaw at just about the time Nicely's program flagged the problem, but did not consider it very important and simply corrected it in later chip manufacturing runs. Nicely, however, was frustrated. He used the Internet to contact others, asking them if they could duplicate the problem.

That let the cat out of the bag. The news spread like wildfire over the Internet, and Intel was flooded with inquiries about the flaw. The company responded that the average user would not be affected; only those with very specialized applications would have a problem, and even so it would arise only once every 27,000 years. This did not reassure the customers who could duplicate the problem in their systems by using a simple equation that was now flashing around the Internet. Soon, the mainstream news media took notice. Now under close scrutiny by the press but still convinced it had only a minor glitch on its hands, Intel decided to replace the defective Pentiums—but only for those who could demonstrate that their applications would generate a problem. Then, at the height of the holiday shopping season, IBM announced that it was suspending all sales of its Pentium systems because Intel had understated the impact of the problem. IBM, producer of a chip that competed with Pentium, estimated that the problem would occur on the average user's system once every twenty-four days. Owners and potential buyers of Pentium systems were now totally confused and angry. Under an onslaught of bad publicity, Intel backed off and announced it would replace anyone's Pentium chip on request.

After the smoke had cleared, it appeared that Intel's estimate of the problem was closer to the truth than IBM's, but even users who will never encounter the flaw know it is there. They certainly know they can get a free replacement; many have, and many more will. At $500 per chip and with two million chips on the market at the time, Intel could have gotten off much more cheaply and with less tarnish on its reputation by simply announcing the flaw when it was first discovered and stating that only the most sophisticated users should be concerned but that anyone who wanted a replacement could get it free. Very few users would have bothered, and bad publicity would have been slight or nonexistent.

I know a lot of planners who would have made the same bad moves had they been in Intel's shoes. They just cannot stand to see a bad decision made, so they are reluctant to trust the public to make the right one. Understanding that the problem is not yours but rather your customer's is one important step toward accepting this risk. Nor is the decision yours, but rather the customer's. If the customer's decision fails to solve the problem, it is not your failure but your customer's. But if the decision you thought was flawed actually solves the problem, the customer succeeds and so do you. Either way, you did your job of giving options and allowing a decision to be made by the person who actually had the problem.

The Craftsman's Tools Principle

This is a concept that I have been using for a long time, but I didn't realize it until I read this commentary by Michael Swaine (1995) in *Dr. Dobbs' Journal:*

> The phenomenon of tool user as tool maker is not unusual in the profession of programming. Well, it may not be unusual in

programming, but it does make programming unusual among professions. Most workers do not create their own tools and work environments; carpenters do not make saws, doctors do not make X-ray machines, and bus drivers do not make buses. For that, they are at the mercy of other professions or trades. But programmers do make programming tools. This distinction is crucially important because it makes programming uniquely capable of self-definition. Or self-redefinition. The ability to change the tools and environment of programming is the ability to change fundamentally the nature of the enterprise. Programmers can redefine what it means to be a programmer. Programming has, as it were, the power to rewrite its own genetic code.

Perhaps it is my computer programming background, but I am constantly creating new tools and reengineering old tools to help with my planning projects. Doing this is a very powerful thing because it can let you redefine the nature of planning and the environment in which you conduct your service. Accepting that I can develop new tools allows me to solve problems in situations where it would be impossible with traditional planning techniques. I have found this particularly true in regard to public participation.

One tool I reengineer frequently is what I call the "issue brief." For clients who are legislative decision makers, time is likely to be very precious and they must deal with dozens of issues at a time. In fact, time is one of their most important resources. These clients will not appreciate inch-thick reports that cover any question that could ever be asked. More valuable to them are short, well-organized, quickly readable condensations. I use an issue brief format to condense complicated projects into a set of key issues for which I can quickly communicate the facts.

The issue brief is just that, brief—one or two pages. It typically has three parts, a short statement of the issue or problem, a brief analysis of why it exists and what its impacts are, and a list of possible alternative responses to it. You may decide to also include a recommendation, but this can weaken the effectiveness of an issue brief. More often I may include a pro-and-con analysis of each alternative.

I have used issue briefs extensively in my work, and it is one of the most valuable tools in my toolbox. I always use the same basic structure of issue, analysis, and alternatives; but I will change the format to suit a particular client's needs. For large groups I will prepare a brief on all the issues. This helps to simplify complex issues and focus debate. I use them regularly when briefing the planning commission, city council, and city manager on my projects. In these cases I typically will only prepare a brief on the key issues about which decisions must be made without a clear consensus. Occasionally I will also include a political analysis of each alternative, identifying who supports each and why.

Why Not?

I hate bureaucracy. Most people I work with learn quickly not to say "You can't do that." Such comments never fail to make me try harder to find some way to "do that." But this trait isn't mere radicalism. It has to do with paradigms.

Paradigms are important. They are the way we cope in a world of information and sensory overload. They help us eliminate extraneous data so we only have to react to information that is important to us. You couldn't drive a car if you didn't embrace a set of paradigms; you would swerve off the road every time if you didn't accept the assumption that cars coming from the opposite direction will stay in their lane.

But sometimes paradigms become barriers to problem solving. Paradigms are assumptions, and usually that's fine; every time we develop alternatives, we leave out the ones that strike us as absurd or unlikely based on our experience and other considerations. If we didn't, the list of alternatives would be endless. Still, things change. If the basis for an assumption is no longer valid because something has changed, part or all of our paradigm is invalid. Paradigms must change when reality changes; the assumption that it is safe to drive on the right side of the road fails if you're on a motoring holiday in England.

Consider an apartment development in the mid 1990s. During the 1960s, federal law made apartment investments such a lucrative tax shelter that even a money-losing project could still provide tremendous tax benefits. This resulted in an explosion of cheap apartment projects all across the country. But Congress changed these laws in the 1980s, and projects that once were assets quickly became liabilities. Defaults and foreclosures were not uncommon, but worse, projects that were losing money declined in quality and became instant slums. This left a sour taste for apartments with residents and community leaders. They shunned apartments as if they were a plague. However, during the early 1990s the economics of apartments changed again. The demand for high-quality, low-maintenance living units began to rise. This created a market for high-rent apartment complexes, and such projects became viable investments. The typical residents of these projects are young, single or married professionals with high disposable incomes. The communities that still view all apartments as detriments are missing out; their paradigm is obsolete. Their failure to reassess their assumption is resulting in a loss of housing opportunities, assessed value, and tax dollars.

Paradigm-busting is a particularly useful technique when faced with "must do" situations in an environment of limited resources. I have survived three such environments in my career. The first was when I worked for the Rice Center, a nonprofit urban research group associated with Rice University in Houston. I joined the center just about the time the economy began to go sour in Texas. I bailed out when rules began to get in the way of doing things better and more cheaply. I admit I was confused; I did not understand why the rules were so important. I went through the classic symptoms: first I felt I was losing control of my environment, then I became frustrated, and finally angry and scared. Ironically, the Rice Center went under several years later and no longer exists.

The second time was in Arlington, Texas. Under the leadership of City Manager Richard Kirchhoff and Planning Director Rose Jacobson, this was a completely different experience. The philosophy was something like, "If you can do it better for less, then hang the rules." We were able not only to cut through a lot of unnecessary bureaucracy, but also to develop some innovative planning approaches. One of these was Arlington's Strategic Comprehensive Plan. Arlington had an old comprehensive plan from the 1960s. Experiencing rapid growth in the late 1970s, the community had attempted to update the plan in 1979, but failed to reach a consensus; essentially the magnitude of the issues had overwhelmed it. By 1985 the old plan was proving inadequate to deal with the pressing issues of growth. Yet the city had limited resources to create an update. So, rather than the traditional comprehensive approach, the city took a strategic approach. First came an inventory of trends and issues; then the community weighed which issues were most critical. The plan then focused on developing alternatives for only the most important issues. This approach helped the community to limit its debate and achieve a consensus on most issues. The resulting plan was adopted unanimously by the planning commission and council with a great deal of praise from all segments of the community. Several years later the American Planning Association recognized Arlington with a national award for its innovative approach to comprehensive planning.

Hearings Are Not for Hearing

This took me a long time to figure out. The bottom line is that the public hearing as we know it today is worthless. Asking a hundred people for the first time (or even second or third time) to debate openly an issue in front of a legislative body, and then have the legislative body digest the debate at the hearing or a subsequent hearing and make a decision, is ludicrous if not impossible—particularly when the legislative body has dozens of decisions to make at each hearing. Actually, it rarely works that way; in most legislative environments, legislators have made a tentative, if not final, decision before they sit to hear public comment. Often those making public comments know this, which is why so many hearings are so contentious. If speakers were not part of the process by which decisions were made before the hearing, they become frustrated and angry. The result is long, unpleasant hearings filled with comments from people who are unhappy because they know what they say has little impact. These, then, are hearings where no one hears.

But decisions do not need to be, and shouldn't be, made in smoke-filled back rooms by the power elite. Hearings can be a place for valid public dialogue, but their structure, focus, and purpose have to be reengineered. In Phoenix, we have concentrated on reengineering our public participation and public hearing process. Our approach has four major elements: reduction of agenda load, extended public debate outside the hearing, focused public debate on consensus and positions, and the use of public hearings to focus on key unresolved issues.

During the 1970s, Phoenix experienced incredible growth that resulted in an enormous number of zoning cases. Most were cut and dried, with little or no public opposition. Yet the sheer number took up a large portion of the planning commission's and city council's time. To combat this, the city created a new system: each zoning case is first considered by a hearing officer, who approves, modifies, or denies the case. If the applicant or a neighbor does not appeal, the planning commission does not hold a hearing and the city council simply ratifies the hearing officer's decision on a consent agenda. If there is an appeal, the normal hearing process occurs. As about 70 percent of cases are not appealed, this has greatly reduced the planning commission's and city council's work load.

Controversial cases or planning projects are now frequently moved outside the public hearing process into a much more informal setting. This allows extended debate, sometimes facilitated by the planning department but often left to the opposing parties to try and resolve their differences. When possible, this takes place before the public hearing. Sometimes during a hearing, however, if it becomes obvious that a case is contentious, the city council will continue it and direct the two parties to work out their differences elsewhere. The implied threat is that if the proponent does not reasonably accommodate concerns, the case will be denied. Conversely, if the opponent does not accept reasonable accommodation, the case will be approved.

When the planning department is involved in such extended public debate, the staff tries to establish points of consensus and to clearly define each group's position on points lacking consensus. All participants have an opportunity to convey their viewpoints to their satisfaction. The staff then tries to build consensus where positions are close, and to establish priorities on issues with no consensus so as to focus debate on the most important issues. A key aspect of this process is documentation. Participants must feel that the documentation generated adequately represents their opinions. Often, participants are asked to draft their own white papers; these are made part of the documentation. This approach to the extended debate also allows the staff to establish clear lines of communication between all involved parties.

Finally, Phoenix restructured its formal public hearing process in an attempt to focus more on key decisions. Documentation created during extended public debate is provided to the legislative body before a public hearing. Staff creates concise briefs on the key issues, including a range of proposed alternatives. These briefs not only help the legislative body focus on the most important decisions they will need to make, but provide a framework in which to organize the public comments that will be heard. Using the contacts developed during the extended public debate, staff tries to help groups and individuals polish their presentations; groups are encouraged to choose a single spokesperson. At this point, most of those participating have a good understanding of the different positions, and can focus their comments on the key elements of difference and try to persuade legislators to their viewpoint. The legislative bodies strongly encourage speakers to be brief and to the point, and not repeat points made by other speakers. The results of all these efforts: hearings that are more productive and less contentious, and at which more people seem satisfied that they are being heard and are part of the decision-making process.

The Urgency of a Deadline

People seem capable of extraordinary things when they are motivated and given a clear deadline. This is certainly true of those involved in public planning efforts, particularly when a diverse set of customers and a complex set of issues must be dealt with. Given unlimited time, people will never find enough time. Give them a mandatory deadline, and they will focus on the matter at hand, either finding common ground or clearly identifying the differences in their positions.

Deadlines can be external or internal. When dealing with public groups, particularly those with opposing interests, an external deadline set by those who make the final decisions can be very effective. Such deadlines work best when all groups see that they are more likely to lose if they don't give their input on time. These deadlines can be legislated into ordinances or simply set as a policy; the more binding they are, the more effective.

Internal deadlines, established by group consensus, can also be effective in team environments. Meeting such deadlines can be a matter of pride to the team, particularly when its progress is being scrutinized from the outside. These deadlines can be reinforced by outside events, such as the requirement to advertise a particular public meeting far enough in advance. In Phoenix, the city in many respects closes down during the summer. Yes, it is dry heat, but 122 degrees is just plain hot! Our city council and most of our planning committees take July and August off, which creates a rush each June to get things done before the break. Miss that deadline, and it's an automatic three-month delay.

All Views Are Valid

Planning is like climbing a mountain to decide which direction to go next. It may be tough to get to the top, but when you do, you can see what lies in all directions; now it's easy to decide which way to go. But imagine getting to the summit only to find the View Police waiting for you. You try to look north, east, and west, but the officer quickly covers your eyes and says, "Sorry, those views are not realistic. The only valid view from here is to the south." You could call it Mount Pointless, since there was no point in climbing it. The same can be said of planning efforts that restrict the discussion of alternatives to only those deemed valid by the Planning Police. Perhaps four people climb the planning mountain to decide which way all should proceed. At the top, each is forced to point in a different direction and none is allowed to discuss what they see with the others. Which way do they head next? Probably in four separate directions, even if three end up falling off a cliff.

I have found that planning projects that involve a variety of clients work best if all viewpoints can be placed on the table for honest discussion. This accomplishes two things. First, it educates everyone about all alternatives. People can then judge for themselves, based on their personal goals, the good and bad points of each alternative, and weigh which is best. Second, it gives people the opportunity to be heard. This is often very important. People want to be given the opportunity to inform others of their viewpoint. They want to feel as if others understand even if they do not agree. When denied this opportunity they become frustrated and often isolate themselves from the process, or, worse, try to throw a loose grenade into the process to kill it.

I frequently use what I call "smart alternatives" to help with this process. A smart alternative is a brief description of an alternative that contains a description, a pro analysis, and a con analysis. The best smart alternatives are short and written in such simple language that they act as a mental icon for the reader; just seeing it again will evoke memory and identification of the issue. The pro and con analyses should be objective, and the language easily understandable to all customers of the process. Frequently short statements can be abstracted from other more lengthy documents that analyze the issue. Smart alternatives work best as a series that represents the full range of alternatives that can be used to address a single issue.

The smart alternative provides a variety of benefits. Including a full range of alternatives helps to define the range of debate. If it becomes obvious during public discussion that an alternative has been left out, a new smart alternative can be added on the spot, using public discussion to define pros and cons. It also provides a focus for debate. People can point to a specific alternative and discuss its merits with everyone knowing exactly what alternative is being discussed. Pros and cons can be added or refuted. It provides a way to claim ownership; people or groups can define their position by stating which alternatives they support or oppose. Lastly, and probably most important, it clearly conveys to your customers that you understand, if not necessarily support, their viewpoints.

In 1992, in response to federal, Native American, and private pressures, Phoenix had to decide the fate of 105 acres of federal land in the heart of the city. The land, occupied by a Native American school that was closing, was to be swapped with a Florida developer for thousands of acres near the Everglades. In exchange, the city would get 20 acres of park and the Native Americans would receive $35 million. The developer hoped to end up with land and permission enough to build as much as ten million square feet of office space. This would have doubled office inventory for the city's downtown and uptown development potential. In a declining office market, this was not considered good for the city, but federal legislation dictated that the issue be settled within an almost impossibly short time: 120 days.

Nevertheless, the city was able to conduct a study to determine appropriate uses with full public and council support within the allotted time. One technique used to manage and focus public participation was smart alternatives. City staff developed five alternatives that represented the range, from maximum to minimum, of development options. Each was objectively described in terms of cost, market impact, and policy implications. These alternatives were then discussed by a variety of groups, who identified the good and bad points of each and eventually took their positions in terms of the alternatives. This allowed the staff to clearly identify points of agreement and disagreement among the different groups. The council was able to narrow its decision down to a key set of points. A study by Arizona State University surveyed most of the participants and found that almost all were satisfied with the process because they felt that their views had been honestly represented and understood, even when the final decision was not what they had desired.

Windows of Opportunity

One of the most common concerns I hear expressed at my workshops on customer service is that focusing on immediate customer problems results in less attention being paid to problems that will become critical in the future. I respond with a "windows of opportunity" approach to planning management. Not all of your attention needs to be focused on current concerns, and in fact doing so is a strategic organizational mistake. Most businesses, whether they deal with goods or services, are constantly conducting research on future products. Some spend as much on research as on actual production because it is the only way they can remain competitive. Long lead times mean that the next generation of products must be under development long before the current line becomes obsolete. Planning organizations must take the same approach.

In our profession, much of what we can accomplish is framed by the political will of our legislative bodies and the public at large. This will changes over time and from issue to issue. Many events can trigger changes in political will, including changes in the economy, natural disasters, cultural changes, aging of the populace, scandal, and human suffering. Some of these can occur quickly, and when they do the political will of a community can change overnight. An excellent example is the Los Angeles earthquake in 1994, which destroyed many key sections of the area's freeways. Until then, most organizations' desire to allow or encourage telecommuting was quite low, but necessity changed that will overnight. Today, even with the freeways reconstructed, the support and acceptance of telecommuting has increased drastically.

We as planners are good at peering into the future and anticipating such needs. We can utilize this skill to our advantage by quietly preparing for such windows of opportunity, these moments when political will suddenly changes. The key to success in such situations is to be prepared to move quickly and strategically. I try to manage the department's work load so that there are constantly a few people spending a small amount of time examining these less pressing issues. With this approach, when a window of opportunity opens, we can quickly throw a proposal through it.

I also use "windows of opportunity" as a metaphor to create deadlines for projects. As long as a project is not critical to your client's needs, attention to it can slip. But such windows typically only are open for a brief time, and that fact can be used to create a sense of urgency for a project. If the window closes before you are done, then likely you will have wasted all your effort.

Chapter Twenty

The Planner as Entrepreneur

Floyd Lapp

More than forty years ago, as part of the Housing Act of 1954, the federal government began funding comprehensive planning at the local level. In subsequent years these funds were made available to other levels of government and new funding programs were created for a variety of functional planning activities. From the mid 1960s to the early 1980s, a considerable part of my planning career was spent utilizing these public funds to prepare plans, programs, and projects for open and space recreation, coastal zone management, housing, and community development. Eligible activities were usually spelled out by the federal or state governments and all you did was follow the rules. However, events of the 1960s and early 1970s had started to shake people's faith in the capacity of government programs, and the effectiveness of city planning came under closer scrutiny. Public-private ventures were an idea whose time had come, and entrepreneurs in local government found plenty of support (Frieden, 1990).

The dictionary defines an entrepreneur as one who assumes the risk and management of a business. This actually embodies three functions. One is investment, or the capitalist role, which furnishes the necessary money for the enterprise; and a second is management, which maintains the enterprise as an organization. The third function is that of the entrepreneur proper, who determines the purpose, the spirit, and the place of the enterprise in the market and the economy (Bellush and Hausknecht, 1968). When many of the public planning funds were diminished or discontinued in the early 1980s, many public sector planners reduced their aspirations or, even worse, they gave up. However, even if the image of government improved and budgets were more balanced, these individuals would not be planning leaders because they lack the initiative and creativity to redesign their job, invent programs and projects, and create a new mission for their agencies. As the public and private sectors continue to come together, it is increasingly important for planners to understand their role as entrepreneurs.

In 1982, the agency I was affiliated with, the Tri-State Regional Planning Commission covering the New York–New Jersey–Connecticut metropolitan area, was terminated because major public funding support was discontinued under the Reagan administration. Tri-State, created in 1962, was the nation's largest metropolitan planning organization with a service area of 8,400 square miles and a population of eighteen million people. The agency was dependent on a federal Department of Housing and Urban Development (HUD) annual grant in excess of $1 million. Born in an era of boundless federal and state funds, it had never sought any other means of support except the local funding match for the federal grant. Unable to replace the lost public funding support in a short period, Tri-State closed its doors after twenty years. I assumed the directorship of a newly formed local organization, the Kingsbridge–Riverdale–Van Cortlandt Development Corporation, in the Bronx. Its mission was housing rehabilitation, economic development, and commercial revitalization in a service area of just a few square miles with just under 100,000 people. The challenge was to transfer my macro involvement in housing and community development at Tri-State to the micro level of the local development corporation. More important, the new organization's blank slate and the memory of the events leading up to Tri-State's passing encouraged me to use my planning skills to become an entrepreneur, initiating programs and projects rather than waiting for someone else to provide the guidance.

I will describe the planner's role as an entrepreneur by using the development corporation's commercial revitalization program as a case study. As a second example, I will discuss new funding and redesign of the transportation planning program at the New York City Department of City Planning, which I have been involved with since 1992.

Commercial Revitalization: Lessons for the Urban Streets

Since the 1970s, commercial revitalization programs have sprouted up in urban centers all across the country with financial and technical assistance from the public and private sectors, such as HUD's Community Development Block Grants, the National Trust for Historic Preservation's Main Street Center, and grants and loans from the banking community. Comprehensive programs usually have three major components: public improvements and street amenities such as upgraded and decorative sidewalks, trees, lights, and the like; storefront renovations; and an ongoing maintenance program to sustain the improvements once they are installed. To implement these programs, local development corporations, in addition to exercising their planning and design skills, play the role of expediters, brokers, or negotiators among merchants, owners, contractors, banks, and permit processing agencies.

A local development corporation, by delivering public dollars to provide street amenities, demonstrates that it can make things happen. Business people who have had a feeling of neglect for years, even decades, can develop a sense of wanting to do something else to keep the ball rolling because someone has finally done something for them.

Our local development corporation used upgraded and decorative sidewalks as the first visible improvement to the business district. To stretch public dollars and provide community participation and pride, a state grant was used to leverage private dollars from property owners on a fifty-fifty basis. The development corporation was also responsible for coordinating work with the contractor, so the arrangement was more like sixty-forty in the property owners' favor. The first phase of the sidewalk program was on a large and highly visible block. The result was a showpiece for all the neighborhood property owners to examine. The product was good and, because of the financial sharing package, the price was right. Soon property owners were lined up to participate. A modest $35,000 state grant triggered an equal investment by property owners, which led in turn to a city grant of close to $70,000, a further equal amount of private money, and finally a commitment of roughly $250,000 from the Bronx borough president and the city to substantially complete the project. Owners even financed sidewalk portions 100 percent when they wrapped around corners, just off the commercial strip. So, a $35,000 state grant yielded $150,000 of private investment and $320,000 of local funding in just one year.

This project established the development corporation's ability to deliver money, raise more money, get things done, and in the process provide a rapid and visible improvement for all the community to see. With increasing credibility, sidewalks paved the way for more delicate involvements with the other facets of the commercial revitalization program.

Storefront renovations and maintenance programs are the components that primarily involve brokering and negotiating. In the case of stable, urban areas, whose economic base is the neighborhood, storefront renovations hold limited if any promise for business growth. Furthermore, very often the merchant is plagued by an uncertain future with a landlord and a distressing environment of litter and crime. In this type of setting, how can the planner sell merchants on a storefront renovation that might cost a few thousand dollars? The local development corporation can offer technical and financial assistance consisting of free design consultation, delivering contractors to the site to get the job done, and providing low-interest bank loans, cash grants, or both. These types of partnerships, which give a sense of getting some things for free and others at low cost, facilitate getting the work done and provide a goal of at least maintaining and upgrading what exists even if the business improvements are minor. The lessons learned through these activities were very clear:

- High visibility makes a difference. Staff, when they are on the street where they can be reached and are seen to be working each day, yield tangible results and show people you are working for them.
- Merchants work best on their own volition. If the seed is planted, the thought is not lost. It is very important to acknowledge work that merchants do on their own.
- Everyone looks for something for nothing, even though they know things don't really work that way. With this mindset, matching programs can be popular and provide very successful leveraging instruments.

- Money talks. Loans are not as popular as up-front cash grants: the latter provide immediate, tangible benefits while the former only help over the long run. Piggybacking both is the best way to go.
- The domino effect usually works. Merchants are more likely to consider repairs and improvements when their neighbors do it first. Therefore, identifying key leaders in various locations in the business district who are willing to initiate improvements can generate a powerful multiplier effect.

Our development corporation used a consultant's analysis to evaluate storefronts, placing each in one of four categories: no improvements, cleaning and repair, renovations, and restoration. The survey was explained and each merchant was introduced to the type of work his storefront required. In areas such as ours, with many small and diverse privately held properties needing moderate rehabilitation, we do not recommend focusing on a common urban design concept. It will probably prove impractical and frustrating, and could yield too much uniformity in shopping districts that thrive on a hodgepodge of exciting signs and colors. However, renovations strived for similar materials and colors wherever possible. If you try to preach a color palette to an urban merchant you're likely to be laughed at. Comprehensive approaches probably work best where many holdings are either publicly owned or, if privately held, are in a few large tracts. Historic preservation areas and gut rehabilitation also call for an urban design concept at the outset. Otherwise, strive for improvements through incrementalism and successive approximations.

Our experience showed that merchant interest in storefront renovations fell into four categories: no interest, where merchants had no capital available and did not want to take a loan; limited interest, where the merchants responded to suggestions by doing their own handiwork; merchants who already had work under way and were expanding their businesses; and merchants who were interested and decided to take part. The merchants who did their work were encouraged by praise whenever a new change became visible on their storefront. It appeared that their handiwork encouraged their neighbors to do similar cleanup work such as painting gates or bulkheads. Those who had their own plans already in motion also caught the eye of their neighbors—there was much comment and in some cases this also encouraged neighbors to put forth a little extra effort. When the merchant was working on his own volition, the work was completed the fastest.

When interest was expressed in work being done, the range of that work was large. Some merchants only wanted new signs; others knew of one particular part of their storefront, such as doors or bulkhead, that needed replacement. This type of work often went quickly. However, when a whole new storefront was the issue, it went slowly. Often even after four or five estimates were obtained, merchants would decide it was too much money and opt to make a few repairs themselves; sometimes this did improve appearances, but often it only postponed work that was still needed. Other merchants, after deciding the cost was high, decided to wait until their lease was up in order to speak with the landlord about a better deal in rent in exchange for the storefront work. Yet others chose to drop out completely. It was apparent that there would be no clamoring in line for this program; due to the many questions about "our half" it became clear that the best way to get people involved was to make them feel they were getting something for close to nothing. It also became apparent that loans were not looked upon as favorably as cash—the work that was done was completed without the help of even one loan.

With regard to the third major component, ongoing maintenance programs, these were just emerging and called for a new partnership involving the local development corporation, chamber of commerce, commercial owners, and renters all organized to provide suburban shopping center management techniques on city streets. This structure takes two approaches: one is organizing key services such as sanitation, parking, and security so they augment the minimal services usually provided by government (especially during an era of cutbacks), and the other is financing mechanisms that can provide the capital to support these services. The financing can be derived by structuring leases so that a portion of the rent is pooled for maintenance. These negotiations can be delicate because of the need to provide a fair-share arrangement. Should contributions be based on sales, front footage, square footage, or some other measure or combination of measures?

The end product of all this effort was a stabilized commercial district, which also attracted a few hundred thousand square feet of new commercial development. Fears of further expansion of South Bronx physical and economic decline were left behind in the process. As an entrepreneur, I learned to mix public and private resources. As I interacted with our customers on the street, their feedback provided the partnership to guide our program. More important, in terms of transferring this experience to other functional areas and places, planners need to recognize that a major way to craft programs and projects will be to inject greater reliance on public and private partnerships and to invent new roles and responsibilities for coordination and funding. With limited staff, partnering and creating shared agendas will enable synergistic results to occur. This is especially crucial because the role of government will continue to change even more dramatically as major political factions continue to embrace downsizing and privatization.

ISTEA: Lessons for Transportation

A planner's training should provide an opportunity to specialize in a variety of functional areas within the framework of a generalist. Since 1991, when I became director of transportation planning for the New York City Department of City Planning, I have had the opportunity to specialize in yet another functional area. Many of my colleagues have only specialized in transportation. All too often specialists become myopic and fail to grasp the relationships of their work. I have viewed my public sector job as a creative business that is constantly looking for new roles, responsibilities, and funding sources for growth and change. Unlike the experience at the development corporation, this story is still unfolding and only has a beginning and middle. However, it is still worth relating as yet another example of the planner's role as an entrepreneur.

Funding for city planning's transportation program for many years had amounted to roughly $1 million annually with minimal relationships to the operating and implementation agencies. In 1991, the Intermodal Surface Transportation Efficiency Act, or ISTEA, came into existence. A new program in ISTEA, Congestion Mitigation Air Quality, or CMAQ, had the potential of expanding city planning's activities into new modes of transportation with strong connections to implementation. The choice was clear: continue with business as usual or consider a major new venture into CMAQ activities. As a nonoperating agency without a capital budget, the only way for city planning to participate would be through partnerships with agencies that had the means to implement plans and programs.

Since 1992, city planning's transportation unit, by selling its role as the agency that provides the planning framework, has been able to create shared agendas in new mobility modes such as bicycle and pedestrian planning and new roles in goods and freight movement.

With regard to bicycles, city planning has produced a greenway plan and bicycle network for allocating CMAQ funds to encourage a new transportation mode for journeys to work and recreation. City planning provides the planning and design expertise and the New York City Department of Transportation (DOT), as the operating agency, takes the lead on implementation either through signage, painting and striping, or actual physical reconstruction. Beginning with a bicycle network development project of $1.5 million for 1991 through 1993, more than $8 million was allocated to plan, design, and implement the program during 1994 and 1995.

For the same period, projects to encourage pedestrians were organized with DOT. Similar to the bicycle network, a $1.8 million project was organized to identify centers of activity throughout the city for street treatments. City planning is responsible for planning and design and DOT for managing the construction contracts. More than $12 million has been proposed for a variety of projects.

In the early 1990s, city planning's Waterfront Plan and Citywide Industry Study identified waterborne and rail freight goods and freight movement opportunities along with the creation, expansion, and revitalization of intermodal facilities. City planning has embarked upon a $1 million study of intermodal goods movement with the Economic Development Corporation. EDC is the city's charter-mandated agency responsible for effectuation.

With CMAQ funds, city planning is also revisiting Manhattan's central business district and downtown Brooklyn parking standards in light of the experience of the past ten to fifteen years and the amendments to the Clean Air Act of 1990. As the custodian of the city's zoning resolution, city planning can promote these changes on its own initiative.

In the process of developing shared agendas with other agencies and creating new programs with new funding sources, city planning's transportation unit has doubled in size from twenty to more than forty staff and tripled its budget while the department of city planning lost more than 100 people because of budget deficits and the lack of any new funding sources.

My experiences in both commercial revitalization and transportation planning have taught me a lot about being a successful planner in an era of scarce resources and changing roles for government. To be a planner who really gets things done, you need to re-create your job tasks by finding new funding sources and new people to work with. Otherwise you and your activities will atrophy.

In my experience, this is as basic as getting planners from different agencies and related players to come together for a common purpose. This sounds nice and easy, but when turf and funding are at stake it's a lot of hard work to get all parties to understand synergism. However, once the understanding occurs, new roles and funding sources facilitate a new business for planners who seek to be entrepreneurs.

Some thirty years ago, the *Journal of the American Institute of Planners* talked about the planner as a bureaucrat (Beckman, 1966). The similarities between politician and planner were discussed; the politician's role was described as that of a broker-mediator. The article concluded that the increasing reliance on planning requirements in federal grant-in-aid legislation, the availability of federal 701 and Community Renewal Program funds, and the expanding budgets for planning agencies all indicated acceptance of the role of planning in the administration of public business.

But for today's planners, the funding sources are less predictable and far more varied, and it is much more challenging to produce results. The only way out is to emerge from bureaucracy into entrepreneurship.

Chapter Twenty-One

Attitude, Professionalism, and Opportunity

William W. Bowdy

To put my comments in context, it is important to understand that most of my planning experience has been in the public sector and in multijurisdictional situations. Such conditions result in having to work with literally hundreds of local elected and appointed officials, all of them primarily interested in reacting to their respective local constituencies and usually less concerned with the problems of the larger community or region. And, since many new officials come on the scene in each of the many jurisdictions every three or four years, the process of education and reeducation is constant and usually cumbersome because of the sheer numbers of people involved. Such situations present a major challenge to planners who must deal with so many councils, commissions, boards, special districts, and others. Coordination and cooperation between so many units of government on any project is a major achievement.

Many of the suggested practices and how-to recommendations that turn up in publications for planners are much more difficult to apply in multijurisdictional situations. This kind of setting greatly challenges planners to effect even the most basic planning concepts or programs, but it may bring out the best in some of us: it forces some innovative thinking about ways to communicate, to seek buy-in, and to find new ways to encourage and implement cooperative efforts. Some techniques of accomplishing these are very simple, but usually take considerable time for the establishment of personal contacts and to build a basic level of trust.

With these thoughts in mind, I concentrate here on three subject areas. Most of this material is uncomplicated, because in my opinion that is how we must offer our thoughts and recommendations to decision and policy makers and to the clients and public we serve. And, due to my background, most of what I discuss has to do with public sector planning issues.

Attitude Toward Service to the Public

Having worked in the public sector almost all of my planning career, I am particularly concerned with how we treat the public and how the public perceives planners and planning. (I suspect the same concerns apply in the private sector as well; clients there are also members of the public.) In my opinion, the customer—the citizen—is the most important person with whom we deal. With permission from the L. L. Bean company, I have adapted and displayed throughout our public offices posters that say the following:

A Customer (Citizen) Is . . .

. . . the most important person ever in this office—in person, by telephone, or by mail.

. . . not dependent on us—we are dependent on him or her.

. . . not an interruption of our work but rather the purpose of it—we are not doing people a favor by serving them; they are doing us a favor by giving us the opportunity to do so.

. . . not someone to argue or match wits with—nobody ever wins an argument with a customer (citizen).

. . . a person who brings us wants, needs, and problems—it is our job to handle them with respect, professionalism, and good results.

Although obviously aimed at day-to-day service to the general public, the spirit of the message conveyed in this poster indicates a basic philosophy in which I most thoroughly believe. A great number of practicing planners handle such service; it brings them into close and continuous contact with the public. The more the planner and the public meet face to face, the more likely a mutual trust and understanding will result. And trust is vital when the planner is attempting to work with the larger public on issues of neighborhood, community, or regional importance.

This need for mutual trust is not limited to planners. It permeates all communication between the public and the governments they rely upon for fair and objective treatment. Today, with "good government" considered an oxymoron by much of the general public and some elements of the media, the need to build or rebuild trust is critical. As Michael Smith-Mello and Peter Schirmer state in *The Context of Change: Trends, Innovations and Forces Affecting Kentucky's Future* (1994, p. 157), "As any manager or public official who has ventured into new, more democratic territory will attest, trust is the essential ingredient in positive, constructive change."

My daily application of this philosophy may be considered naive or unnecessarily severe, but it has worked for me. It has resulted in respect for the public agencies with which I have been affiliated, and I have worked hard to ensure that the entire planning commission staff understands and buys into it. Here are some of the guidelines I use as a planning manager; I consider each of them a matter of common sense.

- Regardless of evening meeting schedules, all staff are expected to arrive on time for work in the morning, either at the office or in the field. They must be available to the public as usual; the public is not swayed by the excuse of overwork.
- Even during a staff meeting, calls from or visits by the public come first. Staff members are expected to leave the meeting immediately and offer assistance. Such interruptions may make time management more of a challenge than usual, but the public comes first.
- When possible, staff should assist the public in the privacy of their offices. This may not always be feasible, but people feel respected whenever they are treated in such a manner.
- All staff shall be trained and alerted to the importance of professional, respectful treatment of callers and visitors to the office. A first contact with our office may be the only contact; it should demonstrate that government employees, especially the planners in this office, care about them.

- Staff members should always be on time for appointments and meetings and should bring whatever they might need, such as audio or visual equipment, with them.
- Customers seeking assistance at the end of the work day must be treated the same as those arriving at the beginning of the day; their problems are just as important.
- Staff members should show respect for their customers through their appearance. Greeting citizens in jeans and T-shirt can send a message of arrogance or insensitivity to their concerns.

Public Service: Perception Is Reality

Unfortunately, public planners are often perceived as nothing more than enforcers of a plan, zoning ordinance, subdivision regulation, building code, or whatever—in other words, as people who stop other people from doing what they want to do. I am convinced that, by using common sense and sensitivity, the planner can instead be viewed as a helper, someone with a job to do but with the willingness to go the extra mile to find answers to problems. Knowing that others may not understand their role, planners need to find ways to overtly show the value and community good that can come from what they do. Partly this is a matter of having good working relationships with customers.

Most problems can be solved if people on one side trust that the other side is willing to listen to their concerns. On the planner's side of this equation, such trust must be earned and constantly pursued. Longevity in the job helps, because trust is usually gained over time and after contact on a number of issues. Eventually the forthright planner becomes known as someone who is trying to help (despite occasional honest mistakes) and becomes trusted by people on both sides of an issue. They will know that what is said at a face-to-face encounter with such a planner will be honored, and that is the planner's clear basis for finding sound solutions to problems. If you are a planning manager, I suggest you surround yourself with capable people and teach them that we are primarily helpers, not enforcers.

Processing Efficiency

Most people who come into contact with planners do so rarely. They often do not know what steps are necessary to get done what they want to do; they may not know what approvals are or how to get them. They need guidance. They need to know how the process works so that they can understand their options. If the planning department is their first contact, the planner has a perfect opportunity to help and, with luck, to gain long-lasting appreciation for it.

The process of applying for a zone change, zoning permit, building permit, or (for that matter) permission to build a new subdivision should be as simple and efficient as possible. Planners should be prepared to give a simple explanation of each process, using graphics or other materials if appropriate, and a complete description of the process should be available as a handout. Actually following a given process may be a little arduous for the customer, depending on how many departments or agencies are involved, but a clear statement of steps that need to be taken and results that can be expected will at least put applicants on the right road. Neither the experienced builder nor the first-time citizen applicant enjoys being surprised by the words "oh, by the way"— signifying, of course, a previously unmentioned step in the process. If there are legal consequences, so much the worse.

A recent federal report, *Standards for Serving the American People, Putting Customers First,* offers suggestions for reducing red tape. One example: "As in most big cities, many people in Atlanta, Georgia, are eligible for several benefits, such as Medicaid, food stamps, and housing. To apply for the various benefits, they had to travel around the city from one agency to another, wait in long lines, and puzzle through a different application form for each program. But now, Atlanta's Common Access Project team has created a single, all purpose application covering six programs. The team reduced 64 pages of forms to eight" (National Performance Review, 1994, p. 45). Since that time, Atlanta has reduced the paperwork even further.

Planners need to strive for such efficiencies so that the processes we create are less cumbersome and so more of our time can be spent on productive pursuits. One way is to keep up with ever-changing information technology. Vast systems for information storage, processing, and quick retrieval, although time-consuming to construct, should finally make us more efficient and allow more face-to-face quality time with customers.

Wherever possible, the one-stop shopping idea is worth pursuing. One department or agency may be given the authority to coordinate all applications so that the interdepartmental process can happen smoothly and the outcomes can be expedited.

Telling and Listening

Much of the planner's work in public or private practice necessitates the public airing of issues. This often takes the form of meetings or hearings at which the members of the general public may hear about and comment upon planning matters of particular concern to them. It is the planner's job to ensure that the issues in question are presented in an accurate and easily understandable fashion. As I said earlier, the best way to offer our thoughts and recommendations to decision and policy makers and to the public we serve is the least complicated way.

Still, some issues are innately complicated. No matter how well we explain them, they are bound to be viewed differently by the applicant, the neighbors, the planning and engineering staff, various special interest groups, the media, and whoever else is paying attention. Regardless, we must ensure that the information we offer allows all these parties, and the decision-making body, to base their opinions and decisions on facts. How often have you heard a presenter at a public meeting apologize because the visual aids are hard to see from the back of the room? I always want to respond, Then why are you showing them? The people in back are just as important and just as interested as those in the front. Why didn't you take more time and prepare your materials properly?

If you're going to be criticized, be criticized on substance, not preparation. Planners are supposed to be good at defining the problem, developing alternative solutions, and offering well-based recommendations. To fall short because of poor communication and presentation is sad, especially given today's computer technology, which makes it much faster and easier to come up with clear, accurate, and easily understandable visual aids. Planner training should include these techniques; fortunately, professional organizations regularly offer programs on them. The American Institute of Certified Planners (AICP), for example, has initiated the Continuing Professional Development Program. It encourages members to take advantage of all types of continuing education and professional development programs, and to keep track of credits earned, to assure employers, clients, and the general public that they are serious about keeping their planning knowledge and skills current so they can offer the best service possible. When I run for various national AICP offices, part of my position statement reads: "The benefits of membership should include the responsibility of keeping current—we owe this assurance to ourselves, to our profession, and to those whom we serve."

In any case, it is a small leap from these very basic concerns, dealing with day-to-day issues, to the much more complicated job of building public interest in the longer-range and more difficult issues of community and regionwide planning and visioning. But however large or small the issue, many of the techniques for approaching the public are the same.

Professionalism and Politics, Politics and Professionalism

The AICP has its Code of Ethics and Professional Conduct and the American Planning Association has its thirteen APA Ethical Principles for Planning. Whatever your capacity as a planner, you need to be constantly vigilant of compliance with ethical standards. Smith-Mello and Schirmer (1994) emphasize it this way in their report on Kentucky: "In an environment where mistrust has historically characterized a relationship, trust must be painstakingly earned through consistent, forthright actions. Workers must believe that managers and corporate officers want what is best for them, as well as the company, just as the citizens of Kentucky must believe in government's commitment to public good. Reinforcing that belief, that fundamental trust in government will require aggressive, consistent efforts to engage and involve citizens at every level in problem solving, policy making and planning, as well as an unyielding commitment to ethical conduct at every level of government" (p. 159).

Planners in both the public and private sector will normally be required to deal with one or more levels of government. This usually means coming in contact with politics. Planners used to be taught to steer clear of any form of politics, that such contact led to unholy alliance, real or perceived. Planning was supposed to be a pure way of looking at long-range ideals toward which the community should strive; politicians were supposed to take care of the nitty-gritty, day-to-day problems of community development. Planning, in other words, should be above politics.

But it has become clear that the planner, like most other players in community growth and development, must at least be aware of the politics of a situation and, more often than not, actually involved in them. It's the only way to ensure that good planning principles are a part of the decision-making process. Planners must constantly urge that short-range proposals fit into the longer-range goals agreed upon by the community. Simultaneously, they must be sensitive to the local official's view of the benefits of such short-range proposals and be capable of negotiating toward acceptable end results. When they cannot win the day, planners still must try to provide input to lessen the negative effects of a decision. All these things are political acts, and all of them are common sense.

Leon Eplan, Anthony Catanese, and many others have stated that planning and politics are not an unnatural combination. I suggest that they are in fact a necessary combination. In *Planning in the Face of Power,* John Forester (1989) puts it simply: "If planners ignore those in power, they assure their own powerlessness" (p. 27). Most decisions are made by officials who are elected via a political process. They are attuned to the politics that helped get them elected and to the mandate they believe was given to them by the electorate. Planners cannot ignore this; the more salient issue is how to deal with the situation. There are too many mixes of planning and politics to detail them all here; at any given time, the planner may be forced to serve many differing ideals and groups. Says Forester: "Local planners often have complex and contradictory duties. They may seek to serve political officials, legal candidates, professional visions, and the concrete requests of particular citizens' groups all at the same time" (p. 82). And as noted, in multijurisdictional situations such problems are further complicated. Yes, the planner must stay aware of and sensitive to the politics of a situation, but trying to keep track of the politics of numerous local government entities is complicated. Often this is exacerbated by the planner's need to consider the total community, even as the governments within it run in different political directions from one another.

In such situations, I suggest finding and building upon issues of a regional or areawide nature that are matters of common concern to all parties and that simply cannot be addressed by a single local government entity. Examples are air quality, water quality, provision of basic water and sewerage service, and transportation. If working together on such issues is successful, it will help build a mutual respect between the participants and they will not be so suspicious and cautious about addressing other more localized common concerns later on. The politically astute planner will be able to recognize the local issues of common appeal and use them to build trust between the entities that come together to work on them.

Again, it is important to recognize that this process takes time and patience; to a degree it depends on the longevity of the participants in a common cause. It also clearly requires awareness of the many federal, state, and local laws and requirements under which such regional and local work must be accomplished. And again, APA and AICP continuing education and professional development programs are a good way to keep current with such important matters. Willingness to help and understanding political reality are important, but so is making sure that the assistance you give is accurate and timely. As I write this chapter, major changes in the power structure of Congress are taking place; this will make it vitally important for planners to keep current with congressional actions as they apply to private property rights, regulation, and a myriad of other planning and land development issues, and to recognize the changing politics of various interest groups in connection with these issues.

There are times when the line grows fuzzy between planners' professional conduct and their personal politics. Perhaps this is more prevalent in the private sector, where planners must assess a potential client's objectives in light of current law and their own ideas of sound planning. At any rate, if there is any serious conflict, the planner's professional ethics must prevail. Unfortunately, some situations are not so clear-cut. To help with such dilemmas, the AICP has made available Carol Barrett's *Everyday Ethics for Practicing Planners* (1995). This manual aims to help the planner determine what the ethical issues of a situation are and how to go about assessing and reaching conclusions. It also offers various scenarios to help planning commissioners assess the ethical issues of matters

that come before them as they fulfill their role in community decision making.

Most planning results are finally deemed, by simple community acceptance or by court test, to be legal and free of ethical conflict. Others, however, are perceived by the public as wrong or as a
violation of the public trust. It is difficult for planners or planning
commissioners to assess what their involvement should be in such
cases. It has been said that if the public perceives an act to be a
conflict of interest, then it is a conflict of interest. The person or
group that proceeds regardless will likely find all their future
actions tainted in the public mind. How can you deal with such
matters? I suggest you examine your position in light of the AICP
Code of Ethics and Professional Conduct or APA Ethical Principles
for Planning, read the ethics manual mentioned above, and if you
still feel uncomfortable, don't take the chance. Do what you honestly believe is right, and if you err, err on the side of sound and
professional ethical behavior.

Recognizing and Acting on Opportunities

Sometimes recognizing an opportunity is easy, sometimes you have
to think about it in terms of what you want to achieve.

One of my earliest experiences was as a brand-new planner
working for a three-county regional planning commission with
some forty planners, engineers, economists, and others. I was directed by my boss to accompany, for my first three months, every
staff member who attended any evening meeting, which meant I
worked almost every night. In addition, he instructed me to say
nothing, just observe. For a young planner eager to display his
knowledge and talents and to be recognized for my abilities, this
was a little humbling.

I learned more in those three months than probably any other
similar period in my professional life, but I likely could have learned
even more had I been more open-minded and less upset about my
lot in life under such a severe directive. I did not recognize or take
full advantage of the opportunity my boss, a seasoned professional,
was offering me. Still, I was able to watch many staff members present ideas, answer questions, deal with problems, and face different
audiences and individuals in many different communities with

many different characteristics. After each such meeting, on the way home, I asked questions of and argued with whichever staff member I was with: Why did you do it that way? Why didn't you answer the question? That sort of thing. Most important, I sat at the back of meeting rooms and watched the reactions of the audience, the city council, the planning commission, and the others. The experience was invaluable, and every staff member I have hired in my later professional life has gone through it too. Many of them confided later in their professional careers that they too found it a most valuable learning process.

Recognizing opportunities and being able to take advantage of them requires planners to have the right attitude and a good grasp of the issues for which they are responsible. It also necessitates, as earlier noted, having an awareness of the politics of the situation, in the many senses of the word.

Another personal experience may help convey my thoughts in this connection. After three years of in-depth study and research and numerous public meetings, the staff of the regional planning commission for which I was working completed the first-ever comprehensive plan for our area of jurisdiction—two counties, thirty-six municipalities, and numerous single-purpose special districts (fire districts, school districts, police districts, sanitation districts, water districts, and the like). Our comprehensive plan contained many recommendations that recognized the limitations of small government units to provide full services and identified how some such services needed to be provided on a wider basis.

Unfortunately, one of the local newspapers misunderstood one recommendation involving volunteer fire departments and suggested that if the comprehensive plan was adopted, the planning commission would have authority to determine the type and amount of fire equipment that could be purchased by each individual volunteer fire department. As anyone who has ever been involved with volunteer fire departments will attest, such a dictate would be entirely unacceptable. By the time appropriate explanations could be offered, much of the value of other parts of the plan was in jeopardy. Litigation was filed questioning the authority of the commission, and many months were required to correct the damage. One lesson I learned well from all this was the importance of making sure the news media are fully aware of whatever is going on. My contact with the media since then has been frequent and open, and it has served me well. We trust each other, even if it came a little late.

After the comprehensive plan identified the need for service provision without constraint of political boundaries, the commission approved my request to allow our staff to prepare a study on government restructuring. The study took a year and a half and included exhaustive visits to other places in the country where consolidation of governments or service had recently occurred. Our study recommended dissolution of all cities and special districts (including our own area planning commission), merger of the two counties, and creation of a consolidated government. The plan was very complex, but suffice it to say that it was supported by the media and by various special interest groups and met with dismay and anger by most elected and appointed local government officials, most of whom visualized loss of their fiefdoms. One comment was: "From those same folks who are advised by our own local 'Zoning Czar' [yours truly] and who gave us the far reaching and unrealistic comprehensive plan, we now get their recommendation to restructure our very government entities to achieve their recommendations!"

I was asked in one public meeting if our recommendations included dissolution and consolidation of all school districts so that high school X would never again play football against high school Y. As you might imagine, I was caught entirely off guard by the question.

I continue to believe that the recommendations of the report had much merit, but neither I nor the commission had thought out the full and far-reaching political implications of our plan. We were poorly prepared to face the public and to sell the merits of such a major set of recommendations, having not solicited strong buy-ins along the way. Lessons learned were many, but clearly it became obvious that careful and well-planned approaches to working with the public (in many different forums) and to elicit early and continuous buy-ins to such plans are often as important, if not more important, than the plans themselves. Understanding and taking advantage of the politics of the situation and being sensitive to the various concerns of the various publics would have been vital if implementation of some of our planning recommendations were to be realized. We need to be major players in such decision making, and we can't be naive about the directions and objectives of the other players. We need to spend quality time in determining our implementation directions, just as we spend quality time in our plan preparations. Lessons learned from the experiences of private enterprise in the selling of major product lines or ideas are worthy of study and possible adaptation. And, I suggest that planning educators need to more thoroughly examine how to incorporate selling techniques into their practice-oriented curricula, just as they teach how to do comprehensive planning.

After two less-than-adept personal experiences, I now offer a successful recent one. It has turned me into a preacher from my bully pulpit, making me urge our profession to wake up, recognize, and take full advantage of a major area of technological advance in which we as planners should be leaders.

In 1985, following a regional health-related problem where causes were, ostensibly, traced to a fractured sanitary sewer line and resulting surface seepage, the county chief executive officer questioned the accuracy and completeness of the region's mapping records of the sanitary and storm sewerage system. Both the manager of the sanitation district and I responded that we were indeed concerned about the completeness and accuracy of our mapping for a system that in some parts was more than a hundred years old. One of the county chief executive's first priorities was to get such information up-to-date and accurate as soon as possible.

My concern was that much of our base mapping had been created in the early 1960s and kept only somewhat current since then. To base new maps on an outdated system seemed less than sensible. I had tried unsuccessfully on a number of occasions to find money to perform a more complete update, but there were always more pressing priorities. For the first time, I became vaguely aware of what I then referred to as "electronic mapping." I quickly became enamored with the possibilities of automated mapping and facilities management (AM/FM) and soon was beginning to be able to spell GIS (geographic information system).

The short version of this story is that we created a partnership of the county legislative body, the sanitation district, the county property valuation administrator (county assessor in most other states), and our planning agency (Northern Kentucky Area Planning Commission), as the lead agency or managing partner (the county water district has since become the fifth partner), to proceed with development of a geographic information system. It was brought on-line in May, 1988. Our system has grown and become constantly more sophisticated. It also had the benefit of construction of GIS-controlled base mapping upon which the sanitary sewerage system (the original and basic reason for such an undertaking) was mapped as a layer of information.

The agreements to proceed with this effort did not happen overnight. It took many months and many meetings of negotiation and politicking to sell this strange new technology, which would have considerable cost and amazing end results but would not offer easily available access and information until a major database of mapping and associated attributes was built. Time estimates for the database to be created and put into use transcended the terms of office of some of the officials involved in approving the budget for it. But we saw an opportunity and took advantage of it: it had become quickly obvious to me that this new technology held promise far beyond just planning-related applications, so we attempted to sell the concepts by emphasizing the potential value and possible end products of many diversified applications, depending on whom we were addressing (one use could be making information on voting precincts readily available; who do you think might be interested in that?).

Our GIS program has been extremely successful, with many applications in place and more becoming obvious each day, including another basic processing efficiency effort upon which we are now working. We will be providing a Public Access Information Center that will allow customers to view property-related information on a computer screen, point and click, and walk out of the office within minutes with a map and related information about any property they might be interested in.

Most important, early recognition of the potentials of GIS for public and private purposes and in many diversified planning and nonplanning ways was of major importance. And then to be able to move quickly and with sensitivity to the needs and desires of other potential users allowed us to get a cutting-edge start to a technology that is becoming more and more commonplace as a tool to assist decision makers as they assess difficult and complex problems.

I remain convinced that our profession has not taken full advantage of the vast potentials of GIS-related applications. I suspect, from conversations I have had over the past few years, that much too shortsighted views of the capabilities of this technology is the big problem. Too many planners seem to be concerned only with planning-related applications of this technology and primarily only with basic graphic or mapping applications and minimally with the vast analytic capabilities. Significant amounts of information, what-ifs, and varying analytic results can be put in the hands of policy makers quickly and easily. Some easy-to-learn, easy-to-use software now permits those same policy makers to have desktop access to such information. The analytic capabilities of this technology are limited only by our limited visions. And it should be very clear by now that GIS is but one of the many tools becoming available as part of the information infrastructure and technology world.

This shortsightedness can be a major deterrent, not just as it applies to GIS and general information technology-related issues, but in most all we do. We need to be more broadly visioned. We need to recognize potential planning applications and deliver immediate results. But most important, we need to recognize how the planner can become the direction setter and a major community player by being able to recognize opportunities and help the community take advantage of such opportunities in broader areas of interest and concern by being timely, proactive, and action oriented. As Fred Bair observed over twenty-five years ago, "If you start planning and planning doesn't start doing things for you in the present, it isn't likely to do much for you in the future" (Bair, 1970, p. 153).

Chapter Twenty-Two

Understanding and Improving the Management of Planning Agencies

Stuart Meck

Let me tell you a story. When I graduated from planning school at Ohio State University in 1971, I joined the Memphis and Shelby County Planning Commission in Memphis, Tennessee. Memphis was a city that had gotten into planning early. Harland Bartholomew, the pioneer city planning consultant from St. Louis, completed one of the nation's first city plans for Memphis in 1924. The city's lush parks were the result of careful long-range acquisition. A parkway in the City Beautiful tradition ringed older neighborhoods.

The joint commission for which I worked employed an executive director, whose appointment was subject to the confirmation of the two city and county chief executives, the city and county legislative bodies, and the commission itself. He was a fine man, a seasoned professional, and a member of the American Institute of Planners.

The planning staff numbered around forty. The majority of the nineteen professional staff members were young college graduates like me and held master's degrees in planning or a related field.

We occupied a half floor in the Memphis City Hall in the city-county civic center complex in spacious, well-lit offices. My first office had an expansive view of the Mississippi River, overlooking Mud Island, now a park and tourist attraction. In the spring, I could see the Mississippi flood as far as the horizon.

The planning commission budget, as I recall, was quite adequate. We did not seem to want for anything. The Xerox machine always worked. The drafting room was efficient. At no time in my life since have I had such a cornucopia of Prisma color markers (still not cheap), Zip-a-tone, and related graphic arts supplies. Enabling legislation posed no limitations. The joint city-county agreement that created the planning commission was very well drawn and clear in describing its responsibilities for planning and development control.

The planning commission members were, at least superficially, pleasant people, the kind with whom you feel comfortable drinking a mint julep at the Memphis country club (where a lot of business was conducted). The Memphis city appointees tended to be businesspeople, wives of wealthy or prominent men, and members of old planter families. County appointees were builders, developers, and real estate brokers. The commission had no community activists as such, and few minorities.

By any traditional test, the Memphis and Shelby County Planning Commission should have been a highly effective planning organization. Everything I had learned in my planning administration class at Ohio State told me that. It had adequate financial and physical resources. It had a trained, competent staff. And it did not have to worry about the multiplicity of governmental units and competing agencies that often made planning difficult in other communities.

Drawn from the crème de la crème of the Memphis community, the planning commissioners themselves should have been influential in shaping public opinion on development issues and in articulating a vision. They should have been people whose views were sought, respected, and heeded by elected officials. After all, that was the classic theory of the planning commission, a product of the governmental reform movement of the 1920s.

Yet the Memphis and Shelby County Planning Commission was not an especially effective or influential organization. From almost the first day, I sensed something was wrong. The county legislative body had held up the executive director's biennial appointment for the second time. Planning commission members, I quickly learned, did not like staff recommendations on rezonings and subdivisions to be made public. Instead, they preferred to receive them privately, in executive session, where they decided individual cases "on their merits." Puzzled over the quixotic and, indeed, often irrational nature of the commission's zoning recommendations, the Memphis City Council periodically requested the original staff reports, but the commission balked at releasing them.

Long-range planning itself had foundered. The commission staff had initiated a series of planning district studies. We thought them important, but the commissioners did not seem particularly interested in discussing them or accelerating them to the public hearing stage. Consequently, the studies went through numerous internal drafts, each of which watered down the studies' specifics, and work sessions were put off. The commission was not terribly interested in citizen participation or social issues, even though the city itself was sharply divided along income and especially racial lines (school desegregation was the big issue then).

A year after I began, the executive director who had hired me resigned to join a mortgage banking firm (he was later to go into land development). I regarded this as some sort of dark omen. One of his deputies, a longtime staff member, was appointed as a replacement. Not much changed, except that the new executive director ordered that we all wear plastic name tags that slipped into our shirt pockets, the idle suggestion of the commission chair. In a subtle act of rebellion, I took to wearing turtlenecks, sans pockets.

Gradually, I came to the conclusion that while there was planning to be done in Memphis and Shelby County, no one had any expectation of the staff doing it with the commission itself leading the charge. Despite a promotion, I left the following year for a planning job in the north. Almost the entire professional staff turned over within two years of my departure.

Frustrated over the commission staff's ability to produce planning documents quickly, the city's chief administrative officer, who worked for the mayor, set up a Policy Planning and Analysis Bureau to administer the then-new federal Community Development Block Grant Program. The city council later created a Center City Commission to plan and implement development projects inside the parkways.

After I left the planning commission itself, it hired the American Society of Planning Officials (ASPO), one of the American Planning Association's predecessor organizations, to undertake a management study. That study, completed in May 1975, was blunt.

The planning commission, it concluded, "has not been a very effective forum for identifying and resolving growth management issues facing city and county government. In part, its organizational structure has hampered it in dealing decisively with development issues involving both governments" (Mosena and Thurow, 1975, p. I-4).

The report went on to criticize almost everything about the commission. The organization's structure distanced it from the center of decision making. Further, the commission had failed to undertake long-range planning, had failed to provide leadership, it said. The resulting land development system was "inefficient, unwieldy, and confusing"(p. I-4). And it was, the report hinted, possibly laced with conflict of interest.

The management study recommended a series of measures to restructure the agency and improve its internal operations. Many were carried out. New staff members were brought in. Some took early retirement. To this day, I still find this early experience disquieting and difficult to rationalize. Why was this planning organization not effective?

Why Planning Agencies Are Different

Public planning agencies are different than other departments and divisions in local and state government. These distinctions enhance their potential for controversy.

Line Versus Staff

Planning agencies tend to combine functions of line workers (those that conduct routine activities like processing water bills and fighting fires) and staff (those that advise other departments, coordinate and help plan their activities, and assist the chief executive officer). The staff function is sometimes shifted out of the planning department into the office of the chief executive officer to give it increased visibility (or to rein it in). When the two functions collide, tension results. Should the chief executive officer want to grease the skids for a development to impress the public or the city council, the planning agency, which often is expected to promote economic development, is supposed to find a way, even if it means ignoring the zoning code's enforcement. In one unpleasant situation some years ago, I recall being harshly upbraided by a supervisor for pointing out that a proposed restaurant chain would violate the zoning code if it followed through with its intention to pave over the entire front yard of a development to squeeze additional parking onto a cramped site. In the interest of attracting the restaurant, I was expected to keep silent about the conflict.

While all line departments plan to one degree or another, the staff function of the planning agency often places it at odds with other government functions, because the planning department is telling other departments how to do their jobs. For example, municipal engineering departments can gold-plate design standards that significantly add to the costs of housing development, precluding lower-cost housing, for which the planning department may be the only internal advocate. (One big-city planning director once told me that when his engineering department made ridiculously onerous recommendations in connection with proposed developments, he did not feel an obligation to defend them. "Let them look out for themselves," he said ruefully.)

Numerous Lay Boards and External Advisors

Planning agencies must also work with large numbers of lay advisory boards and commissions whose advice may depart (sometimes wildly) from the counsel of the planning staff (this was the case in Memphis). Think about the average local government these days and the surfeit of boards (and opinions!): planning commissions, boards of zoning appeals, environmental commissions, neighborhood planning boards, internal technical advisory committees, corridor committees, special plan committees, historic and architectural preservation commissions, and others. This diversity blurs the identity of the customer or client of planning. If you are uncertain who the customer is, then how can you know whether "the customer is always right"?

Few local government departments—the police or finance departments, as examples—have to function under similar conditions. While extensive public participation is a fact of life in local government, the planning agency typically has more than its share. But, regardless of the quality of planning that is being done, when a planning agency does not attend to how this public participation is handled (down to the appearance and organization of agendas, the content of minutes, responsiveness to inquiries), friction occurs. Thus, the success of the planning agency is often gauged by how well the agency manages these numerous constituencies.

Lack of Mystique of Expertise

Although this is changing, planning agencies do not have the mystique of expertise that other departments may have. As an official, if you fail to follow the finance director's advice, you get audited and may have to pay back misappropriated local funds. Ignoring the city attorney means you may go to jail or have an embarrassing and expensive loss in litigation. The engineer can refuse to seal plans for bridges and structures that may collapse. And the police, if they disagree with your behavior, can always reach for their gun, mace, or handcuffs. Similarly, these departments, because of their size and independence (through civil service protection of their employees), may have more clout with the chief executive officer or legislative body. Nothing intimidates a city council more than to have a roomful of police officers and their spouses (and sometimes their children) sitting in the council chamber, jaws set and arms folded, when the salary ordinance comes up for annual review.

But planners can often only invoke "principles of sound planning" (about which there can be a fair degree of debate), an appeal to reason, and the potential for compensatory damages remedy due to a temporary taking (which few laypersons understand). And, of course, everybody is an expert on issues of density, appearance, environmental risk, hazards to small children, property values, and traffic congestion (they drive cars, don't they?).

Enabling Legislation's Impact on Agency Operations

While the missions of other local government agencies are clear (collect taxes, pick up the garbage, respond to and put out fires), there may be considerable difference in what planning agencies do, depending on where they are in the nation. In some states (such as Florida, California, Oregon, and New Jersey), the planning statutes are detailed in both procedures and substance. There, simply following the law will keep the planning agency very busy.

In other states, where the planning statutes are not so fine-grained, the planning agency has more discretion as to what it is to do and how it is to do it. That was the case in Memphis, where the planning agency had a broad menu of responsibilities, but no priorities among them, through the joint city-county agreement creating it.

Regional agencies may have an even more ambiguous charge—to coordinate and cooperate, for example. Or external agencies may prescribe their mission (for example, metropolitan planning organizations, whose programmatic emphasis is dictated by the federal and state departments of transportation and federal statutes and regulations).

A Turbulent Environment

The political environment in which planning agencies operate (like much of government these days) is rapidly changing and, indeed, is a lot more turbulent. In planning's early days, the local government's elected and appointed officials might have come from a stable, relatively unchanging group of longtime residents and businesspeople. Today, particularly in the developing suburbs, participants in local government may come from a more fluid collection of transitory residents (many recent arrivals, some due to business uprootings and relocations), some of whom were elected or appointed on single-purpose platforms (often in opposition to something). Indeed, in suburban, high-growth, environmentally aware areas, elected officials see political stakes in planning decisions and want to keep the process close to them.

Rifts sometimes arise between the old-timers and the arrivistes, and planners and local government managers are placed in the middle of them. Because compromise cannot be reached, and the political leaders do not want to finger themselves as the reason for the strife, the planning agency becomes the object of scorn ("We are unhappy with ourselves and it's your fault"). Add to this tension the new role of state government in many places as an external monitor and critic of local planning (through review and certification of local plans and appeals of local development decisions) and you have another chance for scapegoating.

Jack Be Nimble, Jack Be Quick

It's a tough, mean world out there. Planners and planning agencies must collectively tiptoe through the minefields and alight on the dance floor of opportunity. Even when the staff, financial, and physical resources are ostensibly in place, as in Memphis, being effective in a dynamic, as opposed to a stable, environment means that we change our traditional ways of doing business.

It is important to recognize that not all planning environments are dynamic or require change or innovation. Many planning agencies in such environments are caretakers. They cautiously respond, rather than initiate. That change has implications for the structure of planning organizations and the skills of planners.

Mechanistic Versus Organic Organization

To respond to this new turbulent environment and produce results, we will need a new planning organization, one in which information flows in all directions, not just up and down but to where it is needed. There will be no "one true way" to organize the planning function—the executive dominance model (placing planning in the office of the chief executive officer), for example, or the independent commission. The structure of the new planning organization will constantly redefine itself to respond to the nature of the problem to be solved.

Everyone has a favorite paradigm for portraying this approach. Mine draws from the 1961 work of Tom Burns and Geoffrey Stalker, two British management theorists. Their book, *The Management of Innovation,* was one of the first research studies of why some organizations are successful at adapting to technical and commercial change. They described two contrasting management systems: a mechanistic, or hierarchic, management system appropriate to stable conditions, and an organic, or network, form appropriate to changing conditions. The organic system addressed "fresh problems and unforeseen requirements for action which cannot be taken down or distributed automatically arising from the functional roles defined within a hierarchic structure" (p. 119). The following list of comparisons is adapted from Burns and Stalker (p. 125).

Characteristics of Mechanistic and Organic Organizations

Hierarchic Structure	Network Structure
Vertical communication—information goes up, orders go down.	Lateral communications—information goes where it is needed.
Communications consist of instructions and decisions.	Communications consist of advice and information.

Precise definition of rights, responsibilities with each functional role.	Continual redefinition of individual tasks through interaction with others.
Omniscience attributed to top management.	Omniscience not attributed to top management.
Loyalty to superiors a condition of membership organization.	Commitment to tasks and "technological ethos" greater than loyalty.
Prestige attached to internal knowledge of organization itself.	Prestige attached to affiliations and expertise external to organization.

In most places (depending on the relative stability or turbulence of the organization's environment), the new planning organization will be shallower, less hierarchical; there will be less distance between those at the top of the organization who manage it and those who actually carry out its work. This shrinkage of distance will speed up communications.

Self-Evaluation

The planning agency will need to be what political scientist Aaron Wildavsky calls the "self-evaluating organization" (Shafritzand, 1987, p. 458), one that constantly evaluates its external environment, what it is doing, and how it is doing it. Unlike the Memphis and Shelby County Planning Commission, it will not wait for a crisis of confidence to assess its ability to respond to community planning issues.

Egalitarianism in the Workplace

The new planning organization ideally will treat planners (and, indeed, all employees) as a resource, rather than a commodity. In such an organization, planners will be regarded as an asset with valued skills that must be periodically refreshed through continual retraining, rather than slots to be filled (lest the budget cutters eliminate it).

Finally, the new planning organization will be more egalitarian. The planning problems with which it contends have no intellectual boundaries; they are truly interdisciplinary and they may call for knowledge of computers, geographic information systems, environmental or economic analysis, real estate finance, or transportation and traditional land use planning. The wisdom and the skill to solve them do not necessarily respect academic degrees, chronological age, or organizational hierarchies. The solutions may reside anywhere in the organization. Those who manage it must create a setting in which solutions can surface quickly and be tested.

The New Skills

Typically, graduate and undergraduate planning programs stress the development of technical skills. Today, others are required as well.

Managing for Production

A notable omission in many educational programs is teaching planners to become better managers of both themselves and their subordinates. Management becomes more important as the pressure to produce quickly, on time, mounts. The environment in which many planners now operate requires performance now, instead of long after the need for action passes from the public agenda.

The computer, of course, has greatly enhanced and speeded up the analytical ability of the planner. Planners no longer have the great luxury of spending years collecting data, building complex and cranky computer models of transportation behavior and urban development before arriving at a recommendation. Being useful in the present is replacing being elaborate in the future.

Bargaining and Negotiating

As noted above, it is a fact of life that planning agencies must now work with a variety of formal and informal organizations. Numerous task forces, each one a blend of interest groups, very public and very noisy, now oversee plans and studies. The planner's ability to bargain and negotiate with them to obtain agreement on a direction and, indeed, to get out a product will be paramount.

Angels in the Infrastructure, Guerrillas in the Bureaucracy

The planning agency should have a point of view, should stand for something, and should tack like a sailboat when the wind shifts so it can achieve its objective. It, however, is only one of a number of competing actors in the process by which communities are built, and it must fend for itself. When planners find that the formal planning organizations in local government (the planning commission, for example) fail to respond quickly enough, ignore the changes in its external environment (again, the case in Memphis), or simply do a bad job, they will have to develop skills in bypassing the official structure, manipulating bureaucracies, and establishing informal structures and alliances to get the job done.

Planning agencies, I have argued, are not like other local government organizations. Their staff and line functions may conflict. They must respond to numerous internal and external constituencies and monitors. Sometimes they lack the mystique of expertise or political clout that other public agencies may have. The criteria for gauging their success or failure are disparate and ambiguous. In many places, the political environment in which agencies operate has become a lot more turbulent, in part because local officials see political stakes in the consequences of planning decisions, and want to keep the process close to them. Struggles between old-timers and newcomers in developing communities may result in rifts that are laid at the feet of the planning agency (and other local government managers) to heal.

I urge those who manage and staff planning agencies to recognize and respond to the contemporary pressure to be relevant, to produce results, to have a "bias for action." Planners will need to pay careful attention to the structure of their agencies. They will move toward organizational forms that are shallower and less hierarchical in order to speed up communications. The agencies themselves—only one of a number of factors in the process of community building—will need to constantly reevaluate themselves and their missions. The agency's staff will need to be regarded for what they know, not for where they perch in the pecking order. And when the formal planning organizations such as planning commissions drop the ball and fail to respond to changes in their environment, planners must be prepared to pick it up and deftly maneuver around them to get the job done.

Conclusion: Lessons Learned

Anthony James Catanese

It is alleged that the great Yogi Berra once said, "If you don't know where you're going, you probably won't get there." To which it is further alleged that the great Billy Martin retorted, "Yeah, but you won't get lost." Perhaps these statements, apocryphal or not, have something to say about the nature of planning in America. It is clear that planning is going through a period of great change, even if it is not clear where it is heading. Planners are not lost, however, because the process has become so enmeshed in the American polity that it has created a firm foundation of support. Planning is so institutionalized in American life that its future is secure. The pressing question is whether it will be an effective process within today's political arena.

This book is an attempt to bring together a number of lessons from some of the most successful planners in America. These are people who have fought the wars and are willing to provide lessons for those engaged in such battles or soon to be joining the fray. The intent was not so much to create a scholarly base of information as to give some practical lessons that planners can use in the real world. The approach may be criticized by some formalists, but remember that this book is an effort to go beyond the traditional pedagogy. Its goal is to present straightforward lessons about the skills needed for success from those who have been successful. If some wish to call these "war stories," so be it. There is much to be learned from them.

The real world is a changing one. If anything is real, change is. Families are not the kind that we remember; the demographics

287

indicate a whole new structure of family life in America. That in turn creates a whole new structure of communities in America, perhaps even the decline of communities in some parts of the country. Cities as long envisioned by the great architects and urban designers of America are really not quite like they used to be. The idea of a strong central city where most attributes of culture and society could be concentrated has been negated by urban sprawl. That is a result of communications and transportation improvements, to be sure, but it has also effected basic changes in the lifestyle of Americans. One can sit at a personal computer at home and access the Internet to be part of a global electronic village. This creates intrinsic questions about the very meaning of urban space and community, putting planners in the peculiar position of having to define the future without having much if any way to predict it and only a vague sense of direction. All we really know is where we have been.

Lessons in this book attempt to prepare planners to deal with this changing reality. The approach is one of common sense, gained from experience. By no means are we saying that formal education is useless. That is not at all the case. What we have tried to say, however, is that much can be gleaned from an intelligent discussion of experiences from throughout the nation that have resulted in success.

Practical Lessons

We began this book in Part One with a series of lessons gained about professional effectiveness and the personal success of planners. Norman Whitaker offers suggestions for making planners indispensable to their communities and strategies for increasing their agencies' effectiveness. He believes that individuals must be held accountable for their own success or failure. Perhaps the most important lessons that can be learned from this part is that the ability of planners to be effective is highly correlated with their success as persons. Planning is a profession and carries with it a code of ethics, credentialing standards, and educational foundations. Sergio Rodriguez advises that planners, probably more than most other professionals, need to uphold the trust placed in them, and this requires that, first, they be true to themselves. This should be kept in mind as one examines personal success. Nonetheless, it is quite clear that some planners are successful while others are not.

Rodriguez contends that in order to succeed planners need to be trustworthy, flexible, pragmatic, politically smart, cognizant of their strengths and weaknesses, able in public relations, and capable of adjusting to change.

It would seem that there is an element of risk-taking that is essential for personal success as a planner. Richard Bernhardt notes that once you establish credibility you then have the opportunity and responsibility to demonstrate commitment by taking appropriate risks rooted in the professional ideals of your personal value system. He urges planners to recognize what they stand for and to understand whether their value system is compatible with the job they were hired to do. Most of our successful planners have stated that philosophical commitment to serve the public is essential to this personal success. Perhaps that in itself defines some personality traits for planners. Successful planners must be able to listen, to build trust, and most important, to develop commitments. Paul Bergmann suggests that effectiveness depends on the principles of commitment to meaningful public involvement with ownership and to implementation that produces results. Jim Reid also advocates tapping into the power that can be gained from using an open participatory process and from focusing on implementation.

As Reid makes clear, our academic training does not always provide strong preparations for these lessons. While it is true that scholarly work can help in the development of concepts such as equity planning, it is more important to realize that our education presents a foundation for the commitments that must be made by planners in practice. These are lessons that are indeed learned on the battlefield rather than in the classroom.

In Part Two, we learned many more detailed lessons about politics. Even though, throughout the history of planning in the United States, we have attempted to shield planners from the political process, it is now widely understood that effective planning can only occur within an effective political process. Thus, whether we like it or not, planners must be actively involved in politics. It is clear that this involvement can take different levels. While some planners may be overtly political and rise and fall with their political allegiances, others can be more covertly political. In that sense, planners can affect public policy without becoming thoroughly political. This is not to suggest that there should be guerrillas in the bureaucracy, to use the 1960s rhetoric. What we mean to suggest is that planners can participate in a political process whether they are appointed or part of a civil service system by implementing plans and policies that are consistent with the prevailing political views.

It also is quite clear that the involvement of planners in the political process can mean both success and failure. That is why survival is indeed a major consideration. It was once argued that the average planner should not plan on spending more than three years on a job because their political capital would be used up by then. Today we are somewhat more realistic and think that five to seven years might be adequate for planners who want to get actively involved in effective planning within a political process. Nonetheless, it is quite clear that the political route does have a high job turnover rate compared with the bureaucratic model. Certainly planners can fit into a bureaucratic mold and simply avoid participating in the political process, using as a shield the planning commission as well as technical studies and jargon. Although this does indeed lead to longer survival, it seems to be a clear-cut lesson from all of our successful planners that this is the least effective way to practice.

The political process offers other interesting aspects. Although such concepts as advocacy and equity planning are in decline among planners, they are not gone. There are indeed many planners who believe that it is their primary job to effect redistribution of wealth, especially in urban areas. A more viable approach may be the newer concept of empowerment. The empowerment theory seems to be more consistent with current political arguments for personal responsibility for developing skills to improve one's own life. Empowerment means that people can take part in the decisions that will have a major impact upon how they live. This can indeed be undertaken within a collaborative environment so that professionals and community leaders can work together.

In Part Three we talked about lessons involving values and specific principles for effective planning. Some of the lessons learned here had to do with the orientation to communities and ways of getting involved. The recent development of vision studies is a modern-day equivalent to older concepts of the long-range plan. The development of visions for the future enables communities to interact with professional planners and develop reasonable agreements on the long-term content and character of communities.

While these studies can be fairly criticized for their generality, successful planners can develop clear-cut principles and tools for using the vision process in a participatory democracy.

Along with planning principles, planners have another important set of tools, their technical skills. Professional planners can bring certain techniques and methods to the development of policies and plans to meet the long-range needs of communities. The planner needs both: values tempered by the development of significant technical approaches. These tools are put to use by teaching and developing relationships with political, business, and community leaders. The most important tool to develop may be the skills to be a member of a team. It is clear that the days of the "Lone Ranger planner" striking out to create a personal vision are long gone, if they ever existed. Planners are part of a team that involves many professions and a large number of participants. The ability to work with teams may determine the future success of planners.

In Part Four we talked about an entirely new orientation for planners. Here we discussed a somewhat radical notion that planners are providers of service to customers. In that sense, they are more like business leaders attempting to satisfy the needs and wants of their customers. They develop approaches to providing services that are quite different from the past. They develop new ways of thinking about operating principles for providing superior service. This means that while the customer may not always be right, the customer is there to be satisfied, not regulated. Planners can also benefit from a sense of competition in the free market, finding needs and filling them.

The next logical step is for the planner to become a sort of entrepreneur, a packager of development proposals that satisfy both the public and private sectors. Indeed, a major role of the planner may be to formulate programs that will allow the private sector to implement public plans. In the real world this may be the secret of successful planning. In the current political environment it is unrealistic to assume that higher taxes will be available for the implementation of many public plans. Thus, the planner as an entrepreneur is developing much currency.

Finally, this part also dealt with realities of change within a bureaucracy. Since we have been talking mostly about planners within a public context, we must begin to think about ways of improving upon the management and structure of planning agencies themselves. It is no longer adequate to do business as usual. It is now essential that planners come up with new organizational methods for developing a customer-based service in an efficient and economical manner.

Conservative Times

Conservative trends may be related to worldwide events. The collapse of communism and socialism as viable economic and political strategies has an effect on American planning as well. In some ways the 1994 national elections can be seen as a referendum on government, which government lost. But people do not want to get rid of government, they just want it to be smaller, less intrusive, and more efficient.

As recently as twenty years ago, many planners were interested in socialist theory as a basis for planning practice. What was most difficult about this approach was that it tended to put an emphasis on collective behavior and tried to ignore the reality of individual behavior in American society. America is still the home of the rugged individual. Whether it be a Florida retiree, a yuppie in New York, or a Generation X member in Los Angeles, the tenets of individualism are as strong as they have ever been in American history. This has been enforced by legal opinions relating to land use and development. These changes have become the rallying cry for political elections and the success of conservative politicians. It has become an important part of the civil rights and equal opportunity movement in the United States as well. The fundamental error of the socialist approach to planning was that it seriously underestimated the significance of individual rights in America.

As a result, planners have had to shift their thinking. While there are still some collections of socialist planning thought in a few universities, there are probably no examples of a socialist, collective-based approach to planning in the examples that we have studied. Even equity planning, which uses some of the rhetoric of redistribution of wealth, has become quite tame lately.

Yet there is a dilemma in this. While most people do not support a collective-based approach to planning, there is still enormous support for the planning process. Whether it be political support for growth management in growing states like Florida, Texas, and California; widespread commitment to urban redevelopment in the urban centers of New York, Michigan, and Ohio; or the popularity of protecting and enhancing the environment in states like Colorado and Montana, planning enjoys enormous public support. All of this indicates that the American people support planning and planners. Perhaps it is a dichotomy that while most are opposed to some of the early roots of planning thought, they are very committed to the current thought in planning. This in itself indicates that there is a wide gap between the literature of planning and the practice of planning. It indicates a need for more studies like the one we present here, using examples from the field. This kind of reality-based literature can be useful to help explain the apparent dichotomy between public acceptance of planning and the criticism of early and socialist planning thought.

Lessons About the Future

So what can we learn about successful planning in the real world from America's most successful planners? We can learn that planning as a profession has grown from an idealistic, utopian-based approach to a realistic way of managing the future. We can learn that successful planners must develop a whole new orientation toward their customers, the people who live in the communities they are planning for. Currently we are abandoning the old approach of "the planner and the plannee" and developing a new approach of the planner as a service provider to customers. In a way this brings a new entrepreneurial vocabulary to the public world of planners.

It also shows that planners must get beyond the regulatory mode. For many years the tools of planners were inherently regulatory. We told people what they could and could not do with their land. We tried to decide where one could drive and not drive. We even tried to decide where one could live and where one could work. While much of that was admirable in its objectives, it was not successful in its application. What we have learned today is that planners must be involved in the management of growth and the redevelopment of older areas. We must use concepts from the private sector having to do with efficiency, accountability, and productivity.

While we must be sure that our cities work, we must also be sure that they are wonderful places. While we can point out the serious problems of urban sprawl, we are in no position to tell people where they can live or the ways that they can live. We can educate our customers, however, about better products and services available to them.

We must deal with the reality that planning has to be reinvented. As David Osborne and Ted Gaebler (1992) point out in *Reinventing Government,* it simply is no longer possible to have centralized bureaucracies that dictate to people. While it may have never really worked in America, which is by its very nature a country that fears central control and the loss of freedom, such an approach is totally unacceptable today. For as we must reinvent government, we also must reinvent planning within that context. When one thinks of all the changes in American business and industry, as well as government, it is actually foolish to think that planning cannot change. We must deal with the very hard lessons that have been learned in the private sector. We must require people to work harder, smarter, and provide more services. We must cut unnecessary management and strive for greater productivity. Indeed, with the advent of technology in planning, it may even become a viable goal of planning agencies to minimize the number of employees and increase the efficiency of services. These are hard lessons that do not come easily, but they are probably the key to creating success in planning agencies. Certainly the alternative, developing large central administrations that are intent upon rule-making and regulatory actions, is absurd in modern America.

Clearly, planning profession is in the midst of great change. In this sense we are reinventing planning in America. We are developing new ways of doing things and new ways of thinking about people and communities. Yet we would be remiss to end this discussion without a strong lesson from an earlier real world. The greatest role for planners in America is to develop a vision of the way that things could be. Perhaps the planning profession is uniquely qualified for devising plans for the future that can serve as a beacon for collaboration and teamwork. In that sense, we are very much beholden to Daniel Burnham, the American city planner and architect, for his words more than a hundred years ago. Burnham argued that planners should make big plans, create magic, to draw real interest and inspire action. Without big plans, he said, people would never be excited enough to work towards implementation. While Burnham's work may be somewhat dated, the concept is still a powerful one. Successful planners can develop the vision that will help people get to where they want to be. In that sense, planners can help change the real world for the better.

For too many years we have not dealt with the most important lesson from the real world, which is that implementation is the most important part of planning. We are so concerned with planning theory and the subsequent development of techniques and methods that we pay little attention to the implementation of plans. In too many cases we have essentially stopped the planning process when it entered the implementation realm. For too many years we have left it to others to carry out plans that were really not theirs. The most important lesson that we can learn from successful planners is this, in a rephrasing of Coach Vince Lombardi's motto on winning: implementation isn't everything—it's the only thing.

This is probably the most exciting period in the short history of planning in America. We now have the stories from America's most successful planners to use as lessons to restructure, reinvent, and renew planning practice. We can take a fresh look at the skills of success and the practical tools for making planning work. It is critical that planning education improve, and that it be enriched by teaching lessons from practicing planners. It is through successful planning that we can make America a better place.

Afterword

Planners have the heavy responsibility of helping elected officials resist the pressure to sell out the future. As Alvin Toffler observed in *Future Shock* (1970, p. 483): "Instead of anticipating the problems and opportunities of the future, we lurch from crisis to crisis and our political system is 'future-blind.'" In an age where change is continuing to come with frightening rapidity, future-blindness is a deadly flaw.

In *Reinventing Government* (Osborne and Gaebler, 1992), David Osborne and I audaciously argued that governments at all levels were failing on a massive scale and that reinvention is the only option left. Simply stated, the centralized governmental bureaucracies that successfully evolved in the 1930s and 1940s no longer function well in the rapidly changing, information-rich, knowledge-intensive society and global economy of the 1990s. Looking around, we noted that all institutions in America are struggling to adapt to the hurricane winds of change. We concluded that today's rapidly changing environment demands institutions that are extremely flexible and adaptable. It needs institutions that are responsive to their customers, offering choices of nonstandardized services; that lead by persuasion and incentives rather than commands; that give their employees a sense of meaning and control, even ownership. It means government must empower citizens rather than simply serving them because fostering dependency in the guise of public service is no virtue.

The service that I attempted to provide in writing my book was to synthesize and share the ideas and experiences of the most dynamic, innovative, and entrepreneurial governments across America. In these extraordinary governments I observed that entrepreneurship was the norm and bureaucracy and business as usual was the exception. I learned that most entrepreneurial governments promote competition between service providers. They measure the performance of their agencies, focusing not on inputs but on outcomes. They are driven by their goals—their missions— not by their rules and regulations. They redefine their clients as customers and offer them choices. They prevent problems before they emerge, rather than simply offering services afterward. They put their energies into earning money, not simply spending it. They decentralize authority, embracing participatory management. They prefer market mechanisms to bureaucratic mechanisms. And they focus not simply on providing public services, but on catalyzing all sectors—public, private and voluntary—into action to solve their community's problems.

I have often wondered what would happen to government functions and services if they were all organized according to the principles described above. With respect to the planning function in local government, I now know the answer. What Bruce McClendon and Anthony Catanese have been able to achieve in their book is to provide nothing less than a road map for reinventing the planning profession. Their road map is based on the principles and practices which have been developed by some of America's most innovative and entrepreneurial planners.

In reading this book I was struck by the many similarities between my vision of entrepreneurial government and the experiences and practices of these successful planners. Time and again, different planners would describe and advocate the use of practices that were remarkably consistent with my own ten principles of entrepreneurial government. With great frequency they referenced the notion of empowerment, customer service, prevention rather than cure, market orientation, competition, decentralization of authority, and the role of government as a catalyst.

The good news is that many planners are learning how to use their unique training and skills to help communities focus on the future and to help them anticipate and benefit from change. Planners are becoming more relevant by adapting and reinventing traditional approaches to comprehensive planning to include the most desirable characteristics associated with private sector strategic planning. Planning by local governments is not something you can do once and put on a shelf, but rather a process that must be regularly repeated. The important aspect is not the plan but rather planning itself. By creating consensus around a vision of the future, the community builds a sense of where it is going among all of its members. This allows everyone—not just a few elected officials—to understand what direction they need to take, without waiting for word from the top.

Planners have a critical role to play in reinventing government. This traditional use of planners to promote public participation and involvement in decision making is a valuable role that must be capitalized and expanded upon if we are going to reconnect citizens with their government. Unfortunately I found that American governments tend to be customer-blind while successful businesses are customer-driven. This may be the ultimate indictment of bureaucratic government. Everyone in government must learn to treat their citizens as highly valued customers. Listening to your customer and sharing what is learned with the bureaucracy is an opportunity and essential responsibility for planners. In reading this book I was impressed by the degree to which so many planners understand the importance of customer service and are so committed to the principle of public empowerment.

This book envisions a new paradigm of pragmatic public service that is based on the real world experiences of some of this country's most successful planners. In truth, you don't learn about the skills of success in school but on the job, one day at a time. One day with this practical, hands-on guide to successful practice can save you years of trial and error. I believe the collective experiences of the planners that contributed to this book can provide the catalyst that is needed to shift the existing planning paradigm, to reinvent the basic philosophy of planning, and to restore planners to a position of value and importance in their communities.

May 1996   Ted Gaebler
San Rafael, California

References

Abrams, C. *The Language of Cities*. New York: Viking Penguin, 1971.

Albrecht, K. *At America's Service*. New York: Warner Books, 1992.

Albrecht, K., and Bradford, L. *The Service Advantage*. Homewood, Ill.: Dow Jones–Irwin, 1990.

Altshuler, A. *The City Planning Process*. Ithaca, N.Y.: Cornell University Press, 1965.

American Management Association. *AMA Management Handbook*. New York: American Management Association, 1970.

Bair, F. *Planning Cities*. Chicago: American Society of Planning Officials, 1970.

Barrett, C. *Everyday Ethics for Practicing Planners*. Washington, D.C: American Institute of Certified Planners, 1995.

Baum, H. *Planners and Public Expectations*. Cambridge, Mass.: Schenkman, 1983.

Beckman, N. "The Planner as a Bureaucrat." *Journal of the American Institute of Planners,* 1966, *30*(4), 323–327.

Bellush, J., and Hausknecht, M. "Entrepreneurs and Urban Renewal." *Journal of the American Institute of Planners,* 1968, 289–297.

Birch, E. L. "Chester Rapkin: Planner, Teacher, Scholar." *Journal of the American Planning Association,* 1988, *54*(4), 421.

Brevard County v. *Snyder,* 627 So.2nd 469 (Fla. 1993).

Brooks, M. "Four Critical Junctures in the History of the Urban Planning Profession." *Journal of the American Planning Association,* 1988, *54*(2).

Burns, T., and Stalker, G. M. *The Management of Innovation*. London: Tavistock, 1961.

Byham, W. C., and Cox, J. *Zap! The Lightning of Empowerment*. New York: Fawcett Columbine, 1988.

Carroll, L. *Alice's Adventures in Wonderland*. Austin, Texas: Holt, Rinehart and Winston, 1985. (Originally published 1865.)

Citizens' Goals for the Colorado Springs Community. *Steps to Goals*. Colorado Springs, Colo.: Citizens' Goals for the Colorado Springs Community, 1978.

Clavel, P. *The Progressive City*. New Brunswick, N.J.: Rutgers University Press, 1986.

Collins, J. C., and Porras, J. I. *Built to Last.* New York: HarperBusiness, 1994.

Coonradt, C. *The Game of Work.* Salt Lake City, Utah: Deseret, 1985.

Covey, S. 1989. *The Seven Habits of Highly Effective People.* New York: Simon & Schuster, 1989.

Dolan v. *City of Tigard,* 114 S.Ct. 2317 (1994).

Drucker, P. *Management Tasks, Responsibilities, Practices.* New York: Harper-Collins, 1973.

Drucker, P. *The New Realities: In Government and Politics/In Economics and Business/In Society and World View.* New York: HarperCollins, 1989.

Forester, J. *Planning in the Face of Power.* Berkeley: University of California Press, 1989.

Freidmann, J. *Planning in the Public Domain.* Princeton, N.J.: Princeton University, 1987.

Frieden, B. "Center City Transformed: Planners as Developers." *Journal of the American Planning Association,* 1990, *56*(4), 423–428.

Garfield, C. *Peak Performers.* New York: Avon Books, 1986.

Genge, N. *The Unofficial* X-Files *Companion.* New York: Crown, 1995.

Heskett, J. *Managing in the Service Economy.* Boston: Harvard Business School Press, 1986.

Imundo, L. *The Effective Supervisor Handbook.* (2nd ed.) New York: AMA-COM, 1991.

Ingraham, P. W., and Rosenblum, D. "Political Foundations of the American Federal Service: Rebuilding a Crumbling Base." *Public Administration Review,* Mar.-Apr. 1990.

Kent, T. J., Jr. *The Urban General Plan.* Novato, Calif.: Chandler & Sharp, 1964.

Kestin, H. *21st Century Management.* New York: Atlantic Monthly Press, 1992.

Kouzes, J. M., and Posner, B. Z. *The Leadership Challenge: How to Get Extraordinary Things Done in Organizations.* San Francisco: Jossey-Bass, 1987.

Krueckeberg, D. "Self, Property, and Community in American Planning." Paper presented at the annual conference of the Association of Collegiate Schools of Planning, Philadelphia, Oct. 1993.

Levitt, T. "Marketing Myopia." *Harvard Business Review,* Sept.-Oct. 1975.

Lucas v. *South Carolina Coastal Council,* 112 S.Ct. 2886 (1992).

McClendon, B. W. *Customer Service in Local Government.* Chicago: American Planning Association, 1992.

McClendon, B. W., and Quay, R. *Mastering Change: Winning Strategies for Effective City Planning.* Chicago: American Planning Association, 1988.

McConkey, D. *MBO for Nonprofit Organizations*. New York: AMACOM, 1975.

Miller, T., and Miller, M. "Standards of Excellence: U.S. Residents' Evaluation of Local Government Services." *Public Administration Review,* 1991, *51*(6), 503–514.

Monk, S. "Crisis Center Fund-Raising Drive Reaches Goal." *Graham Leader,* 1982, p. 1.

Mosena, D., and Thurow, C. *Making Joint Planning Work: An Administrative Study of the Memphis and Shelby County Planning Commission*. Chicago: American Society of Planning Officials, 1975.

Murray, C. *In Pursuit of Happiness and Good Government*. New York: Simon & Schuster, 1988.

National Commission on the State and Local Public Service. *Hard Truths/Tough Choices: An Agenda for State and Local Reform*. New York: Rockefeller Institute, 1993.

National Performance Review. *From Red Tape to Results: Creating a Government That Works Better and Costs Less*. Washington, D.C.: U.S. Government Printing Office, 1993.

National Performance Review. *Standards for Serving the American People: Putting Customers First*. Washington, D.C.: U.S. Government Printing Office, 1994.

Nollan v. *California Coastal Commission*, 483 U.S. 825 (1987).

Osborne, D., and Gaebler, T. *Reinventing Government*. Reading, Mass.: Addison-Wesley, 1992.

Palm Beach v. *Wright*, 641 So.2nd 469 (Fla. 1993).

Perloff, H. *Education for Planning: City, State, and Regional*. Baltimore: Johns Hopkins University Press, 1957.

Peters, T. *Liberation Management*. New York: Knopf, 1992.

Peters, T., and Waterman, R., Jr. *In Search of Excellence*. New York: HarperCollins, 1982.

Rybczynski, W. *City Life: Urban Expectations in a New World*. New York: Scribner, 1995.

Sennett, R. *The Conscience of the Eye*. New York: Knopf, 1990.

Shafritzand, J. *Classics of Public Administration*. Belmont, Calif.: Dorsey Press, 1987.

Smith-Mello, M., and Schirmer, P. *The Context of Change: Trends, Innovations and Forces Affecting Kentucky's Future*. Lexington: Kentucky Long-Term Policy Research Center, 1994.

Swaine, M. "The Programmer Paradigm." *Dr. Dobbs' Journal,* 1995, *20*(1), 109.

Tocqueville, A. de. *Democracy in America*. New York: New American Library, 1956. (Originally published 1835.)

Toffler, A. *Future Shock.* New York: Bantam Books, 1970.

Toner, W., Gil, E., and Lucchesi, E. *Planning Made Easy.* Chicago: American Planning Association, 1994.

Waitley, D., and Tucker, R. *Winning the Innovation Game.* Old Tappan, N.J.: Revell, 1986.

Zeithaml, V., Parasuraman, A., and Berry, L. *Delivering Quality Service.* New York: Free Press, 1990.

Index